PRAISE FOR
An Impossible Life

"The writing is gorgeous…a page-turning story that is filled with strong lessons on healing." — *The Book Commentary*

"A fascinating glimpse into the mind of one suffering from bipolar disorder." — *U.S. Review of Books*

"These words left a mark on my heart, and this story is one of my most sacred and special I've ever done." — Dr. Tara Narula, *CBS This Morning*

"This erudite book could prove insightful for patients, caretakers, and therapists alike. Illuminating, impactful writing about coping with mental illness." — *Kirkus Review*

"Sonja's despairing yet hopeful story unveils the inner turmoil of mental illness and recovery." — *Publisher Weekly*

"*An Impossible Life* should be at the top of any reading list." — Diane Donovan, *Midwest Book Review*

"The reader comes away with a sense of empowerment." — *Feathered Quill Book Award*

AN IMPOSSIBLE *Life*

A True Story of Hope & Mental Illness

AN
IMPOSSIBLE
life

RACHAEL SIDDOWAY
& SONJA WASDEN

Cover photo by Whitney Wame, Ivory House Photography
Front cover concept by Emma Wasden
Book cover design by Marisa Jackson for TLC Book Design
Interior layout by Creative Publishing Book Design

Library of Congress Cataloging-in-Publication Data has been applied for.

ISBN: 979-8-9897980-1-8 (pbk.)
ISBN: 979-8-9897980-2-5 (hardcover)
ISBN: 978-1-7336194-6-2 (ebook)

Contents

Rachael Siddoway

Between the covers of this book is my mother's life—quite literally in your hands. Her story, as told on these pages, captures not only the moments she wanted to share, but also the moments that for many years she refused to. While it is true that many good things come anonymously, I find there is direction in the details and more comfort in the chaos when you can put a face to a name, a name to a person, and a person to a story.

Many people, like her, hope to find someone or something to save them—an inspiring quote to hang in the house, a quick fix to pin onto the bulletin board—praying that the advice still brings hope tomorrow. But the next day, you realize the quote was just a prism for looking at life from someone else's perspective. Without the road map sharing how they arrived at that perspective, or how you can find it, because the author is a ghost, the very thing you're terrified of becoming.

My mother's story is told here in unvarnished detail so that her journey will not leave the reader with "author unknown." It is told because the thought of her escaping hell and becoming nothing more than an unknown to the people just entering those fiery gates—that's what terrifies her most.

I may have put in the hours to write this story, but she put in the years and lived it. This story was written in first-person narrative as Sonja. Writing this book with my mother is my love letter to her.

AUTHOR'S NOTE

Sonja Wasden

The events in this book are conveyed to the best of my recollection. Some names have been changed, some dialogue has been recreated, but the events are true stories from my life. While there is information shared about my children, this book does not go into detail about how they felt or their lives. I understand this will leave you with questions. I feel strongly that my daughter and sons should have the right to speak for themselves.

Many people have asked me why I would make myself so vulnerable by publicly sharing such raw and unedited moments from my life. I believe it's important to openly discuss the realities of mental health disorders so that people feel they can not only come forward but also be understood and shown compassion. My hope is that my story will give people who do not suffer from mental health disorders a new perspective, helping them build stronger relationships with those who may suffer. My motivation is that if my story lets one person know they are not alone and helps them connect with the people they love, it has all been worth it.

CHAPTER 1

Emergency Room

Baton Rouge, Louisiana, 2007

"Wait here," the ER nurse said as the door clicked shut behind her.

I fidgeted on the exam table. The paper crinkled under me, occasionally breaking the silence. I did not want to be here. I needed to convince Mitch he was wrong: a seemingly impossible task since he was the authority on every subject in our house. Politics, religion, finances, and worldviews lay at his feet to slice and dice as he saw fit. I knew once I told the doctors everything I was going through, they would agree that it was nothing more than stress. I was positive I'd walk free. I had the gift of persuasion and used it frequently. I could twist problems until they became allies. Whether returning things I had clearly used without a receipt or getting out of a speeding ticket, I knew I could bend people to my will.

Except my husband, Mitch.

Mitch sat in a plastic chair, his back straight and emotions tucked deep inside. For him, there was a proper way to behave at all times, even when trying to commit his wife to the psychiatric hospital against

1

her will. Mitch, a master of the art of projection, displayed a constant image of control and confidence. My blood boiled when I looked at him. *How dare he corner me.*

"Let me write up notes about you and show them to a doctor! Then you'd be sitting where I am right now," I whispered vehemently. "I called Allyson and Mike. They said I could have *you* admitted to the hospital against *your* will, and they're both attorneys. So maybe you're crazy!"

"Okay," he said. My words bounced off him, but I continued sharpening them. I had tried to cut into him and reveal his core throughout our entire marriage, but his stonewall emotions left me craving more.

A different nurse knocked on the door before popping her head in. She stared at me. "Wow! You're stunning."

Since I was a child, my sleek blue-black hair, green eyes, and sharp features often made people take second glances. Plus, I had a knack for putting together an outfit. Give me forty dollars at T.J. Maxx and I'm ready for the Oscars.

I waited for her next question.

"Where are you from?" she asked.

"Utah, but you want to know my nationality. German," I said. "Shocking, I know."

"I would have guessed Persian."

"Maybe an affair somewhere in my heritage." I forced a smile—I wanted this conversation to end. I was mismatched. My outside did not match my inside. It disturbed even me at times. I looked so put together, when internally I was falling apart.

The nurse turned to Mitch. "You can come, they're ready to see her."

I let out a slow, deep breath before I followed the nurse out. Mitch followed without hesitation. It seemed like nothing could ruffle his feathers, whereas I was incapable of a poker face, no matter how hard I tried. When sharing my thoughts and feelings, I was vocal and loud, which would soon be my downfall. The nurse led us through hallways until we entered a room where a COPE (Community Outreach for Psychiatric Emergencies) evaluator was waiting for us.

"Hi, I'm Dr. Warner," she said, ready to shake Mitch's hand. *Perfect, a woman.* I put on my best smile, ready to shake her hand next. *She'll understand my situation.* "Mrs. Wasden, I'm here to evaluate you."

"I don't need to be evaluated." I smiled and leaned back into the stiff chair trying to escape her isolating stare.

"Then what brings you to the emergency room?"

"Just stress." I ticked off each event on my fingers as I recounted them aloud. "I've moved, been living in a house while it's being renovated, recently lost a hundred pounds, and I'm homeschooling my three children."

"Wow, that is a lot."

I straightened up, feeling more confident. *I knew she would understand.*

"Have you ever thought about taking your own life?" she asked.

Living made death look desirable. It was a solemn song few sang out loud. I chose to answer honestly—*it was about time someone did.*

I raised an eyebrow. "Who hasn't?"

"How often?" Her tone, similar to a flight attendant taking a drink order, signaled this was routine for her.

"I don't know—just as much as a normal person does."

"Can you give me an estimate?"

"Seriously? I have no idea. Probably as often as you." For a woman used to openly talking about suicide, she sure asked a lot of rhetorical questions.

"Is it daily? Weekly?"

"Daily."

"In what ways have you thought about suicide?" she asked, writing down everything. I felt uneasy, but knew I needed to get through these questions in order to get home to my kids.

"Jumping off a building, swerving my car into oncoming traffic, taking pills, drowning myself, stabbing myself and bleeding to death and," my favorite, "standing in front of a semitruck and having it run me over." I paused. "But no guns. That's where I draw the line." Mitch had heard me talk about suicide so often—I knew this was nothing new to him.

"Have you ever attempted suicide?" she asked.

I shook my head no.

"And why haven't you tried any of those things?"

"I don't think I could face God if I did."

I was raised in the LDS (Latter-Day Saints) faith, and since childhood I'd obeyed my religious checklist of reading your scriptures, saying your prayers, and going to church like it was a prescription for peace. Members of my church testified that this prescription works, but it left me confused when that promised peace never came for me. I felt all the punishment of a sinner. The Bible talks about weeping, gnashing of teeth, and being cast out into outer darkness, and that's how I felt. I knew we were all sinners, but I had thought about that a lot and concluded I hadn't committed any big sins. I'd prayed a thousand prayers and begged for forgiveness and peace. I didn't understand how I could feel everything the scriptures say about being a damned soul and not be bad. If there were two groups of people, and one group had all the accomplished, righteous, lovely people, and the other group had the drug addicts, prostitutes, and broken souls, I would belong with the broken souls.

"Do you want to die?" Her question caught me off guard. I thought about suicide all the time. The answer should've been obvious. It wasn't. I didn't want to be alive, but I wasn't sure I wanted to be dead either. I just wanted out of the pain. I held her gaze as her question echoed in my mind. *Do I want to die?*

"Yes."

She and Mitch glanced at each other. She looked back at me. I couldn't get a read on her. *Is she on my side?*

Dr. Warner stood up.

"Can I go home now?" I asked.

"I'll be back."

She never came back. Mitch and I waited for ten eternal minutes. We didn't talk. In the silence I grew more anxious. The only sound in the room was the soft hum from the air conditioner. The tension in our marriage had been rising for some time, and Mitch forcing me to the ER wasn't helping. The door opened and a short man with two security guards entered the room. I immediately stood.

"Mrs. Wasden, I'm a crisis worker and we are admitting you to the psychiatric hospital," he stated. I looked at him and then at the two guards. I wanted to run, but my feet felt glued to the floor.

Surely, this was a nightmare and at any moment I would find myself safe in bed at home. I wanted to scream, but all I could get out was a raspy, "I refuse to go."

"You're under the care of a physician, and she's made this decision for you," the short man said.

The room spun. I needed protection. I turned and grabbed Mitch's arm. "Let's go home," I demanded.

He said nothing.

"Mitch, take me home," I pleaded.

He raised his eyebrows at me empathetically but remained silent.

"Mrs. Wasden, we're going to help you get well." The crisis worker stepped toward me.

"But I'm not sick!" I stepped away from him. "I'm stressed! Why won't anyone believe me?" My heart pounded and I was sweating. Hysteria gripped me.

"There is a van outside waiting for you."

The two security guards watched. *I bet they're waiting for me to give them a reason to be here.*

I faced the crisis worker. "You can't force me. I won't go!"

"We have a physician evaluation certificate with your name on it, Mrs. Wasden. So, yes, we can force you. And we will, if necessary."

He held open the door and waited for me to walk out. There was nowhere to run.

"You're making a big mistake. I'm not sick!"

"Mrs. Wasden, you're actually very sick," he responded. "Let's go."

"I am not crazy!" I screamed. I hated his use of *very sick*. I knew what he really meant.

He stood in front of me, arms folded. "No one's saying you're crazy, Mrs. Wasden."

"Yet you're forcing me into the psych ward." I reached out and grabbed Mitch's arm again and shook him. Why wasn't he saying anything? Doing anything? "Help me!" I yelled.

He wrapped his arms around me and whispered, "You can do this. Things will be better, I promise. The sooner you go, the sooner you'll get to come home to the kids and me."

I closed my eyes, not wanting to leave his embrace. I leaned in closer, wanting to disappear into him. But when I opened my eyes, the hospital floor was still beneath me.

"Please don't make me do this. I can get better without going to the psych ward, I promise. I'll do yoga and deep breathing. Please!" I shamelessly begged.

He stepped back and lifted my chin with his thumb, but I kept my eyes down. "Look at me, Sonja."

I looked up and was surprised to see exhaustion hanging heavy in his blue eyes. Mitch looked too weathered and beaten down to help me anymore. Had I been so consumed by my pain that I hadn't noticed him silently suffering beside me? Or had Mitch's "I'm fine" facade fooled me into believing he was? I longed to know his deeper feelings, to understand his hurt, but doubted he'd ever share. At that moment I realized this hospital visit was Mitch running out of ways to make things better.

"Please go. This could save us," he said.

Tears fell from my cheeks as I stared into his unflinching gaze.

I took Mitch in one last time—his fair skin, blond hair, lean figure—before turning around. I straightened my cream silk blouse, twisted my diamond bracelets into place, and held my head high. In my black designer skirt and suede heels with a security guard on each side of me, I walked that long hallway like a runway. I would not be dragged out; I would not go kicking and screaming. If I had to leave, I'd make it look like my choice. Nurses and patients hovered around the scene pretending not to stare. I kept strutting that runway until I stepped inside the back of the van and looked straight through the iron bars separating me from the two men up front. Those bars made me feel like a criminal, convicted of something I didn't do.

How did I get here?

CHAPTER 2

Ten Hours Earlier

"Kids, come downstairs! Omi and Opa's car just pulled up!" I shouted.

My parents' favorite treats sat on the counter—caramel popcorn and powdered-sugar donuts for my dad, and a marzipan Ritter Sport chocolate bar for my mom.

All three kids came down carrying the giant "WELCOME" sign they made from taping seven sheets of printer paper together. Rachael was twelve, Alex was ten, and Lincoln was seven.

"Lincoln, don't bend the corner," Rachael said, taking his hand off the paper.

"Mom! Rachael is being bossy!" Lincoln grabbed his corner back.

I remained deaf to Lincoln's cries.

"*Guys*, we can all carry it." Alex sighed.

"We can, but not if the poster gets ruined," Rachael said. I knew Rachael understood how important it was to me to have company visit.

"That turned out great!" Mitch said, helping place the large sign on the counter.

"They're here!" I yelled.

9

The back door opened, and there stood my mom. At sixty-five, she only had a few white strands interspersed in her brown layered bob. Her small frame was decorated head to toe in red: her favorite color, obvious to anyone who saw her clothes, house, car, nails, or phone case.

"Sonja, is all this for us?" she asked in her thick German accent as her rings that adorned almost every finger clanked against the kitchen counter piled with treats.

"Yep!" I said.

My mom grew up in post-war West Germany as a refugee. She was three years old during World War II and lived in Anklam, which was in East Germany. Russia invaded Anklam and took my grandfather as a prisoner of war, leaving my grandmother to look after their six children, including a newborn baby boy. My grandfather ended up dying in a Russian prison camp. After the war, my grandmother escaped to West Germany with her six children. The baby boy died of starvation. At the age of eighteen, my mom met my dad in Bad Godesberg, Germany, while he was serving a church mission there. At the age of nineteen, knowing very little English, she left her family and country to go to America to marry him.

"Hi, Dad!" I could barely finish greeting him before he picked me up in one of his famous bear hugs.

My dad was a force of nature. His life began on a small farm where he lived in a one-bedroom house with no plumbing, heating, or running water, but plenty of physical abuse, poverty, and alcoholism. Despite all this, he managed a successful marriage, raised seven children, and netted over twenty million dollars working in mergers and acquisitions. He lived large and spent large. From expensive art collections and elaborate hunting trips in Mongolia to his beloved courtside seats for the Utah Jazz, there always seemed a place for his money to go.

I grew up in a 15,000-square-foot home that he designed. Hearts were tucked into every detail of our home—from carvings on the outside of the chimney to the large red stained-glass hearts encircling the kitchen window. My dad was obsessed with hearts and called my mom his double double sweetheart. I think my dad used the idea of true love as a way to heal parts of his broken childhood. But love didn't stop his childhood memories from relentlessly following him around. I remember him spending Christmas and Mother's Day sad in his bedroom. As a child I couldn't figure out why anyone would be sad on Christmas. His father was a truck driver and would be home during the holidays, and that's when he beat his wife. My dad would run with his siblings into the barn, trying to hide from their mother's screams—screams that still echoed through our family history as those holidays crept back up, causing my dad to hide, only now as a man, tucked away in his mansion.

"Now, where are the three people I flew all this way to see?" He tucked his hands behind his suspenders and snapped them against his big belly.

"Opa!" Rachael, Alex, and Lincoln ran into his arms.

"Do you have any happiness gum in there?" Lincoln stuck his hand into my dad's pocket.

My dad was known for his "happiness gum." It was his trademark among the children at church and anywhere in public with strangers. Lincoln gripped two packs of Juicy Fruit and pulled them out with a smile.

My dad stepped back dramatically. "I don't believe this! You're robbing me blind!" He had a permanent laugh in his voice when he talked to his grandchildren. "Do you want Big Red, mint, or Juicy Fruit?" He scooped out three more packs of gum from his pocket and fanned out all the options like cash to Alex and Rachael.

"Big Red," Rachael and Alex said in unison. But there was only one pack of it left.

"You take it," Alex conceded. My dad tossed her the pack.

Alex shrugged. "I'll take mint."

"Go long!" My dad faked a pass and then gently tossed Alex the mint pack. He had all the kids lean in for a secret. "What do you say we have Kids' Day this week?"

"Yes! Yes! Yes!" they all cheered.

"Okay, Kids' Day it is. But it's gotta be our little secret." My dad winked; a chewed toothpick balanced in the corner of his smile.

Kids' Day was a holiday he created, a day where kids got to make the rules. They could wear pajamas all day and eat nothing but sugar. Against his better judgment, he would let them drive his car around the neighborhood. They spent most of the day at Dollar Tree, GameStop, and Walmart, shopping till their little hands were too full to carry anything else. Usually, he would perform a random act of kindness on those outings, like buying groceries for the person in front of him or purchasing a KFC meal for a homeless person. My dad was the personification of love, but in a few short hours, he would become my enemy.

"So, what's the plan?" my mom asked me. She liked to know how the day was going to start and end, even when she had nowhere to be. I think she liked knowing how she'd be fit into the day, made a priority. My dad called her his German princess, and she played the role like it was her birthright, which it could've been. She liked to be called "HRH" because her grandfather, Albert Von Hayn, was a baron—one rank higher than a knight. Her family lost everything in the war. My dad had her family crest made into a stained-glass window that hung in their home.

"We'll go somewhere for lunch and then to the boys' tennis tournament. And I have a church meeting later today. But other than that, there's no plan," I said, filling the boys' water jugs under the kitchen tap. "Boys, give Opa some air. Come load these in the car." I pointed to their tennis bags on the floor.

Mitch clapped his hands together. "Is the gang ready to hit the road?"

"Can I pick where we go to lunch?" Rachael asked, looking up from her notebook where she had been working on her latest fantasy novel.

"Sure, where should we go?" Mitch asked.

My dad leaned over. "IHOP," he whispered into her ear.

"Well, IHOP has great chocolate pancakes," Rachael said, closing her notebook.

"Sounds like a plan. We'll stop there on the way," Mitch agreed.

"You owe me," Rachael mouthed to my dad. He tossed her another pack of gum as we headed down the driveway to the cars.

We drove to IHOP and my parents followed in their rental. We slid onto the blue vinyl benches and looked over sticky menus.

"Hi, I'm Sarah and I'll be your waitress today. Can I get your drink orders?"

"Sarah? Sarah! That is exactly who we asked for!" my dad practically yelled through the restaurant. "We heard you were the best waitress in town, so we asked specifically for you! I'll have a Coke, but take some happiness gum." He handed her a pack of Juicy Fruit, and my kids laughed.

We ate our share of pancakes and omelets and still made it to the tournament early. Alex and Lincoln went to their assigned courts while we found a shaded bench. Mitch, Rachael, and my parents quietly chatted as the sound of tennis balls popped across the court. I didn't contribute. I had prepared too hard for this tournament to casually chat during it. I watched the entire first match with determination because I knew what was at stake. Wimbledon. My sons' tennis had become my most prized obsession. I believed both my sons would become professional tennis players—it was just a matter of time.

"We're going to head back to your house. I'm tired," my mom said halfway through the boys' last match.

"Okay. We'll meet you back at the house when they're done," I said.

"Sonja, you should come with us," my dad said.

I tuned him out, wishing they would stop interrupting the match. Mitch waved his hands in front of my face. "Hello, earth to Sonja."

I pushed his hands away. "Stop, I can't see!"

"You're coming with us," my mom said, standing.

I glanced at her, a bit surprised, then turned my head back to the court.

"You don't see your parents often. Go with them; the tournament's almost over," Mitch encouraged.

"I don't want to go." I kept my eyes on the ball flying over the net. "We'll meet them back at the house when it's done."

"After I flew all this way to spend time with you," my mom complained.

I put up my hands in defeat. "All right, all right. I'll go." My dad had raised us to give my mom what she wanted, when she wanted it. Even in my late thirties, I put her wants before my own. "I'll see you at home." I kissed Mitch goodbye. I followed my parents to the parking lot and climbed into the back seat of their car.

"You're sick, Sonja," my dad said, as soon as my seatbelt clicked.

"Sorry, what?" My eyebrows creased in confusion.

"You're sick," he repeated.

"Is this why you guys came? Because you think I'm sick?"

My mom looked at her lap, quiet as my dad drove out of the parking lot.

"Well, thanks for the visit!" I tried to laugh.

"Sonja, you have been sick for a long time. It's time to get you help," my dad continued.

"No," my voice suddenly stern. I leaned forward and jabbed my dad's arm with my pointer finger as if pushing my words into him. "I'M. NOT. SICK. And I don't need YOUR help."

Neither of them reacted. I felt trapped in the back seat, like a child forced to go to the dentist.

"If this is why you came, you've wasted your time." I was close to screaming.

"Mitch called us. He's going to hospitalize you," my dad stated this as if reporting a weather forecast with 100 percent chance of rain.

My stomach dropped. *Mitch had never mentioned hospitalization to me. Why hadn't he talked to me about this? What other secrets was he keeping?* I refused to look at my parents; instead, I stared out the window as road signs and trees passed. A tingle spread through my entire body. *I bet he's taking me straight to a mental institute. They're in for a surprise if they think I'll go willingly.*

"So Mitch asked you to come?" I clenched my jaw.

"We came because we love you," my dad said.

"Well, I'm not going to the hospital." They needed to know I had a choice in the matter.

My dad changed the subject and filled the car with idle conversation that I chose to ignore. I rolled my window up and down just to break up his sentences before letting their fragments fly out the window.

My dad pulled the car into my driveway, and I relaxed. Well, at least he wasn't entirely out of his mind. *Maybe he remembered I have a church meeting later today?* Relieved, I hopped out of the car.

"Go pack. Mitch will be here soon, and then we're leaving for the hospital." My dad's voice tore through my reality. "I don't know why you look so shocked. Clearly, this is what I've been preparing you for the whole way home."

"I thought I changed your mind." I took in a big gulp of air. "I thought you were bringing me home to stay."

"To pack," he clarified.

I clenched my fists. "I'm not going," I said quietly, hoping it would make them take me seriously. "I'm an adult. You can't force me." My nose flared as my voice steadied.

"Wrong. I can get the police to take you. I can call 911 and have an ambulance take you. I can go in front of a judge and get the right to admit you, and they'll take you," he said. "Or you can go pack, get in the car, and we can take you. You pick."

"I choose none of the above."

I wasn't shocked my dad would corner me into doing what he wanted. The real shock was that Mitch had been a part of it. I could've never predicted he was capable of a forced hospitalization. Mitch pushed for me to "get help" and I refused thousands of times. I thought his most recent push for therapy dried up under my refusal. I couldn't believe Mitch had called my dad to help hospitalize me; though I wasn't surprised my dad rose to the occasion. For how unpredictable my dad could be, one thing remained constant: his love for saving the day, being the hero, rescuing the hurt.

My dad pulled a folder out of the car and raised it like his victory flag. "These documents have all the information to get you hospitalized." When my dad's mind was made up, he was the type to go one step further than his opponent. I never thought that opponent would be me. Even with my dad's folder of damning evidence, and my husband's testimonial, I knew I wasn't crazy.

"Sonja, the psychiatric hospital is happening." His words caused a rush of panic as they echoed in my ears. I snatched the folder from his hands, shuffled through the printed pages, and quickly glanced at the blur of words in front of me.

"Oh no you don't." My dad lunged for the folder. Papers fell to the ground. He scrambled to collect them off the ground as I grabbed a piece with Mitch's name on it. I quickly scanned the letter.

Dear Mitch,

Ever since I returned from visiting Sonja and the children in Baton Rouge last Friday night, I cannot get Sonja off my mind. She has seemed sad ever since your recent move. She seems physically and emotionally overwhelmed. We believe her call on the night of Oct. 11th was a desperate "cry for help." That was the night David called you. I have never seen him so concerned for both Sonja's emotional and physical well-being. David and I have worried that the stress Sonja has been experiencing might cause her to relapse into the tragic health situation she found herself in when she was in Houston. I, too, was scared after hearing her "pleas for help." That is why I made arrangements on such short notice to come visit her and the children.

I can't help but think back to how thrilled David and I were when Sonja visited this summer and expressed how well the entire family was doing in Albuquerque. I believe we would all agree that the move to Baton Rouge is the time when her present health challenges started. David and I keep asking why?

Mitch, most people, even if they never had health challenges, would be overwhelmed by Sonja's unstable circumstances. You are constantly moving your family for the next big promotion. You haven't been able to be there to help carry the burden. You have been gone a lot. She and your children live in a home of chaotic construction. Some of the major concerns we have are the following:

 - *Sonja feels burdened down with the challenges of your children's education.*
 - *Sonja demonstrates such a great love for her children and they remain her #1 concern.*
 - *The family is in a new city with no friends and no support system.*
 - *Sonja constantly has to worry about taking care of the children's needs as well as remodeling the house (we recognize Sonja participated in these decisions, but we do question the timing of those family choices).*

Mitch, Sonja needs your help right now. Our family is willing to assist where they can. As fragile as Sonja is, we find it difficult to believe it is the right thing to do to leave her there alone. We assume you are doing all you can to get permission to join your family as early as possible. PLEASE try to continue to work it out. If it is not possible for you to leave earlier, please let me know as soon as possible and let's discuss your thoughts on how we can provide the most support.

Mitch, Sonja is not aware I am writing you this letter. I'm sure she would be very upset if I asked her for permission. We recognize you, too, must be very concerned.

I hope you will receive this letter in the spirit I have written it as a mother who is very concerned about her daughter, whom she loves very dearly. I look forward to hearing from you.

Love, Omi

As I frantically read the words, I couldn't believe my mom had written it.

"She cares?" I whispered.

"Of course we care." My dad plucked the letter from my hands. I knew my dad cared—he was like me: loud with his feelings; he'd shout he loved me from rooftops. But my mom and I had a complicated relationship. A strained, throw-each-other-jabs type of dialogue that left little room for softer feelings. I looked at her still sitting in the car, trying to pretend most of this wasn't happening. Her need for blinders seemed life preserving with how tightly she kept them on.

"The rest are just notes Mitch wrote detailing your behavior." My dad huffed, tapping the stack back together. *My behavior?*

Just then, Mitch and the kids pulled up next to us. I shot Mitch a glance through the driver window. I hated him for being behind this.

"You've gathered notes on me?! Is this some sort of blackmail?" I yelled as he got out of the car.

Mitch tried to calm me. "Sonja, let's sit down and talk about this."

My mom must have known I wouldn't go easy. "C'mon, kids." She got out of the car and guided them inside the house.

"Are you *both* crazy?" I squared my shoulders, letting the fire in my eyes blaze into my dad and then Mitch. I pushed past them and stormed inside.

"You're going to the hospital," my dad repeated, following me. Mitch headed upstairs with my mom and the kids.

"No, I'm not!" I picked up a kitchen chair and threw it against the wood floor. "I'm not going! I'M NOT!" I screamed so loud my own ears hurt. I wanted to stay in control. It was my pain, and I was greedy. One by one, I threw all the chairs to the ground, each one hitting the floor with a louder bang than the one before. If he wanted a knock-down, drag-out fight, I was up for it. *Fight. Fight. Fight, Sonja!*

My dad didn't flinch. I left the room to hunt down my husband upstairs as my dad continued to follow behind me. I boldly walked up to Mitch. "If you hospitalize me, I will divorce you. It will be *over!*" My voice rang through the house.

It was nothing that he hadn't heard thousands of times before. Divorce was my constant threat. Why did he continue to stay? Did he know, deep down, how much I loved him? Wanted him? Needed him?

He looked me in the eyes, and for the first time in our marriage said, "That's a chance I'm willing to take."

My heart sank deep into my chest. I felt nauseous as tears rolled down my face. I was stuck. I couldn't move. *Wait! Wait, I love you!* But the words wouldn't come. This massive darkness, this burden had always been something we carried together. At times, it felt heavier than Mitch and I could manage, but we had always been a team.

Out of the corner of my eye, I saw my three children staring at me. They had heard everything. My children—my world. I had given every ounce of myself to them. I gave even when I had nothing to offer. Yet there I stood, taking away more of their innocence with every word I yelled. They stood courageously next to my mom, so composed, not one of them shedding a single tear. Rachael held her brothers' hands. Her eyes darted back and forth between me and Mitch. I knew my kids didn't have the luxury to express their own emotions when mine took up all the room in the house. But this time it wasn't my fault. I turned to my dad.

"You did this. You're the reason my family's falling apart."

"Would you just go to the emergency room and talk with a doctor?"

he asked. "Tell them everything, and if they say you can come home, then that will be good enough for us."

I looked back at my kids, and they cautiously met my gaze.

"If you get divorced, I'll live with Mom. Don't worry, Dad, I'll take care of her," Rachael said, determined to be a part of the solution.

"Well, I'm going with Dad," Alex said without a moment's hesitation.

Lincoln said nothing and broke free from the tight circle and ran to me.

"Mom!" he wailed, frantically wrapping his arms around my waist. "Don't go!"

"She needs to go, Lincoln," Rachael said. She walked over and wrapped her arms around Lincoln and me, joining the hug. "Don't worry, Mom. I know you're scared, but everything is going to be okay." It felt like she was the mother and I, her child.

"Really?" I held her tight, hoping to feel her belief.

Alex had moved to stand by Mitch, immoveable. Mitch was his lifeboat in our family's stormy sea. He relied on Mitch more than his brother or sister. He was a serious child. I don't know if he was born that way or created by the environment. I approached him and gently took his face in my hands.

"My little man," I said. Alex didn't move or make a single facial expression; he just gazed at me.

"It's going to be okay, buddy." Mitch said, putting his arm around Alex. Alex looked up at Mitch and stepped closer to him.

"No matter what, we will always be a family. Nothing will sever us," I said. I wouldn't let this hospitalization happen; I wouldn't let them take me away from my children. "You promise if the doctor says I can go home, all this talk about the hospital will stop?" I asked, my eyes never leaving my children's faces.

"I promise." My dad gathered me in his arms.

"But why don't you pack a bag, just in case?" my mom said.

I put a pair of tennis shoes and gray sweats into a bag, just to humor them. I changed into my church clothes, proving I would be in and out of the emergency room in time to attend my meeting, a meeting I would never make.

CHAPTER 3

Involuntarily Committed

The van stopped at the psychiatric hospital, and my thoughts were instantly interrupted.

"Time to get out," one of the guards called back through the bars. The van doors slid open and my heels clicked on the cement as we walked into a brick building. The guard on my right swiped his card and the doors swung open like jaws ready to swallow me whole. I stepped into the hallway, craning my neck back to watch the sunlight slip through a crack in the doors before they locked shut. I felt like I was entering a jail.

Near misses with prison were no stranger to my family: my grandfather almost killed a man, my dad had been indicted five times for securities fraud, and my cousin faked his own death after an elaborate counterfeiting spree. In my family, we have enough material to star in our own version of *Catch Me If You Can*. The problem is, we're no good at subtlety, and we never get away with it.

The guards escorted me into a waiting room where a round dark-haired man sat behind a desk. He motioned for me to surrender my bag. I handed over my bag and waited while his stubby fingers searched through it.

"Give me your necklace," he said, holding out his hand.

I couldn't help but laugh. "Why?"

"It has a string in it. You could harm yourself," he replied.

"Ridiculous," I said under my breath, taking off my pearl necklace and handing it to him.

I watched as he locked away my things and was taken to a white painted concrete room with two beds and a bathroom. Nothing else was in the room except me holding a folded stack of clean sheets and towels balanced against my chest. I felt so alone, and the sterile empty room intensified my sense of isolation. I wondered what Mitch was doing right then and if he was even worried about me. Had he known how horrible this place was before he sent me here? A tall woman in a lab coat entered the room.

"Sonja Wasden?" she read from her clipboard.

"Yes?" I answered, looking up.

"We're ready to start your examination." She took me to an office where a hospital gown lay across a bench. "Take everything off, including underwear, and put on the robe. I'll come back when you've changed."

"Why do I need to be examined?" My voice was quieter than I anticipated.

"I need to chart any bruises or cuts and make sure you're not hiding any drugs or weapons."

"There aren't any weapons or drugs on me. I don't need to take my clothes off to prove that."

She stopped in the doorway and sighed. "We can do this the hard way or the easy way. Your choice. I'll knock before coming in."

I looked at the light-blue robe draped over the bench. *Let's get this over with.* I quickly slipped out of my clothes and tied on the robe. My bare feet awkwardly clenched the cold floor as I waited.

The nurse returned and inspected *every* inch of my body. I felt violated and humiliated. I wondered what she would have done if I refused, but I felt too vulnerable to put up a fight.

Another nurse came into my room that night. She was the first person who smiled at me. She took my vitals then sat next to me.

"Tell me what's happened," she said. My tears seemed to have been waiting for this moment. I started crying and couldn't stop.

"I've been admitted against my will by my husband and father. I don't need to be here. I don't want to be here. I don't belong here," I said, wiping my running nose against my sleeve.

"It will be okay. Everything will become more clear. Take these— they're antipsychotics." She showed me two pills. One was pink, the other blue and white.

"But I'm not psychotic."

"The doctor ordered them. Trust us," she said, her voice full of warmth. "They'll make you sleepy, but your body will adjust." She dropped the pills into my palm, then filled a small paper cup with water. "Here."

I decided to trust her. I swallowed the pills and hoped she knew what she was medicating me with, but regardless, it was too late now. I curled up into a tight protective ball in the middle of the cold hospital bed terrified of what would happen next. I couldn't believe my husband thought I belonged in a mental institution. That didn't seem like something the man I met sixteen years ago would ever believe about me.

CHAPTER 4

Mitch

Mapleton, Utah, 1991

The first time we met, Mitch stood at my parents' front door holding a bundle of strings that led to a dozen colorful balloons. His family had just moved to Mapleton, and his little brother Jon was asking my younger sister Allyson to a high school dance. Mitch was both the chauffeur and delivery boy, as Jon lacked a license and the courage to deliver the balloons himself. His job was to quickly drop off the invitation while Jon waited in the car. Fate would have it that I was visiting my parents that day and answered the door.

"Hi!" I looked at the blond stranger with stone-blue eyes on my doorstep. He stared at me, a bit confused, as if trying to remember why he had come.

"Um…I'm Jon Wasden's delivery boy. He's asking Allyson to a school dance." He gestured to the balloons.

"Oh! How fun!" I laughed. "She's not here right now, but I'll give them to her." I took the balloons and started to shut the door.

"Wait. So who, exactly, are you?"

"Oh, sorry! I'm Sonja, Allyson's older sister."

"I'm Mitch, Jon's older brother."

"Your family just moved here from Texas, right?"

"Yeah, they did."

"So, are you in school?" I fearlessly looked into his eyes.

"I'm a sophomore at Utah Valley Community College, but I want to transfer to BYU," he answered.

"Oh my gosh, I'm a sophomore at BYU!"

"Would you recommend it?"

"Well, to be honest," I said, leaning against the doorframe, "I was forced to go there by my dad. I really wanted to go to Utah State. So can I really recommend a place I never wanted to be?"

He shrugged. "Good point."

"But I can recommend a class. Do you like poetry?"

"Actually, I do. Who's your favorite poet?" he asked.

"Easy. Robert Frost."

"Poem?"

"'The Road Not Taken.'"

"Why?"

"Our choices define our destinies. Your favorite poet?"

"Dylan Thomas."

"Poem?"

"'Do Not Go Gently into The Night.'"

"Why?"

"Death is inevitable, but we shouldn't give into it easily. We should fight for life."

"Agreed."

"Listening to him read his poetry is the only way it should be heard. I own many of his recordings."

"I do love his Welsh accent. Would you like to come in?" I asked.

Mitch looked back at the car and saw Jon reclined in the passenger seat.

"Sure," he said. Stepping inside, Mitch's eyes wandered up to the gold leaf on the ceiling and stained-glass windows. He looked awestruck.

"C'mon, I'll give you a tour." I laughed, finding his wide-eyed reaction amusing. I trotted up one side of the expansive staircase, my black hair swinging behind me. I didn't know why, but I felt completely at ease around Mitch, like we had known each other long before this moment.

He took one step onto the staircase and noticed the large chandelier above us. It was meant to be an attention grabber, with a sky-blue mural of bas-relief horses encircling it.

"Are you coming?" I stood at the top of the staircase, waiting for him.

"Yeah, I'm coming." He ran up to meet me.

I opened a glass door that had a detailed portrait of an Appaloosa stallion etched into its surface. "This is my dad's office."

Mitch looked around the dark wood paneling of the office and the bronze statues of horses and eagles on the shelves and tables. "Your dad must like horses."

"Oh, he loves them. He races Appaloosas." I pointed up a narrow staircase where racing trophies sat on the second story of the office.

I continued the tour through several bedrooms, living spaces, and the indoor swimming pool. I stopped for a moment to sit in our family's telephone booth. "And that's our racquetball court," I said, pointing at an opposing glass wall.

"As one has," Mitch replied with a casual, dry wit.

"You're funny." I smiled. "Come on. I want to show you something really cool." Mitch followed me into a closet as I motioned for him to enter. "I don't normally show people this room, so consider yourself lucky."

"Interesting…" He looked around at the coat hangers. "No offense, but this is one of the more underwhelming rooms of the house."

"Just wait." I slid my fingers around the wood-paneled walls, searching for something. "Ah, here it is." I grabbed a wire hanger and touched it to a metal bolt that secured a coat hook to the wall. *Buzzzzzzzzz.*

A soft vibration buzzed through the wall—and then a single click. I pushed open the wall. Mitch's jaw might as well have fallen to the floor.

"You're kidding," he said. "Don't tell me you have secret rooms, too." He ducked his head under the hangers clinking on the rack and stepped inside the secret room. Stacks of paintings leaned against the walls, and a giant floor safe sat at the back.

"What is all this?" Mitch looked around.

"My dad's art collection. My parents are patrons of the local art museum where a section of the museum was named after my mom: the Ingrid F. Nemelka Christmas Lamb Gallery."

"So what's in the safe? Must be pretty important to be in a secret room."

"I don't know exactly, but my grandpa has some silver bars in there."

"Silver bars?" Mitch said, raising his eyebrows. "I heard the story about your dad's business partner chainsawing his desk in half, and threatening to take everyone down with him if the deal went under."

"Yeah, my dad loves telling that story."

"Does your dad work for the mafia or something?"

"Is that what people in town are saying now?"

"Let's just say I've heard a lot of stories about the Nemelkas. But I've never heard of you."

"Well, now you have." I pointed to the safe. "It's my grandpa's silver. He turned his money into silver and buried it in his backyard. He doesn't trust banks. After my dad got a safe, he dug up the silver and brought it here."

"I think I need to meet your grandpa."

"Maybe one day," I said, stepping out of the closet.

We returned downstairs and sat on a couch in the living room. I asked him question after question, and Mitch happily answered each one. We lost track of time, talking like lifelong friends whose paths had finally crossed again. Thunder sounded from outside, shaking us out of the time warp we had so comfortably been living in.

"I should probably get going," Mitch said. "Jon's been waiting a while."

"Yeah." I stood and walked him to the door. "So, should I be expecting more deliveries from you?"

Mitch shrugged. "That all depends on how well their dance goes."

"Well, then, let's hope it goes well." I crossed my fingers and opened the front door. Warm rain fell onto the pavement outside as Mitch ran back to his car.

Even then, I knew the collision of meeting Mitch was significant; we were like two lightning bolts that finally agreed on a place to strike. I had just met someone who was going to mean something to me. I only hoped I wouldn't have to wait on a storm for us to meet again.

—m—

The phone in my apartment rang interrupting my girl talk with my roommate, Sophie. Sophie popped up from her bed to answer it. She held the phone to her chest. "Sonja, it's for you."

I took the phone. "This is Sonja."

"Hi. It's Mitch." The voice barely came through with all the noise in the background.

"Where are you?" I covered one end of the phone. "It's Mitch," I whispered to her.

"What? The guy you met like six months ago?" Sophie blurted out. I put my finger to my mouth. "Sorry," she whispered.

"I'm at a gas station," he answered over the commotion. I thought maybe his car had broken down.

"Oh, do you need a ride?" I asked.

"No, no. I've been trying to call you for three days. I just pulled over at a gas station pay phone and thought I'd try one last time."

"After six months you call now?"

"You're not someone that's easy to forget."

I smiled to myself. "Our phone has been broken, but it just got fixed." I twisted the phone cord around my wrist.

"I was wondering if you might want to go out with me next weekend. I was thinking maybe Saturday."

"Yes! I'd love to. What are we doing?"

"It's a surprise. I'll pick you up Saturday at six."

I hung up the phone and turned to Sophie. "Mitch just asked me on a date!" As I said the words, my heartbeat caught up with the excitement.

—⁓—

Saturday night at six o'clock, Mitch stood on my doorstep with the same big smile that took my breath away the first time we met.

"You ready?" he asked with his hands behind his back.

"Yes!" I grabbed my coat and closed the door. He backed up, hiding something behind his plaid shirt. "What are you holding?" I peered around him.

"I'm holding in my hands the best date you've ever had." He excitedly revealed two balsa wood airplanes, the kind that cost $1.50 at a toy store and you assemble yourself. Mitch smiled as we walked toward one of the open fields on campus. "Have you ever flown one of these?" he asked, handing me an airplane.

"I can't say that I have." My fingers raced along the smooth wood.

He gave a devilish grin. "Good, then that means I'm going to win."

I rolled my eyes. "We'll see."

Mitch's plane glided past trees, and mine was never far behind. After a few throws and running after the fallen planes, we sat next to each other on the grass a bit out of breath from laughing and running. Spending time with him felt like being with a best friend. I was surprised a first date could feel so comfortable. He placed his hand over mine.

"My dream is complete freedom. I don't want to be tied down by stuff. I want to be able to fit everything I own into my car so I can go anywhere I want," he said.

"Ah, complete freedom. Sign me up!" I said, leaning back on my hands. "On second thought, I think I like my clothes too much to stuff them in a trunk."

Mitch laughed.

"So tell me, what career do you see for yourself?" I asked.

Mitch twirled a blade of grass between his fingers and looked at me. "That's easy. I want to be a history professor."

"I think you'd be good at that." I put my head on his shoulder. We talked for hours, and no topics felt off-limits. By the end of the night, I knew I had found my person. He walked me to the door, and I put my key into the lock.

"Thanks for the date. I had a lot of fun with you," I said.

"Yeah, I get that a lot. All the girls like me. I'm kind of a catch." He shrugged.

His comment caught me off guard. I wasn't sure if he was arrogant and I should be concerned or if he was joking. I just laughed and shook my head.

"I had a great time with you, too," he said and kissed my cheek.

—⟋⟍—

After dating for several weeks, I invited Mitch over to meet my dad. Mitch sat in a deep chair next to our fireplace with hearts chiseled into the stone and wood mantle. The interrogation was about to begin, and I was excited to see how Mitch would do. This family ritual felt so natural to me that I had not even thought to warn him.

I was the fifth child and had already seen my older siblings' dates interrogated. I suspect these simple background checks were my dad's way of preventing poverty, abuse, and potential alcoholics into our family. He had high standards. My siblings married people with impressive accomplishments. My older sister married a man who was number one at his law school. My older brother married Miss Georgia Teen and attended Wharton's MBA Program; my oldest brother had also attended Wharton's MBA program and married our doctor's daughter.

"Where did you grow up?" my dad asked.

"Solvang, California," Mitch replied.

"Do you like Utah?"

"I love it. Growing up, I spent every summer in Scipio working on my grandparents' farm."

"Excellent. Hard work is critical to success." My dad folded his newspaper over his knee. "Do you hunt?"

"No. My brother once took me to shoot jackrabbits, but it didn't take. I usually tried to miss; I just felt bad for them," Mitch admitted. Mitch didn't have to be Sherlock Holmes to know his answer wasn't earning him any style points. Animal heads hung on the walls in the living room and inside the garage. Pheasant, buffalo, king salmon, deer, elk, and various other pelts on display. My brothers weren't casual hunters. Many of their kills were from exotic hunts in Alaska, Africa, and Mongolia.

"And what does your dad do?" my dad asked, leaning back in his chair.

"He was a dentist, but he's retired now."

"Wow. How old was he when he retired?"

"I think forty-two?"

"How does a dentist retire so young? He must've had money somewhere else."

I knew my dad would be impressed that Mitch's parents retired so young. I sat closer to the center of the room to be closer to the interview.

"My parents made some money selling land in California, and we lived on a budget."

"Good. Good. Now, how would you describe your parents?"

"They're hardworking people who value their family and their faith, and most importantly, they love Sonja." He made sure to emphasize this last point.

My dad nodded. "What's your birth order?"

"Fifth."

"Ah, just like Sonja. Tell me your career plan. In detail." My dad crossed his legs.

"After I graduate from college, I want to go to graduate school. I'm thinking about being a history professor."

"What's your GPA?"

"I have a 3.2 GPA, which is honestly a huge improvement from high school," he answered.

There was a pause. I wished Mitch fudged the numbers a little.

"Any extracurricular activities, clubs, or something to save the résumé?"

"My senior year, I tried out for school plays. I won an acting award as one of Texas's best high school actors."

"I don't advise using high school accomplishments on a graduate school application. Doesn't look good. How far have you gone sexually with a girl?"

"Um." Mitch glanced over at me.

I smiled at him encouragingly.

"Um, I've made out."

"And that's it?" My dad raised his eyebrow skeptically. "Removed any clothing?"

"No." Mitch said quickly.

My dad's aim was to leave no stone unturned and make sure he knew exactly what his daughter was getting herself into, and I was glad of it. If my dad was asking the hard questions; it meant I didn't have to.

My dad waited a bit then asked, "What'd you get on the ACT?"

"I never took it."

"But you're going to BYU?"

"I didn't need to take it. I transferred from a community college."

An air of disappointment seemed to settle in. Community colleges were a definite no, but I thought since he had transferred to a four-year college, my dad would let it pass.

"Do you like sports?" My dad changed the topic.

"I watch a little college football."

The conversation continued for hours, Mitch answering each question to the best of his ability, before finally, he leaned forward and announced, "I need to head home to study, but thanks for having me over. It was nice meeting you." I checked the clock. Five hours. That was an acceptable interrogation time—not the shortest, not the longest. I looked to my dad as I stood up to follow Mitch out. He gave me a thumbs-up and I smiled.

"Well, what'd you think?" I asked, walking with Mitch to his car.

"I think your dad questions your choice in men." He managed a smile.

"My dad said you passed!"

"If you say so."

"Well, he did. But my choice is all that matters anyway." I kissed him.

—◆—

On a winter afternoon, six weeks after our wood airplane date, Mitch drove us up Provo Canyon to Aspen Grove. We were listening to "Your Song" by Elton John as snow gently fell. One hand on the steering wheel, the other in mine, Mitch looked over at me.

"I can't imagine life without you," he said. "I've never felt this way about anyone I've dated. All the stupid, clichéd things people say about love really do feel true." He parked the car in the unplowed parking lot. The wind whistled outside as he stroked his thumb across the back of my hand. "I don't see this ending."

There was silence as I reflected on what he just said. I kept my gaze on his hand clasped around mine. "Me either," I replied.

When we were together, I felt the same peace and warmth I felt in those rare moments when I was entirely centered. Watching the sunrise through the mountains—when the reds and oranges swelled in the sky, and the quaking aspen trees reminded me how simple and good life could be. With Mitch, it was the same. He was my personal, constant alpenglow, and I wanted to feel this way forever. He had brushed a breeze through my life that made me feel alive and secure.

He looked at me. "So, you think we're going to get married?"

"Yes." I laughed.

He grabbed my small, cold hands. "If I've only been sure about one thing in my whole life, it's that I want to marry you," he said.

I beamed as white flurries danced behind him. All I could think was, *I'm going to be his wife.*

CHAPTER 5

Psych Ward, Day One

"Breakfast is ready," a nurse called into my room.

I opened my eyes to the room's bare white ceiling. *Ugh, it wasn't a dream.* The people here were part of a group I didn't want to belong to. I wanted to stay in my room all day so I didn't have to join the group out there, but I knew it wouldn't be long before another nurse noticed I hadn't left. Still, I lay on my back, letting the minutes slowly roll by.

"Sonja, come out for breakfast." The nurse came back to my doorway, hand on her hip.

"I'm not hungry," I lied.

"I'm not leaving until you come out. You have to eat with your medication." The firmness in her voice told me I wasn't the first patient to refuse her that day. I got out of bed and stopped at the doorframe. "Come on," she insisted, walking ahead of me. She looked back several times making sure I was following. "Breakfast is right over there." She pointed to a metal cart with food on it. I entered the main living area and stayed a few feet behind the last person in line. The room was quieter than I expected. The tables were filled with people of all ages eating and mostly keeping to themselves. *How many of them were admitted by mistake, like me?* I stepped forward in line and scanned the food options. Nothing looked safe except the oatmeal. I got a bowl, passing bruised fruits and hard donuts on my way out of line.

I looked for an empty seat and quickly realized there were few. I sat beside a blonde girl playing with a deck of cards.

"Hi," I said.

She turned her head to glance at me. The other half of her hair was pink. She went back to her cards. I took a bite of oatmeal and scooted to the edge of my chair in the other direction.

Diagonally from me sat a gray-haired man, chanting, "The man in the mirror is a handsome man. The man in the mirror is me." He hunched over a piece of paper and vigorously wrote the words as he spoke louder and louder. "The man in the mirror is a handsome man. The man in the mirror is me. The man in the mirror is a handsome man! The man in the mirror is me!" He caught me staring and paused.

I smiled at him. He looked down and returned to his writing and repetitious chanting. *I'll try sitting at a different table tomorrow.*

"Line up for meds!" the nurse yelled.

People shuffled into the conference room like soldiers gathering shoulder to shoulder before their general. I squeezed into line and watched the people in front of me. The nurse handed each of us a small paper cup with pills inside; we obediently swallowed and opened our mouths for the nurse to look inside. My cup had the same pills from the night before. Antipsychotics meant nothing to me at the time, but later they would mean everything to me. They would both torture me and save my life.

I went to my room and felt a brand of sleepiness I had never experienced before. It slowly took control of my whole body as I slipped unconscious. The next thing I knew, I was woken and escorted to the conference room again.

A man walked in and sat in a chair next to me. "I'm Dr. Barry. I'll be your psychiatrist while you're here."

"What time is it?"

"Three o'clock."

"I've slept all day?"

"Yes. That's one of the medicine's side effects. Your body will adjust," he said. "So, you're renovating a house." He raised his eyebrows. "That's ambitious."

"That's why I'm so stressed. Most of the flooring has been ripped out, and we have to tiptoe up the stairs so we don't step on the nails sticking through the wood. Also, we eat off cardboard boxes that haven't been opened yet and live in a constant cloud of sawdust."

"And you're homeschooling your kids?" Dr. Barry commented, looking through my file.

"Yes, because the public schools are pretty rough here in Louisiana. I thought enrolling them in magnet schools would be better, but boy, was I wrong." I slid my hands down my lap. "When we got to my sons' school, I thought I took a wrong turn. The school was right next to boarded-up houses and people sitting on their porches selling drugs. And at my daughter's school, we witnessed a student pushed up against his locker getting handcuffed. The armed guards patrolling the hallways weren't exactly a comfort."

"Why aren't your kids in private school? Your husband is vice president of a hospital."

"By the time we moved here, they were full. Right now, we're on a waiting list. I feel *tremendous* pressure to educate my kids, so they can compete in college."

"I'm sure you and your husband will figure it out," he said. His eyes briefly scanned the last parts of my file. "Let's talk about why you're here."

"I'm sure it's all in your notes."

He closed the folder and looked at me. "Do you want to die?"

"Yeah, I do, like most people."

"So you believe the majority of people are suicidal then."

"It's just part of life. I've recently thought it might be nice to fly to an orphanage in a remote part of Africa to help take care of the kids and drink some of the water there. I might get dysentery or a mosquito bite that gives me malaria and die. God couldn't judge me for that."

"You realize that's the reason you're here? Because you're suicidal."

"I don't belong here."

"No one belongs here. This place is just a pit stop." He looked at me and smiled. "The only permanent residents are the doctors, so I'm the only person who *belongs* here."

"I don't need a 'pit stop.' I'm stressed, but I'm not crazy."

Dr. Barry paused and propped his chin onto his palm. "You know, Sonja, I've read your file a few times, and I can't help but think you must know you're sick."

I sat up. "Excuse me?"

"I've been doing this a long time, and most untreated people with a mental illness believe life is brutal and hell for everyone, even though it's not. Have you ever felt that?"

"I know life *is* hell for everyone. Is this a trick question?" I looked at him. "And to be clear, I'm nothing like the rest of the patients here. And you shouldn't assume I am."

Dr. Barry glanced at his pad and wrote a few notes. "I think we're done for today." He got up and left the conference room, and I sat terrified.

On my way back to my room, a man came out of his room with a packed duffel over his shoulder. He stopped and introduced himself.

"Hey, newbie, I'm Doug."

"I'm Sonja. Are you leaving?" I looked at his bag.

He smiled. "Yeah, I've only been here two days."

My eyes widened. "You're leaving after two days?"

"Yeah, I was taking care of my sick father and got depressed so I checked myself into this place."

"I want to get out of here ASAP," I said.

"Don't worry. You'll be one of those who gets out real quick, I can tell."

"I hope you're right."

"The only warning I have for you is *Janet*. She's one of the counselors here, and she's a real bitch. Pray you don't get her. Trust me, two days tops!" He slapped me on my back.

I continued down the hallway, feeling more hopeful. *I can survive two days,* I thought. The problem was the doctors wouldn't be evaluating how I appeared on the outside like Doug had. They would go much deeper, looking inside of me, digging around where they were not wanted.

"Your roommate just arrived," a nurse said, stepping out of my room.

"Oh," was all my nerves allowed me to reply. I opened the door and saw a short slim woman folding T-shirts on the spare bed. "Hi, I'm Sonja."

She dropped the shirt in her hands and turned around. "Oh, hi! I'm Sydney!" Her crystal-blue eyes shined back at me. She stood calm and self-assured.

We didn't shake hands; we only smiled. There was a knock at the door.

"It's time for introductions in the conference room," the nurse informed us. Sydney and I walked out into the room where fifteen people sat in a circle on the floor.

"We're all going to introduce ourselves and say what brought us here." The nurse signaled for the man next to her to start.

"M-m-my n-n-name is Brent." He paused. "I-I-I'm here because of schizophrenia."

A woman in her sixties fidgeted in her seat. "I struggle with suicidal feelings and drugs. I shot my son-in-law with a rifle because he cheated on my daughter. Luckily, he survived. I was high as a kite when it happened."

Next, it was Sydney's turn. I wondered what had brought her here.

"I'm Sydney, and I'm here because I attempted suicide."

Wow, she attempted it. I had contemplated, even fantasized about suicide millions of times, but never tried it. Before I could process her answer, the room grew quiet, and the nurse leading the discussion stopped her notetaking and looked up at me.

"Oh, sorry. I'm Sonja, and I'm here because of stress."

The nurse scribbled more notes, and the next person continued. Depression, drugs, schizophrenia, attempted suicide, bipolar disorder, and electric shock treatment were just a few of the reasons mentioned. At the end, everyone stood and held hands for a prayer I had never heard but will never forget.

God grant me the serenity
to accept the things I cannot change,
the courage to change the things I can,
and the wisdom to know the difference.

—⁓—

That night, Sydney and I brushed our teeth in the shared bathroom and climbed into our beds. We had gone through most of that day without talking to each other.

"What did you do before you came here?" I asked in the dark room.

"I'm an elementary school teacher. What about you?" She asked.

"I'm a mom. I have three kids."

"I don't have kids. Is it nice?"

"Yeah." For a moment it felt like we were two lonely girls at a summer camp, but something in the air of this place made even small moments feel heavy.

I turned over on my side as the meds forced my eyes closed. My heart burned from missing my kids. I could've never predicted my life path would include being committed to a psychiatric hospital. Life had been slowly diminishing my naiveté and youthful innocence, and I wondered if I was losing the ability to see the sparkle life once offered me. I silently cried myself to sleep as I reflected on the poor choices Mitch and I had made and the poor choices that life made for us.

CHAPTER 6

Growing Pains

1992-1996

We rented a bedroom in a seventy-year-old man's house for the duration of Mitch's summer internship in Washington, D.C. Mitch worked in the National Archives abstracting CW veterans' pension records to find out why some lived longer than others. He looked at income, stress, nutrition, and battle injuries. It introduced him to epidemiology, the study of disease in populations. The study was headed by Dr. Robert Fogel, an economic historian from the University of Chicago who had won the Nobel Prize in Economics that year.

"What are you getting ready for?" Mitch asked.

"Just life. I like achieving a certain look each day. Fashion is one of my favorite things. Anyone who really knows me could tell you that." I looked back at him as I continued fixing my hairstyle to complement my outfit.

He hugged me from behind. "I'm learning all the secrets you failed to divulge in courtship."

I laughed, draping my wrists behind his neck. "You look too good to belong in this run-down room. Like a China doll in a pawn shop."

Many people told us how hard the first year of marriage could be, but ours felt light. I knew we were one of those nauseatingly chummy couples that didn't fight and were too affectionate in public, but I loved it. We learned how to work together, how to anticipate each other's needs, and how to just be us. During this internship, Mitch realized he was more interested in the public health aspects of the study than the history aspects, so he decided to pursue healthcare administration.

After the internship, we returned to BYU to continue our studies— Mitch in history and me in humanities. He started studying for the GMAT to apply for graduate school, and I wasted no time signing him up for a test-prep course with Kaplan.

"Look what I bought you!" I said holding a fishbowl full of fish from the pet store.

"What in the world?" He looked up from the glossy-papered Kaplan book confused.

He hadn't asked for a pet, but I knew some company would help him during the long stretches of studying. Water sloshed from side to side as I made my way over to him. I set the fishbowl on the table, and Mitch moved his textbook a few inches to avoid a small splash of water.

"What's this for?" He looked into the bowl of swimming goldfish.

"Study buddies," I proudly said. "You have so much studying ahead of you, with the GMAT and keeping your grades up, so I wanted to give you reinforcements." I tapped the glass, and fish scales flashed metallic shades of orange. "These little guys will be here with you for every minute of your studying. You won't ever have to do it alone."

"I love them. They look like a hardy crew." He smiled at the fish.

"The hardiest." I kissed him.

"I applied to over fifteen graduate schools. Even the top five, but I doubt I'll get in,"

"Of course you can! Don't say that. The top five are all real possibilities." I scolded his disbelief.

After waiting to hear back for months, he realized I was right when he checked our mailbox.

"I got invited to interview with the University of Michigan. They're the number one school in healthcare administration!" he yelled, holding his letter.

"Of course you did," I nodded.

"Wait. How will we afford the airfare to get me there?" He dropped the letter on the counter.

"You could take the train," I suggested.

He sat. "That would take days."

"That's okay." I shrugged. "Whatever gets you there. You've worked too hard to let travel arrangements stop you."

That night, we bought him a ticket from Provo to Ann Arbor and spent the night visualizing how the interview would go. Before bed, I saw Mitch look at his fish tank on the table and smile. "We did it," he whispered.

After his interview, the school told him they wanted students who'd take their time at the school seriously and that they liked both his résumé and his tenacity, which he demonstrated by spending days on a train just for the interview. His acceptance letter to University of Michigan came several weeks later.

"I knew they'd love you," I said.

"That's because you're a woman who believes things into existence." He kissed me.

Five months later and six months pregnant, we packed up our little lives and moved to Ann Arbor for Mitch's master's in healthcare administration. "Welcome to Michigan!" Mitch cheered as we sped past the state sign. Sitting in our un-air-conditioned-U-Haul, I leaned forward on my lap as another wave of nausea hit me.

"Yay," I moaned, my face between my knees.

"How are we holding up?" Mitch rubbed my back.

"We? Who is we? *I* am not great."

As we drove closer to our new apartment—and farther from my childhood home—the more I shrank. This would be the first time I had ever lived more than twenty minutes away from my parents, and on top of all that, I was going to be a mom. Those facts sank in deep, making me feel weighed down, but not grounded. Like my life was a large mess I was too weak to organize and put away. We planned on living off credit cards until we could get established, so part-time jobs and student loans would have to get us through the next two years. I felt unstable financially, emotionally, and physically. I held my breath as larger-than-life tidal waves were curling above me. Mitch seemed untouched. The excitement around our new life rang clear and true for him, like it had the day the acceptance letter came.

"We're in our new neighborhooooood," Mitch excitedly sang.

I looked over the dashboard and saw children playing on a playground surrounded by cookie-cutter on-campus housing. Each home's slight variations and close spacing had clearly been designed to get the most out of the dough.

Mitch and I sat on the floor in our new apartment among the cardboard boxes in silence as I cried.

"Are you hungry?" he asked.

"We don't have any food." I sniffed, tiredly leaning my face on top of my knees.

He patted my back. "Let's go to Denny's and get something." He grabbed the keys and put on his shoes before I could oppose. I felt comforted we had a resolute plan, even if it was just for dinner.

We sat at a table in Denny's waiting for our waitress. "Can you order for me?" I asked Mitch. "I need to call my dad real quick."

"Sure. Don't take too long."

I could talk with my dad for hours. He had a way of knowing what to say when I felt lost. He understood me in ways no one else in my family did. My dad was one of the rare people who understood the radio frequency I was tuned into. He heard it, too. It was like there was thick radio static clouding my inner dialogue, making me work extra hard to hear common sense. I often felt confused and yearned for a concrete sense of clarity. When I listened to other people talk, it seemed they had a clear sense of their reality; their radios were dialed in and playing the news without interruption. Their news could be upsetting or cut in and out occasionally, but it wasn't set on a station that was halfway in, halfway out. For me, reality was close enough to hear but far enough away to question what it was saying. Feeling understood and accepted by my dad was the foundation of our close relationship.

I dialed our home number from a pay phone. I didn't have enough pocket change, so I called collect. I gripped the black handle as it rang, waiting for someone to accept the charges.

"Hello?" My mom's voice echoed into the phone.

"Mom!" I perked up. I could hear familiar background noises of my mom cooking, and it added to the homesickness. "Is Dad home?" I asked.

"No, but did you make it to Michigan already?"

I planned on being strong and letting my mom know we got here safely, and everything was fine. I didn't feel comfortable opening up to her, but I broke hearing her voice.

"Mom," I sobbed. I wanted to be back in my old life. It was better than this. As a kid, I dreamed of getting married and having a family, but now I wanted to take it all back. As an adult, I dreamed of being a kid again.

"Sonja, what's wrong?"

"I want to be a sixteen-year-old again. Sleeping in my room with nothing to worry about except my weekend plans and—"

"You'll be fine, Sonja," my mom cut in.

"I'm scared. I'm scared to be a mom. We have no health insurance, no jobs, no money," I cried.

"Sonja, life is hard for everyone. You're not the only one. You want to know what's hard? Having a child die. Or my neighbor just lost her husband to a brain tumor. That's hard, Sonja. Oh no! My chicken on the stove is burning. I've got to go, but give me your number once your phone is hooked up. Love you." The call ended.

As usual, no time for tears. She would not sympathize. When she did, it was more to pacify me. As a teenager, when I complained about homework or having a fight with a friend, my mom told me life would get easier once I was married and a mom. Even in my twenties, I believed her, which was part of the reason my situation felt unbearable. Where was my happily ever after? Marriage and having a baby weren't solving my problems. What did I do wrong?

I held the phone and rested my forehead against the plastic. In some areas, I was tougher than most people; in others, I was weaker. My "real life" was waiting for me to live in it, but I was unprepared. I needed to get it together. I returned to Mitch, my eyes red. He wrapped me in his arms.

"I don't think I can do this," I said.

"Sonja, of course you can. I married Superwoman." I leaned into Mitch's chest and teared up again. "We can do this." He pressed his lips against my forehead. "We should probably start job searching, so we can get health insurance." He looked at me gently, hoping the statement wouldn't upset me.

"We qualify for government help," I pointed out.

"Welfare is for people that literally have no options. We still have options."

"We're broke, with a baby on the way, and I haven't even seen a doctor yet. What if there's something wrong with our baby?"

"Government help is out of the question." Mitch grew up in a family who believed taking any type of government help went against their morals.

"Mitch, even with jobs, we still qualify for government programs. I'm a humanities major. There aren't many jobs in my field with health benefits. We can't afford to have this baby."

"I know it's scary. Can we at least try?"

In the following days, Mitch and I applied for as many jobs as we could find. Mitch got a job at a warehouse, loading trucks for Kmart. It was part time with no benefits and didn't pay nearly enough. I saw an opening for a part-time phlebotomist with hours from 5 a.m. to 9 a.m. that offered full health insurance benefits. If I got this job, we'd have health insurance and Mitch could watch our baby while I worked. Determined to find out who oversaw the phlebotomy department and secure the job, I took a bus to the University of Michigan.

Two big obstacles waited for me: I had no experience as a phlebotomist, and I was terrified of needles. My stomach clenched at the thought of ever putting one into a human. Our desperate need for health insurance and to see a doctor for my unborn baby drove me forward. My baby would be here in less than three months. I feared something could be wrong and it would be all my fault.

The hospital felt like navigating terminals in a major airport. I finally found the phlebotomy department and walked into a room with plastic-wrapped needles and empty vials resting on metal trays. I took a big breath and turned to the only staff member in the room.

"Is the person in charge of the phlebotomy department here?" I asked.

"She just left, but she'll be back. I can't promise when, though. I can take a message for her?"

I glanced at a counter where tubes of blood were lying, waiting to be sent to the lab. I felt faint and took a deep breath. I hated the sight of blood.

"No, it's okay. I'll wait."

I sat in one of the blue plastic chairs feeling entirely out of my element. I turned my back to the needles and vials, deciding that staring at the bare wall was a better option. *How am I going to get this job? I studied art. I have no medical background. And if I do get the job, how am I going to do it without fainting?* I rested my hands on my pregnant stomach and let out another big breath. Just the thought of drawing someone's blood made me sick. I waited for three hours before a woman walked into the lab.

"That's her," the staffer informed me.

I quickly stood. "You must be the head of the phlebotomy department!" I reached for the woman's hand.

"Yes, I am." She looked at me, a bit perplexed, but accepted my firm handshake.

"I'm Sonja Wasden, and I need to work here. I don't have any experience, but I will get any certificate or training I need to become a phlebotomist!" She widened her eyes and stepped back a bit; my enthusiasm seemed to take her by surprise.

"Normally we don't hire people who haven't been trained, but on very rare occasions we've trained our staff."

I grabbed hold of my sliver of a chance. "I'll do whatever it takes to be part of that rare few. I'm a hundred percent committed."

"Have you filled out an application?"

"Yes, I have." I nodded.

"I'll look over your application and get back to you in two weeks."

I left hoping I had made a good impression on her, since my application wasn't going to set me apart in the least. But I did get a call back for an interview for a waitress position at Olive Garden.

"What days would you be available to work?" the manager asked me, tapping his pen.

"All the days!" I eagerly responded. "Except Sundays. I can't work Sundays because of my religion, but I promise I'll work hard."

The manager paused and rubbed his chin. "Usually new staff without seniority pick up holidays and weekends. But you seem like you'd be good with customers, so I'll take a chance on you."

"Thank you so much. You won't be sorry!" I shook his hand vigorously.

My first day of waitressing, I tied my brown apron over my very pregnant stomach and started waiting on customers. That day, four tables asked about the alcoholic drinks. Since I didn't grow up around alcohol, I didn't know any beer or wine names. I had never even tasted alcohol. I stared at customers, bewildered each time I took down a drink order.

My manager finally pulled me aside a few hours into my first shift. "Jeez, who doesn't know what a Heineken or Bloody Mary is? Where have you been hiding…under a rock? Go home and memorize these!" He handed me the Olive Garden drink menu.

Despite my swollen ankles and lack of knowledge about alcohol, working at Olive Garden was a great way to keep my mind distracted. I was still waiting to hear back from the hospital about the phlebotomist job. Back home, I sat on our couch, quizzing myself on specialty beers.

"Stella Artois, Corona, Heineken."

"What are you doing?" Mitch laughed, picking up one of my flash cards.

"Trying to keep my job." I flipped over the next card. "Peroni."

"Let me help you." He took the stack of cards and quizzed me. "All right, there are six specialty beers, and three of them are in green bottles. Which three?"

"I don't know, Stella Artois?"

"Yep, that's one." He waited for the next two while holding the flash card up to his nose.

I shrugged. I had no idea.

"Okay, let's try a memorization trick. Green is the color of aliens, and the last two beers have foreign names."

"Heineken and Peroni?"

Mitch nodded. He quizzed me on margaritas, wines, and cocktails, and by the end of the night, I felt like a pro. Because of my drink knowledge, I kept my job at Olive Garden, which meant my new after-work routine consisted of Mitch and me sitting on the living room floor counting my tips.

One afternoon, while we sat with bowls of cereal in our laps, stacking quarters and dollar bills in separate piles, the phone rang. Mitch got up to answer it.

"Hello? Yes, she's here." Mitch handed me the phone. "It's the hospital!" he whispered.

I stood in shock as the department manager on the line gave me the best news ever.

"Thank you! Thank you so much! I'll be there!" I hung up the phone and jumped in Mitch's lap, knocking over a pile of quarters. "I got the job!" I screamed.

It felt like we had won the lottery.

I showed up in a white lab coat for my first day, and to my surprise, got to practice on a fake arm. *Thank God.* Every day, the needles and equipment got less frightening. After five weeks, my trainer informed me I needed to practice on a coworker. Joe volunteered. He sat in the chair, and I tied the tourniquet around his upper arm. I felt for a good vein, tore open an alcohol swab and uncapped a needle. My hands were shaking as I hovered the needle over his bulging vein.

"Any moment now, Sonja. My arm is getting a little numb," Joe said.

"I need a minute." I set down the needle and took off the tourniquet.

"You can do this." My trainer patted my back. *Just turn your brain off and do it,* I thought. I retied the tourniquet, picked the needle back up, and felt for a vein. "Stop. You need to open a new needle since you set that one on the counter," she reminded me.

"It's okay, Sonja. Even if you miss, just go for it," Joe encouraged.

I uncapped a new needle, felt for a vein, swabbed his arm with the alcohol, and stuck the needle into his arm.

"I did it!" I was half relieved and half panicked. I looked down at my hand holding the needle in his arm. Horrified, I quickly pulled it out. Blood sprayed out of Joe's arm. He ripped off the tourniquet and grabbed a handful of gauze.

"What happened?" my trainer yelled. I looked at the bloody needle in my shaking hand and set it down. My chest collapsed.

"She left the tourniquet on." Joe laughed, wiping up his arm, the table, and the tray next to him.

"I'm so sorry." My voice shook.

"You need more practice," my trainer stated.

"Am I fired?"

"No. We'll send you to the outpatient area to learn how to draw blood on healthy people. You aren't ready to work with sick people."

She was right. I needed more training, but I was not going down as a quitter. I came home that night totally unprepared for what was going to happen next.

"I quit my job," Mitch said.

"Why?" I could barely get any words out.

"I just can't do it anymore. It's terrible!"

"Mitch, we really need the money. Can't you stick it out a little longer?"

"Now that you're waitressing and got the phlebotomy job, we'll be able to figure it out."

I felt used. Mitch watched me ice my swollen ankles after work each day and knew how scared I was drawing people's blood. *Why does he get a free pass?* He was the one not letting me get government help, yet he was the one that got to quit his job.

"So what will you do all day?" I asked.

"I'll study and prepare for the fall semester to start."

"*Okay,*" I sighed, and my shoulders slumped. Mitch didn't seem to notice my defeat. I felt dismissed but didn't say so to him. I knew how to fight my way toward success, but I didn't know how to be my own advocate.

While Mitch prepared for fall classes, I learned to tolerate needles and become a good phlebotomist. Eventually, I could draw blood on even the most difficult patients. One man dying from cancer had hard veins from chemotherapy. He told me if he had a bag of gold coins, he would give them to me because, unlike other phlebotomists, I only had to poke him once. The triumph of overcoming my fear of blood and needles got tucked deep away in my heart. At the time, I didn't know I would face fears of a far greater magnitude. Yet this small victory was evidence: even when desperate, I could do hard things.

I stood balancing Rachael—now over a year old—on my hip, six months pregnant with our second child. Tears streamed down my face as an older gentleman looked over our only car, a red Chevy Nova. "This car will be perfect for my son." The man beamed.

We had run out of money, and our credit cards were maxed out. Mitch was about to graduate and had a fellowship lined up with Lovelace Hospital in Albuquerque, New Mexico. We had no idea how to get to Albuquerque from Michigan or how he would commute to work, but we were out of options. Mitch had too much pride to ask his parents for help. They believed in doing things for yourself. My parents lived in a multimillion-dollar home, which was mortgaged to the hilt. With my dad, it was always feast or famine; unfortunately for us, it was a famine time in his life. It also didn't help that my dad was going through a multiyear lawsuit with the federal government, charged with thirty-four counts of mail fraud and money laundering. My dad would call us regularly to remind us of the financial drain of the lawsuit and the high cost to upkeep their home and Appaloosa ranch. It didn't matter how many times he was indicted, I believed my dad was on the right side of the law.

"Your dad called me. He wants us to take out credit cards and send him the money!" Mitch panicked. The proposed solution was to have each family member take out credit cards in their name and send as much cash as possible to him.

"Don't worry, we're not doing that." I tried pushing his worry away.

"Sonja, aren't you worried about him? With the lawsuits and his spending habits?"

"That's just dad. Don't worry about it. He always comes through." My dad constantly teetered on the edge of insolvency—spending money before he had it. It was as though the tension of being broke gave him meaning to make the next deal. The thrill of the next battle to be waged defined his existence. I could still hear his King Kong routine when I visited—something he did for as long as I could remember. When he woke up, he'd pound on his chest and give a gorilla-like call, letting the world know he was coming. Living on the edge was the only place he felt at home.

"You know your dad isn't completely innocent."

"Don't say that! Yes, he is." I bit back. "The government has been after him for years!"

"My point exactly."

"Stop! My dad said he is innocent. I believe him."

"Sonja, come on. You don't believe there's even an ounce of truth in the charges?"

"Not an ounce. My dad is a man of integrity."

"Unbelievable." Mitch shook his head. "Your dad's whole situation just stresses me out." He ran a hand through his hair. "I could never be calm if that were my life."

"Then be grateful we're only poor." I kissed him on my way to bed.

After Mitch's graduation, his parents gave us their blue Honda Civic, which had over two hundred thousand miles on it and a trunk that was strapped down with duct tape. It was a beater we were thrilled to own.

CHAPTER 7

Psych Ward, Day Two

"My name is Janet, and I'll be your counselor," a tree trunk of a woman said, standing with her feet firmly planted in the center of the conference room. *The nurse I was warned about. Just my luck.* I couldn't help but roll my eyes.

Five minutes into class a drug-induced sleep overwhelmed me. I was only two hours into my morning. I didn't want to sleep, but the more I fought it, the more I panicked. The feeling, like a lazy river, tugged me into sleep against my will. *I have to leave, or I'll pass out in front of everyone.* I ran out of the conference room back to my room where I collapsed on my bed, shaking and crying. I realized this was just another battle I was losing as sleep overtook me.

Once I woke, I took a deep breath and sat up. In control of my body again, I stepped out into the empty conference room. Today was different, the room was empty. *Where did everyone go?* I glanced at the clock and did a double take. It was 1 p.m. *I woke up before outside time.* Everyone's favorite part of the day happened once a day for thirty minutes.

People walked out of their classes and headed for the doors. I perked up and followed the flow. I needed fresh air, to feel the sun on my face, to see the sky.

"If you have your name on the board, you aren't allowed to join outside time," Janet announced. "Allison, Jared, Brad," she listed off. Those people left the group and went back to their rooms. I was one foot out the door when she shouted, "Sonja!" I turned around, convinced it wasn't me. *Is there another Sonja?* I waited for someone else to appear then stepped my other foot out the door.

"Sonja!" Janet yelled after me.

"Me?" I said, pulling my foot back inside.

"Yes, you. Your name is on the board."

It couldn't be true. But sure enough, as I looked at the board, there was my name. Sonja W. I approached the nurse's desk.

"Why is my name on the board? I haven't broken any rules," I asked a nurse.

"You didn't attend your classes," the nurse said.

I laughed. "You're kidding."

"No." Janet stormed over. "She's not allowed to go outside," Janet flared her nostrils.

"But that's because you guys drugged me! I was passed out in my room!" My cheeks felt hot.

"You're not allowed to go outside. You missed class. Sorry," the nurse said. She didn't look sorry.

"And here I thought depressed people were supposed to be in nature." I glared at her.

"Are you saying you're depressed?" Janet raised an eyebrow, getting ready to add that information to my file.

I was ready to explode. I was being treated like a child who couldn't go out for recess. The only difference was I hadn't done anything wrong! "I don't know why I'm here! I could just as easily be drugged and sleep at my own house!" I stormed off to my room and slammed the door shut.

Sydney quietly opened the door. "Don't worry, Sonja. Tomorrow you'll get outside time. I'll make sure of it." She smiled. I was a little embarrassed she had seen all that.

"Thanks. But you shouldn't be here. You're going to miss outside time. Go. Clock's ticking," I said.

She hugged me before she left.

The next day, Sydney tried to keep her promise. She and Brent tried carrying me down the hall to my classes. My wobbly legs took sleepy steps as they supported either side of me. I fought to keep my eyes open and mumbled "thank you," but we didn't make it far. I passed out on a bench, and the nurses put me back in my bed.

"You looked like a drunk," Sydney told me after I woke up. "Have you ever been drunk?"

"Nope. Never."

"Never?" She laughed.

"I don't need to drink. One time, I went to a karaoke diner with my husband and some friends. They dared me to go up and sing. I went and belted out ABBA's song, 'Waterloo.' I was horrible. That didn't stop me. People began to stand and cheer for me. Our friends were laughing so hard they were crying. After the song, I walked back to our table, high-fiving people as I went, and a guy yelled to the waiter, 'I want whatever she's drinking!'"

"Well, there you have it: you're a sober drunk." Sydney shook my shoulder.

—⟁—

That night was visiting hours. I only had to wait twenty more minutes to see Mitch. My children weren't allowed to visit, and my dad had already flown home for work. I sat watching the clock, waiting for it to be 6:30 p.m. Then the sleepy feeling washed over me. The after-dinner drugs were kicking in. *Just fifteen more minutes.* Then I saw Mitch walk through the door. *Please God, help me stay awake,* I prayed. It wasn't working; my eyelids were slipping. In anger, I forced myself to the nurse's desk.

"How could you give me pills before visiting hours? How could you do it?" I was barely getting the words out. The nurse said nothing. I was sliding down to the floor with my fingers gripping the desk, trying to stand, but my body just kept on sliding.

The next thing I heard was Mitch's soft voice. "Sonja?"

Was it really him? I opened my eyes. There he was at my bedside. I wanted to jump out of my bed and throw myself into his arms, but my body remained completely still. I tried to tell him everything about this place and what they had done to me, but not a single word came out. My eyelids kept dropping. I fought to lift them over and over. It was a blur, but I saw Janet walk in and tell Mitch he wasn't allowed in patients' rooms. He kissed my hand as he got up to leave.

"Waaaaaiiiitt." The word came out slow. I tried with everything I had to get out of bed. I was desperate to stay awake. I had to talk to him. I needed to hear how the kids were doing.

Mitch helped me up, but I couldn't keep my body upright. Like a rag doll slipping through his fingers, I was falling asleep on him. Sleep won, and Mitch vanished as quickly as he came.

On the next visit, I learned that Mitch talked to the nurses that evening asking if they could allow me to take my medicine after visiting hours. They agreed. But my morning meds were nonnegotiable.

CHAPTER 8

Save Myself

Mandeville, Louisiana, 1999

Steak knives were my favorite. I kept them all over the house: on my nightstand in a wooden box, on my computer desk under a stack of papers, on a high shelf by the couch in the living room, and in my bathroom drawer. My knives were such an essential part of my existence. When Rachael was five years old, she would take the knives and hide them from me: waging a battle she was never going to win. I was willing to do anything to make the pain stop.

I reached for the steak knife on my desk and cut the bottoms of my feet. The sting shifted my attention, giving me temporary relief from my emotional torment. The emotions returned, rolling me through an angry sea as I fought for air. I held my knees and curled into the fetal position. My body shook as I cried out in anguish. Praying for the pain to pass, praying to have the strength to endure it, didn't stop the pain from raging on. I cut deeper, wanting that sweet sting to fight off the undercurrent pulling me down. Weapon in hand, I was winning the battle. I cut until I could take a breath, and then cut until I could relax. But there was no real end to this type of war.

I grabbed a towel off the desk and wiped the blood from my feet and bandaged up my battle wounds. I put on socks to hide the Band-Aids and stood. *Oh, crap, I must have cut too deep.* I limped out of the computer room. I told people I suffered from a severe case of ingrown toenails, a lie which covered up my random limping episodes. I rinsed off the knife and watched my blood swirl down the drain. Another move, another town, another baby. What next?

Moving was one of the things that triggered my pain. We left Albuquerque for Mandeville, Louisiana, where I had my third child, Lincoln. Doctors thought my depression stemmed from the baby blues, but I knew my pain ran much deeper.

The next morning, I sat nursing Lincoln with the newspapers spread out on the kitchen table and a highlighter in my hand. My new favorite pastime was collecting obituaries. Mitch carefully watched me as he ate his breakfast.

"Most of these people died in their early eighties," I informed him, highlighting people's names and their cause of death.

"Well, then you still have a lot of life to live."

"I wish I was already eighty, then I would wake up knowing I could die any day."

"I'm glad you're not. We still need and want you around."

"I think you and the kids would be better off without me."

Mitch got up from the table, took my face in his hands, and looked into my eyes. "We love you, Sonja."

I looked away from him and continued highlighting obituaries. "I feel like Earth is God's classroom, and he decides when his students get to go home. Even though my hand is raised, pleading for him to pick me, he keeps picking other people. It's not fair."

I could tell Mitch didn't know what to say. My obsession with death concerned him, and he started coming with me to my postnatal doctor appointments.

"The depression medicine isn't working," he told my doctor.

The doctor turned to me and said, "Sonja, tell me how you have been feeling."

"I'm struggling. The emotional pain is back. I have little energy, and I can't get motivated to do most things," I replied.

"Sonja is saying she wants to die," Mitch informed the doctor.

"Have you made any plans to harm yourself?" the doctor asked.

"Of course not!" I glared at Mitch, upset he shared this information.

"Let's try another antidepressant and see how that goes." The doctor pulled out his prescription pad.

"I don't know if it's related to Sonja's depression, but she also has become obsessed with having everything clean, to the point she used Clorox to clean our carpets and ruined them," Mitch added.

"Wow!" The doctor said.

"They were dirty; I was just trying to get it cleaned quickly, for the lowest price!" I countered.

"On the way to church you power-washed the inside of our van! You and the kids came to church drenched," Mitch said.

"That sounds like obsessive-compulsive disorder to me. But a trained therapist would be best at diagnosing it. I will give you a referral." The doctor nodded at me.

I got evaluated to keep the peace and received a confirmed diagnosis of obsessive-compulsive disorder. Despite Mitch's effort to get me therapy, I refused. I didn't feel comfortable talking to a stranger about my problems and didn't want to air my dirty laundry. I feared being judged and was scared of what might be discovered. Plus, therapists were expensive and offered no guarantee they could help. Therapy felt like such a foreign concept to me that I fell victim to the many reasons people don't see therapists.

I lay in bed as warm yellows and oranges fell heavy on my eyelids, causing me to wake. I blinked sunlight through my lashes and reached out to feel its warmth, but to no avail. My soul stayed frozen no matter how warm a day looked. My moods were impenetrable. I took a deep breath and stepped out of bed in the clothes I'd been wearing the last four days. *Look at you already dressed and ready to go,* I told my reflection, trying to be positive.

Lincoln's fingers gripped the top of his crib, tucked in the corner of my bedroom. In the slurred speech of a one-year-old, he cheerfully called, "Momma!"

My hope, my joy, my only reason for fighting each day, hour, and sometimes minute—my children were my constant reminder that I had a purpose, that others needed me, that this suffering had to be endured, no matter what.

"Good morning, Linky!" I kissed his pillowy cheek.

I could hear the living room TV before opening the bedroom door. Rachael and Alex were sitting side by side on the floor watching the movie *Balto*. Each wore a pair of Rachael's pajamas. She wore her blue Princess Jasmine nightgown, and Alex wore a pink nightgown with lace trim and a kitten on the front.

"Looking cute." I rubbed Alex's hair and walked into the kitchen.

"Mommy, I'm hungry," he called after me.

"All right, one second!" I cut two big slices out of the chocolate cake on the counter, placed them on a plate, and set it on the floor with two forks. Aside from the sugar, it was not a half-bad breakfast. There were eggs, flour, and milk in there. Not much different than homemade cinnamon rolls, in my opinion. I bounced Lincoln in my arms as we watched *Balto* and his team of huskies race through the snow.

Speaking of pets, where in the world is our cat? I looked out the kitchen window and saw our orange cat, Tiger, outside perched over the giant storage bin that doubled as our goldfish aquarium. He slid his tail back and forth across the pavement before standing on his hind legs and striking a fish out of the container. The shiny fish slapped against the cement and flopped around in a small puddle.

"Not again," I moaned, setting Lincoln in his highchair. I opened the porch door. The fish was already gone. Tiger walked inside, weaving his furry body between my legs, purring proudly, as if thanking me for buying Rachael fifteen goldfish for her birthday. We were now at seven and on a steady decline. The credits rolled on the TV in front of my kids' chocolate-frosted faces.

"Go put some real clothes on, and then we can release Rachael's butterflies," I instructed.

Rachael's eyes got huge. "Yeah!" she and Alex screamed in unison before they took off running down the hall.

I also got Rachael a butterfly hatchery for her birthday. It was an animal-themed birthday, after all. The butterflies emerged from their chrysalises before bed the night before, so I told them we would get them out in the morning.

"We're dressed and ready!" Rachael chimed, sliding across the kitchen floor in her socks.

"We're ready, we're ready, we're reaaaadyyy!" Alex screamed, a four-year-old jumping bean bouncing out of control.

I opened the top cupboard where I hid the enclosure of butterflies and pulled it down. Instantly, Rachael and Alex flocked to the container. They couldn't stop touching the mesh walls as we all walked to the playroom.

"Okay, you guys ready?" I asked.

"Yes!" they yelled, jumping.

I opened the cage, and two painted lady butterflies flew out, then another, and another, until the room danced with butterfly confetti. One landed on Rachael's shirt and one on her face. Alex wasn't one to wait for them to land on him. He liked to catch them in his hands. I put a butterfly on my finger and brought it down to Lincoln.

"Look, a butterfly." I held it in front of him, and he looked up at me, laughing.

The doorbell rang. *Who could that be?* I had invited the sister missionaries over for lunch, but it couldn't already be noon. I opened the front door, and sure enough, there were two name-tag-wearing missionaries on my porch. Missionaries lived on a budget and had limited time, so members of our church usually invited them over for meals.

"Sisters, come in!" I welcomed, holding Lincoln on my hip.

"Good afternoon, Sister Wasden." They cheerily smiled. "Shoes on or off?"

"Off, please. You can just leave them by the door. Kids, come to the table!"

Rachael and Alex came running into the kitchen with butterflies on their shirts.

"Mommy, look! All the butterflies are on us!" Alex shouted.

"Where did you get all those?" one of the missionaries asked.

"For my birthday. Want to hold one?" Rachael reached her finger out with a butterfly resting on it.

"Sure." She held out her hand, forming a bridge from Rachael's to hers.

I had lost track of time and didn't have anything prepared for lunch. Thankfully, I had some shredded chicken warming in the oven for the kids. I needed more than one course, so I set a bowl of popcorn on the table, next to a pan of cake batter I hadn't had a chance to bake.

"Come take a seat." I ushered them to the table.

"Thanks for lunch, Sister Wasden," the sisters said, looking over the food.

My kids served themselves handfuls of popcorn and spoonfuls of cake batter, as if this were their daily meal. The sisters watched and politely copied them, spooning batter onto their plates that soon pooled into their popcorn.

Pain filled my chest. It was not brought on by anything; it just came. Daily. The recurring agony chugged through my veins with each heartbeat. Pain pulsed in me as I watched the missionaries eat with my kids. I needed something to disrupt the emotional wave about to pull me under, and I needed it fast.

"Have you ever eaten cat?" I asked as Tiger jumped onto the table and sniffed Lincoln's tray of salty popcorn.

"No, I haven't," one of the sisters answered. She looked at Tiger stepping over people's plates.

"Well, today will be a first then," I said casually.

The oven beeped and I got up to check it. The sisters were quiet for a while, hoping I would clarify. But I let them linger in their uncertainty.

"Wait, are you cooking *this* cat?" one of them finally asked.

"No, no." I laughed, pulling out a pan of shredded chicken from the oven.

"Oh." The sisters looked at each other in relief and laughed, too.

"I cooked his brother." I placed the steaming-hot pan in front of them. "Ran over him this morning, which gave me plenty of time to skin him in preparation for our lunch." I ran my hands down my lap. "Now, who would like to say the blessing?"

The sisters' faces went white.

"Me!" Alex said, standing on his chair. We all folded our arms, and Alex stood while he prayed. "Dear Heavenly Father, thanks for the butterflies and the yummy cake."

"And the cat," I chimed in.

"And the cat. Amen."

The sisters hesitantly spooned small piles of chicken onto their plates and looked at me before picking up their forks.

"Don't worry. You can start. I still have to dish the kids' up," I encouraged, even though I knew etiquette was not the reason behind their hesitation. I served my kids, watching the sisters slowly chew as they inspected every taste that hit their tongues. It probably didn't help that Tiger circled between our guests' feet while they tried not to focus on what they were eating, but like good missionaries, they ate every last bite.

"Thanks for lunch," both sisters said as they got up to leave.

"Oh, it was my pleasure."

And it was.

—ɱ—

I took the kids grocery shopping after the sisters left since there wasn't much in my pantry. Alex and Rachael struggled to follow me through the aisles of Walmart without getting distracted while Lincoln stood in the grocery cart, wearing nothing but a diaper. Whenever I put a new item into the cart, he giggled and dropped on his bum, smashing the food.

I was too exhausted to care. Gathering up my kids I successfully made it to the checkout line. I stacked boxes of mac and cheese on the conveyor belt, and Rachael imitated me by heaping on Hershey bars from the candy rack beside us.

"No, Rachael, we're not buying those," I said, stuffing them back into the cardboard box.

Alex decided to try Rachael's technique with Push Pops, which encouraged her to try again. Every time I turned around, there were little mounds of candy slapped onto the conveyor belt. Lincoln clapped and stomped the bread under his bare feet.

"Guys, please stop." I took the flattened bread from under Lincoln, and the cashier scanned it. I tossed up the rest of the groceries and got out my wallet. Rachael and Alex sat between a pile of shared candy on the floor.

"Please put the candy back!" I pleaded, looking at the line of people trying to move up but couldn't because of my sugar trolls.

The cashier glanced up at me, and I forced a smile. She continued scanning items as I tapped my credit card impatiently on the counter. I felt like a disorganized mom on display. *They're definitely judging me. I'm judging me.* I paid for the groceries as Alex tugged on my leg calling my name over and over.

"What?" I looked down at him, and he was pointing at Lincoln. "What is it?" I looked up and saw Lincoln standing in the cart, holding his diaper in one hand, peeing over the side of the cart like a Victorian cherub fountain.

"We need a custodian at cashier number four," the cashier said into the intercom.

The speaker clicked off and I waited until a custodian wheeled a mop through the line. Humiliated, I grabbed some paper towels from the custodian's cart.

"Don't worry. I'll clean it up," I said, rushing to kneel on the floor.

I threw yellow paper towels into his trash can as he proceeded to sanitize the area. I needed out. With the pee cleaned and my cart full of bought groceries, I was ready to bolt.

"Mom, I'm thirsty," Rachael complained.

"Me too!" Alex said, pushing on my leg.

I snatched a water bottle out of the refrigerated display by the checkout line.

"I just need to quickly buy this," I pleaded with the cashier.

"No, you'll have to go to the back of the line." She pointed to the long line of people waiting to check out.

My eyes widened. "Are you kidding?"

She reiterated, "Please go to the back of the line."

The cashier started scanning the next person's items. I looked down the line of people, then back at my diaper-less kid. I already felt judged, so this was as good a time as any to sin. I opened the water bottle, smiled at the cashier, raised the bottle to the people in line like I was toasting them, and took a drink.

"Mom, it's a sin to steal," Rachael said, pulling on my shirt.

"Yes, it is. We'll repent later. Here's your water." I held out the bottle to her.

"No, that's sinful water," she insisted.

"I'm telling Dad what you did," Alex said.

I rolled my eyes and walked to the doors. A range of emotions ran through my body. I yelled, "I'm shoplifting! Arrest me!" None of the employees stopped me as I pushed my cart out the doors.

Living life had become increasingly difficult, even when the situation wasn't. Having people over for lunch or a basic task like grocery shopping pushed me over the edge. I asked myself the same questions I had pondered for thirteen years: *God, why am I in so much pain? Is it because I am a sinner? Is this some kind of divine Biblical punishment? Is it because I'm not a good enough person, mom, wife, daughter, sister, friend?* And most importantly, *Does God not care about me? Why does he not answer my prayers? Am I not worth saving?* The resounding answer I felt was that God was in no rush to help me. I had to save myself.

—⟋⟍—

"I just had another great idea!" I threw a hand on Mitch's shoulder. Energy pulsed through me like a live wire.

"For your *Wrap It Up* book?" he asked, looking over at the dozens of colorfully wrapped boxes stacked in the corner of our family room. I had the idea to create a picture book displaying different ways to wrap gifts. The boxes were empty, but each had tightly pressed corners, different paper themes, and styles of bows.

"No, no. That project is almost done. I just need to photograph some more bows. This is a new idea," I said.

"When do we get to open the gifts?" Rachael asked for the hundredth time.

"Soon. But remember there's nothing in them."

"I know," she sighed.

"So what's the idea?" Mitch asked, pouring himself a bowl of cereal.

I bit my lip. "I've invented something."

"Well, let's hear it."

"I was vacuuming the house and kept thinking about how I hate running into baseboards and furniture with the vacuum head. Even when you're careful, the vacuum scratches and marks stuff up." I paused to make sure he was following.

"Yeah. So…what's the invention?"

"Vacuum Bra." I smiled.

"What?" Mitch about choked on his Raisin Bran, trying not to laugh.

"It's a cushioned cover you put on the front of your vacuum to stop the corners from scraping things. It's so practical."

Mitch nodded as if thinking the idea through. "That's actually not a bad idea."

"Right? I don't know how I come up with all these ideas. They just come to me!" I slapped my arms at my side. "The only problem is there's not enough time in the day to focus on all my creations."

"That's a good problem to have." Mitch smiled, leaning in to kiss me. "I love seeing you happy."

A week later Mitch came home from work in a panic.

"Someone's opened a credit card in my name! This is identity theft," Mitch said, coming into the kitchen to show me a paper statement. I looked up from the dishes and my eyes landed on the $10,000 cash advance charge. *Oh no, it already came.*

"How did this happen?!" I could hear the anxiety in his voice.

"Okay, don't be mad." I turned off the faucet and faced him.

"That sounds exactly like the kind of thing someone says right before their husband gets mad." He put down the paper.

"I had one of my great ideas again"—I shifted my stance and got serious—"but it didn't go the way I planned."

"What?" He pressed his eyebrows together.

"I lost some money in the stock market, but I'll get it back! I'm learning how it works," I explained.

"When did you start buying stocks?"

"Our friends were making money in the dot-com stocks, and we were missing out! I put us in the game. And maybe that was risky, but if our friends are capable of winning in the stock market, then so are we!" I tightened my fist, refusing to back down.

"Sonja, this is *our* money; you can't make decisions like that without telling me."

"Maybe some of my ideas come at a cost, but all important things involve risk. We needed to take massive action," I said, feeling like our kitchen was an auditorium for motivational speakers and I was tonight's keynote. "If you do what you've always done, you'll get what you've always gotten."

Mitch sighed. "Are you quoting Tony Robbins? Sonja, just tell me how much money we lost."

"I'm not totally sure. But we can turn it around. Look, every problem is a gift, and without problems, we wouldn't grow."

"Stop quoting Tony Robbins! How—how did this happen?" He closed his eyes.

"I called a stockbroker who told me about some stocks that were going up, so I sold our mutual fund to buy them. It turned out he was right—the stock went way up, and all of a sudden, we had over nine thousand dollars! It almost doubled our money! This stockbroker knew what he was doing. I can't explain it. It just *felt* right. Like I knew in my bones we couldn't lose!" I cheered, reliving the moment.

"But we did lose," Mitch interrupted. "We went from having nine thousand to owing ten thousand!" he snapped at me. His tone caught me off guard.

"Calm down," I scolded him. "If we borrowed money, we could make more, so I took out some credit cards to get cash advances and used that to buy more stock. I got an introductory rate, where we didn't have to pay interest for six months, which would give us time to make more money. Then the stockbroker told me about this thing where I could buy stock on the margin and use our existing stock as collateral to buy other stocks." I explained each detail of my clever process, making sure to emphasize how I not only had the gumption to pull this off but the brains. It was clear Mitch couldn't believe what he was hearing. Neither could I—my pre-rehearsed speech sounded even better aloud than in my head.

"I can't trust you." He clenched his jaw.

"What?" I jumped back. Keeping him out of the loop didn't make me deceitful. It made me practical. I felt I didn't have time for his concerns and cautions to get in the way of my brilliance.

"Don't ever do this again! You're being just like your dad—risking everything to win big or lose it all!" he snapped.

"That is not true." I held a firm finger at him. "I was being savvy. And the outcome was out of my control. I went out on a limb to benefit us. I took the time to educate myself and try to make us money. So what if I hit a bump in the road? I put us in the race! Mitchell, I'd rather be in the race and crash then not ever step foot on the track!"

"How many credit cards did you take out?" he asked.

"I don't remember."

Mitch dropped his head. "Give me all the credit cards and just… go. I need you to leave so I can figure this out."

My eyes looked up to meet the pain in his. "Okay, I'm sorry. I thought I was helping," I said, my hands up in the air like white flags.

He looked away from me. "I need you to go—really, go. I can't process anything until I know how financially at risk we are."

That night, I paced our bedroom, occasionally listening through the door as Mitch talked with six credit card companies over the phone.

"And how much is on the card?" I heard Mitch rush them along. There was a pause and then he let out an audible gasp, like he had been punched in the gut. "Eighty thousand!" his voice rose. Once he hung up, I creaked the bedroom door open and peered through the crack. I saw him sitting on the wood floor of our family room crying. I had never seen Mitch cry. Not at our children's births, or at funerals, weddings, movies. Making him show raw emotions was like moving a boulder. When we were engaged, I asked him, "When was the last time you cried?" He told me the last time he remembered crying was when he was twelve.

I closed our bedroom door and waited for Mitch, but he didn't come to bed. Money had not been an issue in our marriage until this moment. We had struggled financially early on, but neither of us had ever overspent or done anything risky like this.

He cashed out what little he had in his 401(k) to pay a portion of the debt, but it was going to take years to make even a dent in it. Mitch started going to work with a different type of vigor than before. There was only one way out: he needed raises, he needed promotions, and he needed bonuses. The $80,000 in credit card debt that I created almost overnight erased Mitch's trust in me and his sense of safety. He said I had always been an open book, which is what made the secrets more blindsiding. It was the first time that deep hurt and love coexisted in our marriage.

CHAPTER 9

Psych Ward, Day Three

"Tell me about your childhood," Dr. Barry asked as we sat in our corner of the conference room for another one-on-one meeting.

"I grew up in a loving home with six siblings whom I adore. My mom made home-cooked meals and kept a clean house. My dad spent hours teaching us life skills in front of his whiteboard like he was a coach grilling us about the right plays to make in life," I said proudly. "I spent my summers in Utah, tubing down the canal and lying on the grass looking at the clouds. And I loved playing night games like kick the can with my friends. I had a perfect childhood." This had always been my answer, and I believed every detail of it.

Dr. Barry smiled. "That sounds ideal."

"It was." I smiled back. "I'm lucky."

"Why do you cut yourself?" He flipped through more of my file.

"Doctor, don't tell me you don't understand why people cut. It's completely logical," I said, annoyed at his question.

"Explain how hurting yourself on purpose is logical."

"Because you're in so much emotional pain, the physical pain interrupts it. I'm trying to get out of the pain that is worse, not inflict more."

"Would you be okay if your children self-harmed?"

"Absolutely not!"

"Then why is it okay for you to do it? Why aren't you using different methods to handle your pain?"

"I haven't found any. But I've searched. Trust me, I've been searching. I never said I thought it was right to self-harm. I only explained why it makes sense."

"Do you think there might be something—even in the smallest degree—wrong with you?" Dr. Barry asked, setting down his pen to look at me.

"To a small degree, everyone has something wrong with them."

"Right, but I'm talking about outside the average quirks and struggles."

I had felt like something was off for twenty-three years, but I also knew I was not insane. The fact that my husband and dad thought bringing me to a psych ward was necessary shocked me. Just because I didn't feel normal didn't mean I needed to be here.

"Maybe." I knew in a place like this, the smallest admission could lead to a lifetime diagnosis, and I was not going to set myself up for that.

"It's the sickness, Sonja. People who are sick self-harm." Dr. Barry felt the need to spell it out for me.

"I'm not sick!" I panicked, trying to steal the words back from him.

He sighed and looked at me like I was a child refusing to fill an aching cavity. "Do you think you feel threatened by the idea of being mentally ill…because you know it's true?"

Rage filled me in that moment. "I don't know what I have, but I know—whatever it is—it's not going to be cured by being here!"

"Do you sleep well?" Dr. Barry continued.

I breathed in and out, trying to relax. "That's all I do since I've been here."

"What about before you came?"

"I slept a few hours at night. I woke up a lot, and sleeping pills were no help. My mind has a hard time shutting down," I explained.

"The medicine will help with that."

"When do I get to go home?" I held back tears. I hated this. Being questioned about my life, my thoughts, and then having a stranger tell me what it all meant. The invasion of my privacy felt unnecessary and belittling.

"Soon enough," he said.

A few hours later visiting hours started. I stood as close to the entrance doors as the guards would allow me. Each time they looked away, I inched myself closer. Occasionally, the doors would open and a visitor walked in. Each time the metal door swung wide, I stood a little taller, thinking this time it had to be Mitch. But the longer I didn't see him, the more I thought he wasn't coming.

Maybe our fights were worse than I realized and he decided to throw in the towel. Our days had become so predictable: the morning fight as he left for work, the afternoon fight on the phone during his lunch, and the evening fight when he got home. It seemed like fighting composed most of our relationship. I was so uncomfortable with life, I lashed out at the people most involved in mine, thinking they must be the cause. *I* wasn't doing things to cause myself emotional pain, so it must have been coming from the choices of the people around me.

I waited longer and longer wondering, *What if time away from me made Mitch happier? What if this is where our life together ends?*

The massive doors pushed open again and there he stood: my everything, my rock. I ran into his arms. It was the only time I felt safe in that place. He tried to let go, but I wouldn't let him. I needed a few more minutes.

"Sorry I'm late," he said. I pulled away looking at his crisp white dress shirt, black wool pants, and Italian leather loafers.

"You look nice." I smiled, smelling his familiar musky cologne.

"My staff meeting went longer than I expected." He kissed the top of my head.

"All that matters is you're here now." I snuggled in closer.

"How do you feel? Are they helping you?"

"Take me home with you." I hugged him tighter.

"Let's sit down." He walked us to the nearest couch to sit, and he plopped his head on top of mine.

"I don't like it here," I said.

"I know. But do you feel any better?"

"I don't want to talk about it."

Mitch didn't ask any more questions and let me sit with him in silence. I had been questioned and probed enough, I just wanted to be with him. With my head on his shoulder, I wondered what the next steps for us would be. I was in a hospital that Mitch thought was supposed to help us solve something, but I wasn't sure what that something was or how long it would take to solve.

I looked up at him. "What's going to happen to us?"

"I don't know"—he combed his fingers through my hair—"but we'll be okay." He rested his head back on mine, and I wanted to believe him, but I was scared Mitch might be considering leaving me for good.

When we were young, I was full of light and laughed easily, and Mitch was calm with moments of clever wit. We were so far away from those optimistic kids, and I wondered if we could ever get back to that place again.

"Visiting hours are over," a nurse came from the front desk to inform us. Mitch saw a flash of concern on my face.

"I better go," Mitch said, standing up. I gripped his arm and held on tight.

"I want to go home with you," I said.

"Don't worry, you'll be home soon." He kissed me.

I waited by the doors as Mitch walked himself out. He turned around and we stood facing each other as the massive doors slowly shut between us. Mitch waved to me one last time, and I was separated from what I wanted most.

CHAPTER 10

A Date with Destiny

Mandeville, Louisiana, 2000

I had hoarding tendencies in the way I shopped for clothes and the way I shopped for food. I bought in bulk and stashed it all away in our closet for safekeeping. Food had become one of my pain relievers. I ate until I felt sick and lay in bed reading romance novels until I felt well enough to eat again.

"Ugh, you're hiding donuts again!" Mitch held up a T-shirt dusted in white powder. "My clothes have powdered sugar all over them."

"Does me being fat bother you?" I asked as I shoved the food into an empty laundry basket to hide from the kids.

"I don't care if I have an overweight wife. I care if I have a happy wife," Mitch said, brushing cookie crumbs off the sheets.

"Well, do you think I'm happy?"

He paused. "I think you're in pain and you're coping through food," he answered.

"Food does make me feel better," I admitted.

"I know, but being overweight is one thing; abusing your body is something completely different. Our family needs a healthy mom."

He had told me he worried that soon I wouldn't only be dealing with emotional issues, but physical ones as well.

"I've tried dozens of weight-loss programs, and none of them work. I just keep gaining weight."

"You need to focus on taking care of yourself," he said, and I could tell he wondered if it was even possible.

At 3 a.m., I slid out of bed, trying not to make a sound. Mitch was a light sleeper, and I didn't want to reveal my latest plan to win my battle with overeating. My toes made it to the floor and I cautiously pulled my packed bag from under the bed. To prevent it from hitting something in the dark, I held it close to my stomach, which bulged out over the elastic band of my skirt. I took one step toward the door, and the floorboards creaked.

"Sonja, what are you doing?" Mitch squinted through the dark.

I froze. He flipped on the lights. Sleepily, he walked up behind me and looked at the bag. I carefully turned around to face him, wishing I could hide the evidence of my travel plans and say I was just getting a drink.

"Are you leaving me?" He creased his eyebrows.

"No! Of course not. I left a note by the bed."

"Then what's this?" He took the bag and lifted it in the air.

"I can explain." I looked over at the red numbers glowing on our alarm clock. "But I have to explain fast because I still need to buy a ticket at the airport."

"Where are you going at three in the morning?" He was fully awake now.

"Tony Robbins is going to be at the QVC Home Shopping Network headquarters in Pennsylvania to sell his Personal Power program. I need to convince the QVC people to let me talk to him. Mitch, he can help me!"

"Sonja, you're scaring me." He sat at the edge of the bed and ran his fingers through the top of his hair. "The QVC people are not going to let you in to talk to Tony Robbins." He blinked repeatedly as if trying to figure out if he was still asleep.

"I'll find a way. If I have to wait outside all day until he comes out, I will. He's the only person who can help me."

"And why would he help a stranger waiting on the street?"

"He has a big heart."

Mitch put his hand over his forehead. "Sonja, he's there to sell a product, not give you a free coaching session. Tony Robbins is famous. If you show up stalking him, they'll call security on you, or worse, arrest you."

"It seems like he cares about people when he talks on his tapes," I countered.

"He has thousands of people begging for his help. It won't work."

"I have to go. Mitch, this is my big chance!" I picked up my bag from the floor.

"This is extreme and impulsive behavior, Sonja. I can't let you go."

I missed my plane that morning, but I wasn't sad. I was confident I would meet Tony Robbins. I just had to wait for Mitch to get out of the way.

A few hours later, Mitch got ready for work. I pretended to sleep as he kissed my head on his way out, but as soon as the front door closed, I jumped out of bed and got moving.

Tony had live seminars all over the country. I had to convince Mitch to pay for one I could go to. *But how do I get Tony's attention?* That was the question. I wrote him a personal letter and then dialed the QVC number in West Chester, Pennsylvania.

"Hi, this is Sonja Wasden. I'm going to be working with Tony Robbins at his Date with Destiny seminar coming up. And I forgot to mail him an important document." *I was going to be working with him. He just didn't know it yet.*

"Wait. What's your name again?" the woman on the phone asked.

"Sonja Wasden. Look, this document needs to be in Tony's hands by tomorrow. I know he's going to be there to promote his Personal Power program. Would you be kind enough to give it to him?"

She hesitated.

"This is crucial. Tony has to have this document in his hands tomorrow or I'm in trouble! I can FedEx it to you personally, and then you can see it's only a letter. Will you help me?"

"I guess I can do that."

"Promise me you won't forget? It's important."

"Okay, I'll make sure Tony gets it," she promised.

Freedom was finally within my grasp. I spent hours writing and editing my letter, hoping to convince him to help me. I stepped away from the FedEx counter after mailing my letter to QVC headquarters, believing I was finally on my way to overcoming my obsession with food.

After much debate, Mitch agreed to let me go to the Date with Destiny seminar in Florida. I think he realized I was going to go no matter what, so he might as well support me so I didn't try to disappear in the middle of the night again.

As I entered the auditorium, energy vibrated off the walls and music played as smoke floated off the sides of the stage. Dancers moved under flashing lights, and two massive TVs showed people skiing off cliffs and dirt biking. The room was filled with hundreds of people dancing to the music. Today was the day I'd find out if my letter worked.

"Have you ever been to one of these before?" the woman sitting next to me asked.

"No, this is my first time," I replied. In that moment, I felt shy. I wasn't dancing or screaming. I just clapped my hands to the beat of the music and watched the frenzy. A man walked out into the energetic chaos to introduce Tony.

"Give it up for Tony Robbins!" his voice rang through the speakers. Music blasted and Tony Robbins came running in through the side entrance, forcefully clapping his large hands. The audience members lost their minds. The woman next to me elbowed my arm and screamed, "There he is!"

I smiled. The music faded out and Tony adjusted his microphone.

"Thank you for that kind introduction," he said, facing the announcer. "And thank you for being here at Date with Destiny!" he cheered into the microphone, and the crowd cheered with him. The woman next to me was very good at this whole screaming thing.

"Now, I received a letter." Tony held my letter high above his head.

Holy shit. I was stunned. I hoped it would happen, but not this soon and not publicly. I thought we'd talk privately after the show. "What have I done?" I whispered to myself.

"'Dear Tony, I'm writing to you because I think you're my last chance at being helped,'" he read to the crowd.

My neck and cheeks burned with embarrassment. I reread and edited that letter so many times, I knew what was coming next. I cringed in my seat before he got to the personal parts. Listening to the audience's reactions made me wish I hadn't been so descriptive. I wasn't sure I could match my face with the person who had written all those things he just read. But I would never see these people again, and I had to be brave. I had gotten this far, after all.

On his tapes, Tony told numerous stories about changing people's lives with his seminars. My heart beat with nervous excitement at the thought of being one of his miracle stories. Realizing my plan had worked made me excited and terrified at the same time—mostly terrified. He was finally getting to the end of the letter.

"Whoever wrote this letter, stand up!" Tony pumped his arms, encouraging the crowd to cheer. Music played for my introduction.

I froze. I couldn't stand, not in front of all those people. I kept telling myself I would never see them again and this might be the price to pay for being cured. My sweaty palms gripped the sides of my chair. I wasn't sure if it was in preparation to keep me in my seat or to get out of it, but either way, I sat frozen.

He looked at the bottom of the letter for my name. "Sonja! Stand up!" he yelled.

The music played its entire loop again as I remained glued to the chair. The longer I waited, the more embarrassing it felt to stand. My heart sank to the bottom of my shoes. Tears slowly streamed down my face. I couldn't do it.

He shrugged his shoulders. "Oh well," he said, and moved on.

On my way back to my hotel room, a thought came crashing down on me: *I came all this way for help and might go home without any.* I let my opportunity pass right by me. I took my duffel bag and filled it with my junk food—chips, candy, and chocolate. I zipped it up and frantically pressed the elevator button down to the lobby.

"Deliver this to Tony Robbins's room." I tossed the bag onto the front desk. The employee eyed the bag before reaching for it.

"Wait!" I grabbed a pen off the counter and scribbled down my message for Tony on a hotel notepad.

Here's my food. I'm ready. –Sonja

—⟁—

That night, Tony brought out my bag of junk food and dumped it out on the stage.

"'Here's my food. I'm ready. Sonja,'" he read off the note. "Well, Sonja, come on up!"

The music started up again. It was a tune I was getting to know all too well. This was it: Tony was going to perform NLP on me, and I would be cured of my overeating.

The women sitting next to me stared as I stood up and walked down the aisle. The crowd's eyes locked on me, and I could feel my face getting warm. I made it to the stage and stood next to a smiling Tony Robbins.

"Sonja, you've gained an incredible amount of weight. What do you think is causing it?" Tony asked.

"Well, I don't know if I would call it incredible," I replied. The crowd hummed a soft chuckle. "But I would say I eat because it fills me up in a way life can't."

"What I'm hearing is you've turned to food because you lack something. There's an essential need you have, but it's not being filled, so you eat. Would you say that's correct?" He looked directly into my eyes as we stood on display under the blinding lights.

I held on to my jean overalls for some sense of stability as I processed his question and responded, "Yes," into the microphone.

"Do you know what you're missing in life that food temporarily fills for you?"

"I'm not sure. Maybe comfort, maybe a small piece of enjoyment?" My hands slightly shook, and Tony turned back to the audience.

"When we lack something, the obvious reaction is to fill it with something. The problem is we usually don't spend enough time investigating our need before we choose something to fill it with." He paused and looked back at me. "So while you may say you don't know what you're lacking, I have to wonder, from reading your letter, if your problem might stem from your relationship with your father. Heal that relationship and see how you feel about food after."

The crowd cheered before I could say anything. I was ushered off the stage. *My dad? Did he play a part in my overeating?* Tony's answer left me confused. I didn't see how my eating and Dad were correlated.

I stayed for the rest of the conference and used the techniques of NLP to consciously link pain to the idea of overeating and pleasure to the idea of being thin and healthy. I began living Tony's mantra of, "Nothing tastes as good as healthy feels."

The process made an impact, and I lost weight. I thought losing the weight would lift my emotional pain, but even as the pounds came off, the emotional pain remained. As the stresses of my life increased, I became less capable of following the steps Tony taught me. I gained all the weight back and more.

I knew what Tony did helped millions of people, but my problems seemed to run deeper than the average person's. It was only treating my symptoms, not the root cause, like giving a cancer patient an energy drink because they felt fatigued. Something else was stopping my progress, but I couldn't figure out what. I wasn't convinced my relationship with my dad was the source of my pain. But if not that, then what?

CHAPTER 11

Psych Ward, Day Four

"The quicker you learn how to cooperate with us, the quicker you'll go home." Janet stood in the doorway of my room. The word *home* caught my attention. I sat on my bed, feeling the morning meds drawing the curtains inside my mind. "Come to class now!" she demanded.

"I'll try." I stumbled to the conference room, hoping a small fraction of Janet's humane side would take pity on me. It didn't. I hobbled over to the table and took my seat.

"Okay, let's begin." Janet took control of the room. A man in the front row with tattoos up his arms blinked wide awake. I wondered if they were giving him any meds. If so, you'd never know it. "Why are you here?" Janet tapped the table in front of him.

"Uh, I partied on my birthday and took some sleeping pills to sleep off the drugs and alcohol, but my sister saw me passed out next to an open pill bottle. She thought I tried to kill myself and called 911. She totally misread the situation, but it's getting worked out. I'll be out soon."

"What have you learned from being here?" she asked him.

He picked at his fingernails. "Nothing."

"I *said*, what have you learned?" She pursed her lips, but he was just as stubborn as she was.

He leaned back in his chair and sighed. "I told you: nothing." He stared straight into her eyes, and she squirmed under his gaze. It was clear she no longer held the power in the room.

"If you don't tell me what you've learned, I'm not letting you out of here. I have the power to do that, you know." Her threat fell flat.

"Fuck this." The man got up and left the room.

Another patient followed him out, but before leaving, turned around and flipped off Janet. She ignored the situation and talked to the rest of us. I had moved to the corner of the room, where I stood bouncing and rocking, trying to keep myself awake. I didn't want to pass out on the table in front of everyone.

"A needle was left in my room," a patient informed Janet.

"No, there was not. You imagined it," she said.

"There really is a needle in my room. I think a nurse left it by accident," the patient insisted.

"You have to trust me. Your disease, your schizophrenia, is playing games with your mind. There is no needle there." She brushed him off.

I wondered why she wouldn't go look in his room just to make sure. There absolutely could have been a needle in his room, left from his roommate's daily shots.

"Just because he has schizophrenia doesn't mean he imagines everything." I heard my voice land in the center of the room.

"Sonja, what's wrong with you? Are you having a panic attack?" Janet peered at me shaking in the corner.

"No, I'm trying"—my eyelids continued to fall even though I was only halfway through my sentence—"to keep myself awake."

"Oh, good. Keep doing that," she replied.

I wanted to scream at her, *Take some of my medicine, while I stand there and tell you to come to class and stay awake!* What was wrong with her? She was in the wrong profession if she thought this was the care we needed.

"Forget it." I walked out and headed straight for my room. I was not about to disgrace myself again by having nurses carry me to bed. I was an adult and could walk there myself. On my way to my room, I saw Brent running down the hall.

"Brent?" I called after him.

He blazed past me in a full sprint. "I'M GOING TO LIGHT MYSELF ON FIIIIRRRRRE!" he screamed.

Two men ran after him, quickly restrained him, and pushed a needle into his arm. Brent fell limp and they dragged him back into his room. My eyelids dropped again and I knew I was about to get knocked out by the medication. I pushed open my door and collapsed on the bed. As I fell into a sleepy haze, I kept thinking about Brent being dragged across the brown linoleum. He and I weren't so different. I could lose it that same way at any given moment.

—ɯ—

Brent was sitting at a table with head down, drawing on a piece of paper. It was already three in the afternoon, and I had just woken up.

"Do you want to tell me some more historical facts?" I asked as I took the seat beside Brent, who had his head angled down as he drew on a piece of paper.

"No," he solemnly replied.

"You really should go on *Jeopardy*. You would win."

Brent lifted his head slightly. "I-I-I have th-thought about it."

I think most people ignored him because he had a hard time speaking; his stutter could make it hard to understand him, but it didn't detract from his genius. I could ask him about any event in history and he knew the day, month, and year it happened.

I looked at his picture. "What are you drawing?"

"Th-th-is is you." He pointed to the rose he colored. "Th-th-is is me." He moved his finger down to the weeds.

"No. It's not, Brent." I took his paper and drew a daisy next to the rose. "That's you. We're all just different flowers."

Brent looked at the addition to his picture and traced his finger over the daisy.

"Wait out here until dinner starts," I heard Janet say to a new patient. She had cranberry hair and a disapproving scowl. She sat at the table across from me and I noticed her arms were covered in razor cuts. I stared at her arms, amazed at how many scars she left out in the open.

"What?" she demanded.

Startled, I looked away. "Oh, nothing."

I understood cutting, but cutting and letting the whole world see? That was brave. I continued to sneak glances at her. To me, she was no different than a soldier bearing the marks of battle. She didn't hide the evidence of past pain. I wondered what that kind of openness felt like but never planned on trying it out.

—◊◊◊—

Allyson walked in during visiting hours and hugged me with a big smile on her face. "Surprise, lucky lady!"

I looked up at her. "Allyson! What are you doing here?" She was my younger sister, and best friend. We had matching black hair and light skin, but the weirdest similarity we shared was our voice. Whenever she called, my kids thought I was on the phone. Even though we looked and sounded similar, our personalities were entirely different. My mother always referred to her as the peacemaker, whereas I was the kid giving the peacemaker a purpose.

"I came down the day after you were admitted, to help Mom with the kids." She untied the belt around her red raincoat, gripped it like a lasso, and swung it into her other hand. "So when do I get to break you out of here? I'm sure you've been keeping track of the nurses' rounds."

I laughed. "I can't tell you how happy I am that you're here." I hugged her again.

Her presence gave me strength. Allyson had always been the emotionally strong one of the two of us. When I was nine and she was six, we waited in our room for our dad to come spank us for riding our bikes through our neighborhood before getting our chores finished. I started crying before he even came to our room, but Allyson was laughing. She told me to laugh through the spanking because that made it hurt less. I could never get myself to do it. I sobbed before, during, and after the discipline. Whereas she laughed through it.

Her positive attitude followed her as she grew up, a permanent fixture of her personality. Even in high school, when she was overweight, the bullying didn't affect her. Because of her dark hair and light skin, kids called her "Shamu." She told me guys were intimidated by her intelligence, and that's why she didn't get asked out. She was so self-assured, her boyfriend ended up being one of the most popular guys in high school. Her positive attitude willed good things to happen to her, and she treated negativity like background noise. I loved that about her; I just wished I could've done the same.

"How are the kids?" I asked, sitting back down.

"They're good. Excited for you to come home."

"And Mitch?"

"He's been strong. I did notice that your house is a mess, but all your pillowcases are ironed." She raised an eyebrow.

"I have my priorities straight."

"Clearly!" She laughed. Then the seriousness of my situation swallowed up her laughter, and we sat together in heavy silence.

"Allyson, what am I supposed to do when I get out of here? I don't want to be sent back."

"Sonja,"—she placed her hand on mine—"I don't know anyone more capable of handling hard things than you. When you get out of here, you're going to continue being an amazing person, but you need to take care of yourself."

"I only have enough in me to take care of my kids."

"You'll get to a point where you can do both," she encouraged.

"What would I do without you?" I squeezed her hand.

"You don't need to worry about that. I'll always be here for you."

Despite our epic fights growing up, Allyson and I developed a friendship no number of unshared clothes or Scotch tape room dividers could sever.

CHAPTER 12

Falling Behind

Sugar Land, Texas, 2002

"Your daughter's going to have to repeat third grade. There's no possible way she can catch up," Rachael's principal said. The words *your daughter* and *no possible way* caught my attention.

"Of course she can," I replied, sitting across the table from him and my daughter's elementary school teacher.

In third grade Rachael was struggling to read at a kindergarten level. After getting her tested, we finally knew what was wrong: she was dyslexic.

"While I appreciate your enthusiasm, you have to understand there's no way she'll pass the state test in April," he assured me.

I smiled. "Don't worry, she'll pass."

He pulled out of piece of paper and drew a stick person representing Rachael and put other stick people far ahead of her, representing the other students. He drew lines showing improvement happening on both sides at the same speed. Since Rachael's line was farther back, it didn't matter that she was improving because the other students were, too. They were always ahead of her.

"She can't make up that much ground. Even if she progresses, she'll always be the one behind." The principal pointed to the paper.

"I see what you're trying to say, but she will go on to fourth grade. We'll catch up. There's always a way, and I'll find it," I insisted.

"Mrs. Wasden, in all my twenty-five years of being a teacher and principal, when a child is this far behind, they never catch up."

"No! We will—"

"She. Will. Never. Catch. Up," he repeated.

"Thank you for your advice, but I guess you'll have to wait and see," I told him.

He stood his ground. "No, Mrs. Wasden, I won't."

I stood, unconvinced, and he followed my lead and stood, too. I held out my hand and he shook it. I walked out of his office, committed to getting Rachael up to grade level. I had full faith in my daughter and her ability. I was angry at the principal's attitude. It was no wonder students didn't reach their full potential when the principals didn't believe in them. I would teach him a lesson he would never forget: faith, grit, and hard work were miracle workers.

"Come sit down, Rachy." Mitch patted the couch. Rachael sat and looked at me with hopeful eyes. She knew I couldn't keep important information to myself.

"It's not a big deal." I pulled my feet up on the couch.

"Sonja, yes it is." Mitch looked at me. He was attempting to take over the meeting. "Rachael, you have dyslexia," he said.

"What's that?" she asked.

"It means your brain processes things differently than most people, which is why reading and spelling are harder for you. When your brain looks at words or hears sounds, it's absorbing the information in a different way," Mitch explained.

"So it's not 'cause I'm stupid?" Rachael asked, looking relieved.

"No, not at all! People with dyslexia often have a higher level of emotional intelligence! Like empathy and people skills. That's invaluable!" I jumped in.

"How?" Rachael asked.

"Most people use three areas on the left side of the brain to process language. You use the right side." Mitch touched the top of her head.

"Oh"—she nodded—"I don't get it."

"Dyslexia is like a superpower." I sat up, excited. "You know how some animals are better at seeing in the dark, or hearing sounds far away?"

"Yeah."

"Well, just like some kids are *really* good at reading, you're *really* good at creativity, having original thoughts, and noticing people's emotions. The brain God gave you makes you different than most people," I said, giving her my best "You're the chosen one" speech.

"Wait, so I *am* special?" Rachael looked at me then Mitch.

"Yes." I nodded.

"I knew it!" She pulled her fists down in victory.

"Dyslexia comes with gifts and things to overcome. Math and reading are harder for you," Mitch said.

"That's fine. I don't like those things anyway." Rachael shrugged. "I want to be an author and zookeeper. I'll use my gifts to do those things. I love dyslexia!" She beamed, like her whole destiny was finally figured out.

"You need to learn to read and write to be an author," Mitch said.

"No, I don't. I can just tell you my stories and you can write them down for other people to read. My gift is thinking up the words, not writing them down," Rachael said.

"Not being able to read or write is hard. I'll be honest, that part of dyslexia sucks," I interjected, "But! If you're able to overcome these weaknesses, all you'll be left with is the gifts. Dyslexia will become your superpower and you will publish hundreds of books," I said, totally unaware that at twenty-three, my daughter would be the one to write my life story.

Her eyes widened with excitement. "Okay, how do I overcome the weakness? I want to get to the author part of this plan as soon as possible."

"It will require a lot of tutoring and hard work, but I'll be by your side for all of it. You won't have to go through it alone," I assured her.

"I'll be here for you too, Rachy." Mitch smiled at her.

"But there is a villain in every story. And your life is no exception," I said, tilting my chin down to her.

"Who's my villain?" Rachael asked.

"Your principal," I replied darkly.

"Sonja, don't say that," Mitch spoke up.

"Shhh." I put my fingers over his lips. "We have to tell her the truth. In order for her to be the heroine of her own story, she must know who her enemies are. How else will she defeat them?"

"Why is my principal my enemy?" Rachael squinted.

"He doesn't think you'll be able to pass third grade because you're dyslexic. He is a hundred percent certain you'll have to repeat third grade!"

"He is? Why doesn't he think I'll pass?"

"He doesn't believe in the gifts." I shook my head, disappointed.

"Most adults don't." Rachael nodded, like her principal was being all too predictable.

"So how are you feeling, Rach?" Mitch checked in.

"I just found out I'm a special hero with a villain! I'm so lucky to be dyslexic," she squealed with excitement.

Mitch shook his head, a bit amused, a bit concerned.

"We're going to teach your principal a very important lesson, Rachael." I looked into her eyes with an intensity that made me feel unstoppable.

—◦◦◦—

Rachael had seven months to catch up before state testing, but dyslexia wasn't the only obstacle we were facing. My emotional pain and exhaustion burned so hot that some nights I thought I was dying. Taking care of my kids' basic needs felt like crawling over broken glass, but I dug even deeper, giving more of myself to save my daughter from falling behind.

Before school in the morning, Rachael and I studied for an hour while she sat on my bed. Her hair perfectly gelled into pigtails, mine greased in a bun, we reviewed flash cards. After school, we visited THINKERS, a specialized program for children with dyslexia, auditory processing deficiency, and poor memory retention. Rachael had all three. I paid for every course they suggested and bought all the take-home programs. A teacher named Sophie worked with Rachael on a cognitive enhancement program called PACE, often referred to as "Mental Boot Camp." Rachael spent two hours every day in Sophie's office working on auditory analysis and processing speed. Sophie called out words and Rachael spelled the sounds—nonsense words like *gr* or *eck*. After tutoring at THINKERS, Rachael worked with a retired teacher who cut dozens of words in half. She'd call out a word and Rachael tried to spell it by piecing the fragments together.

By the end of the day, Rachael and I were worn out, but we still had homework to do from her teachers at school. Many nights, I found Rachael asleep at the kitchen table, her little cheek pressed against her big textbook. Mitch would carry her to bed, and for the next seven months, we continued this rigorous schedule.

I took my kids to lessons like any mother would, but I didn't look like every other mother. I had stains on my clothes, which I hadn't changed in weeks. Mitch knew not to bring up things like that; otherwise, an epic argument would ensue. Putting on fresh ones didn't seem like a good place to spend my limited energy with what was at stake for my daughter.

As I dropped my kids off at school, a friend of Alex's asked me, "Why don't you change your clothes?"

"I do," I lied. "I buy six of the same shirt and skirts." That part was true.

"Then why do they all have the same dirty spots?"

He had me there. Leave it to kids to tell the bold truth.

"I don't know." What else could I say?

"My mom counts the number of days you wear the same outfit. She said you're on day nine," he informed me. It felt like someone had punched me in the stomach. I didn't want to face the fact that people noticed my struggles. I'm sure the grease in my hair could not be missed, but I told myself it looked like I had gel in my hair—another justification, another lie. One would think having people notice would encourage me to change my clothes. It didn't. Basic grooming was too much work. I had to save every ounce of energy for my kids, so I sacrificed what other people thought of me. It had to be done. I pretended no one could see there was something wrong with me. I was fine. I was the fun mom who planned museum trips, sleepovers at the zoo, swim parties, and other activities for my kids and their friends. Once I claimed we were a homeschooling group (which we weren't at the time) to get the Houston Zoo to bring its Zoo Mobile full of live animals to one of our swim parties.

At the time, I told myself lots of people didn't shower for weeks or change their clothes. Even if most of them were homeless, they were still people.

"When was the last time you showered?" Mitch asked me that night.

"I don't remember…maybe two weeks? But it's fine." I rolled over in bed.

He pulled back the covers. "No, it's time for a bath."

"No!" I yanked them back on, annoyed.

"Come on." He sat me up.

"I will tomorrow," I bargained.

"Nope." He went into the bathroom and got the tub running.

"Mitch, no. Seriously, not today," I begged.

"Come on." He undressed me, starting with my socks. He guided me to the bathtub, and I sat in the warm water.

"Are we conditioning or just shampooing your hair today?" he asked.

"Just shampoo," I grumbled.

"Lean back." He poured shampoo on my head and scrubbed the grease out of my hair. Alex walked in and saw Mitch bathing me and quickly went back into our bedroom.

"So, Dad," he yelled from the bedroom, "is this something I'll need to do for my wife?"

"I don't know, buddy. Maybe," Mitch told him.

Is it bad that my kids know I can't function on my own?

"Okay, other one," Mitch instructed as he shaved my legs. The smell of soap washed out my stink. "Lean forward." He scrubbed my back before rinsing and wrapping my body in a towel. I leaned on him as he helped me put on underwear and a black shirt and skirt. Putting on pajamas was a waste of time, so I went to bed in clothes I would wear the next day.

"Mitch, I don't know why this is so hard for me," I said as he put me back in bed and got my toothbrush and a cup of water.

"Open," he said, hovering the toothbrush by my mouth. I opened and sleepily shut my eyes as he brushed. I took a big sip of water, swished it in my mouth, and spat it back into the cup like it was a portable sink.

"Feel better?" he asked.

"I do." I slunk deeper into bed. "I use all the energy I have on the kids, and then I'm left with nothing for me or you. But I love you. You know that, right?" My eyes searched inside his, and I saw the flecks of light blue that had once made my heart stop.

"I know, Sonja." He kissed my forehead.

"Thank you, Mitch." I sighed, leaning into him. "I feel so much better." But my energy deficit was so large, he alone could not fill it. Mitch took me to see dozens of doctors during this time. Every one of them diagnosed me with severe depression, which meant I was put on different depression medicines with little success. Most doctors recommended therapy, which Mitch was a big supporter of, but I continued to outrightly refuse it.

Mitch's strength, patience, and love fed my bottomless soul. We were a team, but we were both running on fumes. The reason I had energy for my children was because in many ways, I was drawing it from my husband. I couldn't let my kids down. That would be the ultimate blow to my self-esteem.

The day of the state test, I knelt with Rachael and we said a prayer. "Dear God, Rachael and I have done everything we could. Please send angels to help her as she takes this test. Amen."

"Do you really think angels will help me?" she asked.

"Of course!"

"But what if I haven't been good enough?"

"God doesn't ask for perfection, just your best. And you have definitely given that. Have some faith. It's in God's hands now."

Several weeks later, I got a call from the principal. "Mrs. Wasden, I got the state test results and sorted through them to look at Rachael's first."

I gripped the phone tighter.

"I believe an apology is in order. She passed."

Silence.

Slowly, it registered in my brain what he said. *We passed? We did it!*

"Thank you! Thank you so much for calling and letting us know!" I screamed with excitement and hung up the phone.

I picked up Rachael from school that day, and her teacher was crying. No one could believe she passed. As we walked home, I gripped her hand. "I'm so proud of you," I said.

"The angels helped," Rachael said.

"Yes, they did! And we taught your principal the truest lesson there is: faith and hard work move mountains."

That day, Rachael learned she could overcome difficult trials, but what kind of example was I? I taught my children that with God, all things are possible. Did I really believe that? I did for other people, but I doubted it for myself. I was hanging by a thread that could snap at any moment. *Where is God for me? Why isn't He sending angels to help me?*

CHAPTER 13

Psych Ward, Day Five

"Someone in this room is stealing crayons, and it needs to stop!" Janet looked out at the sea of patients. "Tell me who it is, and we will restock the crayons."

Everyone had been summoned to the conference room for a meeting, and the longer Janet talked, the more I couldn't believe this was the reason. I looked side to side to see if anyone would fess up. Everyone knew someone was stealing the crayons at the drawing table. First, all the blue crayons went, then red, then green. The theft caused some of the patients to lose their patience when trying to color. People complained that only brown and orange crayons were left. Today, the browns were stolen.

"For those of you who don't know me, I'm Janet Cooper, an important counselor here. So cooperating with me is in each of your best interests. So, who is the thief?" Janet demanded.

A young man sitting behind me giggled, and another patient to my right joined in.

Janet pointed to them. "Are you the thieves?"

They giggled harder and nodded their heads.

"Stop laughing," she scolded them, which only made them laugh harder. "This is *not* funny. Give me the stolen crayons!"

A different patient shot her hand up. "It's me, I stole them!"

"No, I'm the crayon thief!" another patient confessed.

"You four go to your rooms! This will not be tolerated." Janet yelled over the laughter.

They got up and left, laughing the whole way. I felt laughter surfacing in my chest. I put my hand over my mouth to stop it.

A man in the front row jumped up. "After I leave here, I'm going to jail, so with nothing to lose, I might as well confess. I stole the blue crayons."

More and more of us laughed, and Janet kept dismissing people to their rooms as they confessed to stealing the crayons. There ended up being three of us left. I was proud I made it to the final three. But in the end, I couldn't control myself and burst out laughing, too. I was immediately dismissed to my room. Sydney and I sat on our beds.

"Who do you think really stole the crayons?" I asked.

"Maybe it was Janet," Sydney suggested.

"I swear this place is like an elementary school. You teach at one— what do you think?"

"Yeah, this place isn't so different—makes me feel right at home."

"Do you like being a schoolteacher?" I asked.

"Yeah, I do. I have this treasure box filled with stickers and little toys that the kids can purchase with the 'golden bucks' they earn for good behavior. It's fun." She smiled.

"I bet they miss you."

"Do you like being a mom?" Sydney asked.

"I love it. I miss my kids so much."

My heart was breaking. I hated that the hospital didn't allow children to visit, even if they knew their parent's situation, and mine did. I would say I didn't believe in putting up facades for children, but the truth was I didn't know how to. My kids understood with an abnormal amount of clarity what I was experiencing. I viewed my children as my equals and assumed they could handle themselves with adult matters. They gave me few reasons to believe otherwise.

"What are they like?" she asked.

"Rachael is artistic and wants to be a writer. She is my best friend. We have girls' nights and watch movies and eat chocolate in my bed. But she's also my sounding board. She sees situations clearly, so I rely on her perspective. She also helps me take care of the house and my sons. She's like their second mother, and at times, mine."

"How old is she?"

"Twelve."

"Wow. She sounds like a very mature twelve-year-old. What are your sons like?"

"Alex is my opposite. If I'm an open book, he's a locked diary. He's an old soul, and Rachael often jokes that he was born eighty years old even though he's ten. He wants homecooked meals and a structured family life, which, well, I definitely fall short of. Lincoln is the most like me. We share an emotional intensity that makes us understand each other but also can't stand each other. He is loud and vocal, shares his thoughts freely, and is open with his emotions and fears. He can have a conversation with anyone, no matter their age. His social skills at seven are better than mine."

"Sometimes I wonder if I had kids what they'd be like," Sydney said. Someone knocked on the door.

"Sonja, it's time for you to meet with Dr. Barry," a nurse interrupted.

"Again?" I said.

"Yes, you meet with him every day."

I quietly followed her to the room where Dr. Barry sat, waiting for me.

"Good afternoon." He straightened his white coat.

I sat and forced a smile while I braced myself for more questions.

"Would you say you're impulsive?" He clicked his pen, ready to write down a list of crazy behaviors, no doubt.

"No," I answered, hoping to disappoint him.

"So it says here that you and the kids were late to church, but you decided you had to pull into a car wash and power wash your car."

"So what? It was filthy. I didn't want to be that family that drives a car so dirty that kids write 'wash me' on the windows."

"But after washing the outside, you power washed the inside of the van, too? Does that strike you as impulsive?"

"Not really." I shrugged.

"Did it destroy the van?"

"Well…yeah," I admitted. "I didn't realize the water would rot the electrical wiring and seat fabric." I hoped he would see the situation for what it was—an honest mistake—and not some radical behavior.

"It also says here that you gained and then lost over one hundred pounds. When did you start gaining weight?"

"After I had my third baby, I started eating a lot."

"What caused your eating habits to change so dramatically?"

"I don't know. I was just hungrier. I used to eat all my kids' Halloween candy in one night. I always replaced it, and the candy was on sale the day after anyway."

"Would your kids get upset?"

"No, they were used to it. Whenever we had any desserts in the house, my kids begged me to save them a single piece to share. Of course, I'd eat the whole thing, so we'd drive to the store and buy another one. No big deal."

"How do you think that affected your children?"

"It didn't affect them," I straightened up, finding his question offensive.

"Sonja, there's no way your children haven't been affected by your illness."

"First, I'm not ill. Second, I would protect my children at all costs, even from myself!"

"I don't doubt that. But all parents harm their kids in some way. Even if they don't want to see it." Dr. Barry's comment stung as I considered the possibility of his statement.

CHAPTER 14

Hungry

Sugar Land, Texas, 2006

The warm Texas sun felt good against my face. I wore my traditional long black skirt and white T-shirt. My hair was pulled up into a bun by three scrunchies, multiple pens stabbed through it. I liked having pens on hand for abrupt note-taking. Our house was within walking distance to the local H-E-B grocery, and when the kids were at school, I self-medicated with food.

I walked into the store, and my bare feet loved the cold floor after the hot cement. I filled my cart with king-size candy bars—Snickers, Twix, and Hershey's were my favorites. I anxiously ripped open the Twix wrapper, devouring it as I dropped a bag of Swedish Fish into the cart. I scanned the aisles looking for other edible pain relievers. A chocolate cake, a bag of Cheetos, corn chips, and a jar of Tostitos cheese dip were on the menu that day. I opened the bag of Cheetos and shoved them into my mouth faster than I could chew. The hole inside was so deep and hard to fill, but it didn't stop me from trying.

As I licked Cheeto dust off each finger, I scanned the donut section. I grabbed a glazed donut from the bakery case and took a bite. *Yep, yummy.* I put the half-eaten donut into a pastry box. A chocolate-covered donut with sprinkles couldn't be missed. I grabbed it and ate the whole thing standing there. The sugar rush was awesome. I took ten other donuts and bit into each one of them as I placed them into the box. I parked my cart at a closed checkout aisle, took my food out, and set it on the floor. I wasn't hungry in a traditional sense, but starving in an, "I can't get the food inside me fast enough" sort of way. If others were watching, they would have thought I hadn't seen food in months. But my figure suggested something else.

I sat on the floor next to the magazine rack and pulled out several magazines. A few H-E-B workers walked past me, recognizing me from my frequent visits. Picking up the top magazine in my stack, I flopped it open on my lap, opened the donut box, and ate every last one. *Mmmmm, so good.* The headline on the magazine stated that Carnie Wilson had lost 150 pounds after getting gastric bypass surgery. I cracked open the cheese dip jar and flipped the page to continue reading her success story. *Was this my answer?*

I wanted to get the surgery after reading her story but had no way to pay for it. I brainstormed how I could make this happen as I flipped through the pages. I dipped my chips, crunching through half the bag before finishing magazine two. Some cheese sauce spilled on my T-shirt. It wasn't as effortless as I made it look to eat on the hard store floor. I scraped the yellow sauce off my shirt with a chip, but it stained the collar. I closed the lid to the jar and put the plastic top back on the eaten cake tray. I stood, brushing some chocolate cake crumbs off me, and pushed my cart to an open cashier. I placed the empty candy bar wrappers on the conveyor belt. The cashier looked up at me as he scanned them. He opened the donut box and saw nothing but glaze stains inside.

"There were twelve," I informed him.

He closed the box and typed in the number. He proceeded to bag the candy bar wrappers, the empty jar of cheese, cake tray, and donut box.

"Your total will be $23.48," he said. I dug my hand into my smelly, stained shirt and reached inside my bra for the credit card. He looked at it and paused. He grabbed a plastic bag from his rack, placed his hand into the bag like a makeshift glove, and used it to reach for the card.

"Would you like your receipt?" he asked, even though there was nothing left to return.

I shoved the credit card back into my bra. "No, thanks."

I was fat and getting fatter each day. I gained weight proportionally, which isn't as useful as it sounds. The fat became so contagious, I was suddenly fat everywhere. My eyes were the first things to disappear, and it became hard to distinguish what was a leg and what was an arm. I went to the doctor when a large lump appeared on the back of my neck. I thought I had a cancerous growth, but without any testing, the doctor assured me it was just fat.

I needed help to control my overeating; I couldn't do it alone. I rushed home to start my research on gastric bypass surgery. I was a woman on a mission. I needed a job that would give me great health insurance since our current insurance wouldn't cover the surgery. I got a part-time job at a hospital as a phlebotomist. Once again, my career as a phlebotomist was paying dividends when it came to health insurance coverage.

One big roadblock was in order to be a candidate for the surgery, most patients had to have a body mass index (BMI) of 40, and I was at a 38. I made an appointment with a gastric bypass surgeon that week and needed to fix the problem quickly. I knew I couldn't eat my way to a BMI of 40 in a week, but I tried. To guarantee success, I purchased twelve ankle weights at Walmart.

"What are you doing?" Mitch blinked. The kids held ankle weights up to my body as I duct-taped them in place.

"Hold it right there, Lincoln," I said, biting off a strip of duct tape as our five-year-old struggled to hold the weight in place on my thigh.

"Mom's going to a doctor's appointment, and they're going to weigh her," Rachael explained.

"She doesn't weigh enough," Alex said.

"What doctor's appointment?" Mitch asked.

"I'm going to get gastric bypass and I need to make sure I qualify," I said.

"Sonja, don't do that; it's dishonest," Mitch said. "There's no way they won't notice."

"Mitchell, just stop! This is purely a formality," I snapped. "It's not like I won't get heavier on my own. Without this surgery, my weight will keep climbing to the weight they want."

"And how are you going to pay for the surgery?" he asked.

"That's why I got the job at the hospital. Insurance covers it." I smiled, pleased with myself.

"Well, don't make the kids a part of it."

"Do you *really* want to fight about this right now?!" I dropped my skirt, ready to go to war.

He looked at the kids and let it go. There were many times Mitch had to choose to either go to war and destroy the household in the process or let me be. He knew I'd do what I thought was best, even if he thought it was irrational. When people asked Mitch why he let me garden in my underwear or grocery shop barefoot, he tried to tell them it wasn't a matter of him "letting me." He had no more control over me than a stranger.

Before my appointment, I dropped some weights into my coat pockets for safe measure and waddled into the doctor's office.

"Remove your coat and step on the scale," the nurse instructed.

With my heart pounding, I gently laid my ten-pound coat on the chair and stepped on the scale.

My nerves and the struggle of moving were making me sweat and gasp for air. I needed this. This was my last hope to lose weight. I had tried everything! The number flickered on screen. The nurse wrote down "248" on her clipboard. I relaxed and stepped off the scale. I qualified even without all the weights. I learned that typically a BMI of 35 or higher will qualify you for gastric bypass surgery, with other health problems, which I had.

On the day of the surgery, I was weighed again, but this time I didn't have my weights with me. The number "238" flashed before my eyes. "Wow, you've lost some weight before the surgery!" the nurse congratulated me.

Soon, I was in the pre-op hospital bed, in a gown with an IV dripping into my arm as I waited to be taken to surgery. I felt nervous, but relieved. My stomach was going to be made a smaller size. There'd be no way to shove the amount of food down like I used to. I was morbidly obese and at risk for diabetes. I had to get well for my kids. I thought of them coming home from school and seeing the Valentine's Day bags full of gifts I had left.

The staff worker wheeled me into the operating room. It was ice cold and all my excitement turned into nerves. *Maybe this is my solution; it helped Carnie Wilson!* I thought before going under.

My recovery was slow and arduous, and fitting several moves into the mix didn't help. Three months post-surgery, we followed Mitch from Texas to Albuquerque for a job. Six months later, we left Albuquerque and moved to Baton Rouge, Louisiana, for another promotion. Mitch was now a vice president of a hospital that was in the Ochsner Health System—a company he'd worked for previously.

I developed an intense sensitivity to sugar. I tried to eat three Skittles and instantly threw up. My diet was restrictive, but the surgery worked. I lost over a hundred pounds in a year, and with time, my diet normalized.

The darkness remained, but solving my weight removed a pain point. When I looked in the mirror, my reflection looked like me. I was no longer lost under the blanket of self-destructive behavior. Although I still had pain, when I looked in the mirror I saw Sonja, and I never wanted to lose her again. I saw many people eat through their gastric bypass surgery and gain all the weight back, but I didn't. Why did it work for me? Was it because I knew this was my final option? Was it because I never drank soda? Was the fear of getting fat again keeping me from overeating? There are so many unanswered questions in the world, and this is one of them. For whatever the reason, this was a miracle I didn't need an answer to.

A few years after my gastric bypass surgery, I went to my niece's wedding back in Sugar Land, Texas. At the wedding reception, I saw one of my old friends. I hugged her and asked how she was doing. She looked at me, confused, and asked who I was. I couldn't believe it! We had been close friends for four years. When I told her who I was, she slapped her hand against her chest in shock. "When Mitch put his arm around you, I thought he divorced you and got remarried," she told me. I didn't know what to say. Now, I was the one shocked. I had deluded myself into believing people didn't notice my weight gain or weight loss. I lived in a reality I could cope with, and oftentimes, that reality lacked any sort of truth.

CHAPTER 15

Psych Ward, Day Six

"Sonja, there's an urgent meeting you need to attend." The nurse walked me to a room I hadn't been to before. "Go in," he instructed.

I opened the door and saw Mitch sitting next to my mom. Janet had them pinned with her gaze as she sat on her throne and shifted her eyes in my direction.

"Sit down, Sonja," Janet commanded.

Regardless of her off-putting demeanor, Mitch seemed relieved to be here. *Was it good news?* My mom was silent and stoic. She was hard to read, and like usual, I struggled to know her real feelings and thoughts. I sat on the other side of Mitch and anxiously took his hand. He was my only source of comfort.

Janet wasted no time saying, "Sonja's mentally ill. She's bipolar." She spoke as if I weren't in the room. The words dropped like bombshells around us.

Mitch let out an audible breath. "Finally," he said. I looked at him, confused.

"I hate to break it to you, honey, but Janet is the least trustworthy person in this room," I said.

"Sonja, you are bipolar," Janet said.

"What the hell do you mean I'm bipolar? You've known me for six days. Have we even had a proper conversation, a real heart-to-heart?" I paused after posing my questions, knowing she wouldn't answer. "No, we haven't!"

"Sonja—" My mom tried interrupting me, but I couldn't be stopped. They had to know this wasn't going to be a cut-and-dry meeting.

"How irresponsible of you, labeling me mentally ill. Are you even a doctor? Are you qualified to make that diagnosis?" I turned to Mitch. He looked at me like I was burning down our victory flag. "You don't think I'm bipolar, do you?"

He hesitated. "I don't know."

"Your doctor diagnosed you, Sonja. You *are* bipolar." Janet appeared to enjoy saying it a little too much.

"Then where's my doctor? Why is he not telling me my diagnosis? A real classy place you've got here. Real professional, Janet."

"It's a lifelong illness. You have to accept it." She stiffened.

"And what if I don't?" I leaned forward in my chair, my eyes locked on her. "You think you're going to hand me a life sentence without a peep from me? NOT A CHANCE IN HELL!" I screamed.

"This family meeting is over!" Janet stood. "You're not leaving here until you accept it. Do you hear me? You're not leaving this hospital until you admit you're bipolar!" She opened the door. "Nurses, come get Sonja."

I grabbed on to Mitch's arm, but he sat as still as possible, his jaw clenched.

"Don't let her get away with this!" I begged as two female nurses grabbed my wrists and pulled me off him. "Mitch, help me!" I cried, thrashing against the attempts they made to remove me.

"I am," he choked up as they pried me off him.

"Mitch, this place is terrible! They're lying to you!" In a wild attempt to claw out of their hands, I saw Mitch flinch. "Please, stop them!" I shouted trying to get his attention, but he barely looked at me as they yanked me through the doorway.

They dragged and locked me in a holding room. I pounded my fists against the door. "Mitch! I'm in here!" I screamed for hours. I leaned against the wall, exhausted, wondering what they were telling him and my mom about me. Was Mitch asking them to let me out, or agreeing that I should stay longer? Hours passed, and no one came to release me. I personally knew five people with mental illness who died from suicide. Some were family, some friends or neighbors. The illness showed no mercy. If there is a definition of hell, I believed mental illness was it.

That night, I was let out and brought to Dr. Barry. My bones felt hollow, my body like a husk devoid of anything meaningful inside. I sat quietly, trying to figure out how I could put myself back together into something resembling a successful wife and mother.

"Sonja, you have to understand you are bipolar," Dr. Barry repeated.

I was far away, and Dr. Barry beckoned me into the present moment.

"Are you listening to me?" he tried again. "Bipolar disorder is a genetic illness, and it runs in your family. I have a folder here of your family history. Your dad is diagnosed as bipolar. Your aunt is bipolar. Some cousins. How can you not see it's entirely plausible you have it, too?"

"One of those cousins had a vision he needed to convert Tiger Woods to Christianity. I haven't had any visions. Nor am I interested in converting anyone to any religion."

"I never said you were delusional."

I was terrified of having the same illness as my grandfather, father, aunt, and some cousins. Their horrible experiences with the illness filled my mind: jail, bizarre visions, bankruptcy, attempted suicides.

"I *refuse* to belong to a group of people deemed crazy and violent." I looked at him. "I can't be bipolar."

"Well, you are. You've had manic and depressive episodes, a reduced need for sleep, and you've lost touch with reality. Sonja, you've been extremely suicidal." He sighed. "There have been many times I was unsure what diagnosis to give my patients, but with you, I'm certain. You're bipolar."

His confidence in my diagnosis absorbed any fight I had left to deny it. I already knew I'd been living in hell. He had just put a name to it—*bipolar*. That diagnosis slammed the doors on any possibility I could live a normal life. He stole that from me. He was asking me to live an impossible life. I knew he was speaking a truth I had to face. I closed my eyes and mustered courage from every corner of my being to accept this new reality: I would battle this illness for the rest of my life. It wasn't curable, and that was a fact I knew all too well.

"You're right. It's a family illness, and I guess I got nailed with it."

"Sonja, what illness do you have?" he pressed.

I knew what he wanted. I felt bile rising in my throat, leaving a slow, burning sensation in its path. My hands gripped each side of the chair until my knuckles turned white. My teeth clamped down on my lower lip, holding back the words from being uttered until it bled. An internal battle was being fought. Thoughts of my husband and children ached in my heart, and it was no contest. I knew who would win. Them. I will always choose them.

"I am bipolar."

—◊◊◊—

Later that night, Mitch sat on the couch in the psych ward, waiting while I discussed my diagnosis with Dr. Barry. I saw him pacing the waiting room when I walked toward him. I stopped, standing toe to toe with him. Despite holding my chin high in the air, I was certain my eyes showed the fear.

"Fine. I'll accept I'm bipolar," I declared.

"Really?" Mitch looked at me.

Eyes blazing, I asked, "My question is, are you willing to fight this illness with me?"

He took my hands in his. "When have I not fought your battles with you?"

"This morning with Janet."

"And before then?" he asked.

"Never."

"Then you should know you don't need to ask. I'll stand by your side." He kissed my fingers, which were ice cold.

"I know if I want to keep my family, I have to acknowledge I have a mental illness."

"That's definitely a step in the right direction."

"My twenty-year-old self is grieving the life I thought I'd have. I spent so much energy dreaming and planning my future; I was so excited for it. I never thought this would be where I ended up. My dreams have all gone up in smoke," I said.

"Letting things burn isn't always destructive. Sometimes letting something go up in flames is cleansing. Gives you a fresh start." He was trying to reframe our situation. "I know you crave freedom, but you need to find some type of freedom within your mental illness."

"I just need time."

I later found out my situation wasn't all that uncommon. A survey by the National Depressive and Manic-Depressive Association reported almost 70% of people with bipolar disorder are initially misdiagnosed, and more than one-third remain misdiagnosed for ten years or longer.[1]

My mental illness didn't show up one day and display all the symptoms at once for family members and doctors to evaluate. They appeared in fragmented pieces building gradually over time, making it hard to grasp the stark difference between where I started and now. For years,

---

1. Singh, Tanvir, and Muhammad Rajput. "Misdiagnosis of bipolar disorder." *Psychiatry (Edgmont)* 3, no. 10 (2006): 57–63.

I wondered what tugged me off course, refusing to consider mental illness as an option, but now, I knew. *Bipolar disorder.*

—⟋⟋⟋—

My final day in the psych ward, I paced in front of the double doors while everyone else was at breakfast. I was too excited about going home to eat. Mitch would be coming through the doors any minute. The minutes passed like sand rolling through syrup, but when I heard the buzzer, I knew it was him. The doors opened, and he stood between them, holding cream roses. He looked excited and nervous, and with the flowers, he looked like he was about to take me on a date. I ran into his arms, almost knocking him over.

He wrapped me in a hug. "Ready to go home?"

The word *home* hit me, and I hugged him harder. "Yes, please!"

He handed me the cream roses, which were my favorite.

"Thank you, Mitch."

"I've missed you." His lips brushed mine, and I pressed into him, pushing our lips together. He gripped the small of my back, and I could feel his heart beating under my palm.

I loved this man. We were connected in a thousand ways I never wanted to break. It would be my life's goal to keep him. Although Mitch could be irritable, arrogant, and impatient—he was the person I needed him to be when it mattered most. I felt he was a gift from my otherwise silent God.

We walked outside to our car, and not a single tree or branch I passed went unnoticed. Stepping outside into a parking lot felt like such a luxury. It was a freedom I wouldn't take lightly again.

My mom, Allyson, and the three kids were waiting for me when I walked into the house. I dropped my bag and opened my arms wide toward my kids, and they rushed into them.

"It's good to have you back," Mitch said, seeing how excited the kids were to have me home.

"You don't look tired anymore," Lincoln said, looking up at me as he touched my face.

"I finally got to sleep." I smiled easily—a smile the kids hadn't seen in a long time.

"Look what I drew while you were gone." Rachael flopped open her messy sketchbook to a drawing of a black bear catching salmon.

I tapped my finger on the bear. "We will have to get a frame for that one. It's good, like really good."

"*And* I wrote seven chapters while you were gone! My book is starting to take a surprising turn. I think you'll be shocked," she added.

I hugged her. "I can't wait to read it. I'm so proud of you investing in your talents." I rested my head on hers. Rachael was my vacation and my home. She was easy to know and didn't demand much. She was my everything, and equally, I was hers.

Alex stood near me. His posture was stiff as he watched me in silence. He was quiet, I was loud. He was calm, I was chaotic. He was private, I was public. He liked routine and I was incapable of it. I hoped he'd want a relationship with me once he grew up and moved out. I often didn't know what he thought of me.

"Hi, Mom," he finally said as I leaned in for a personal hug. He cautiously took my hand. "Come look at the fort Dad and I made in the playroom."

"Mom, hold my hand, too! I missed you!" Lincoln tugged on my other hand.

"Okay," I laughed, following them upstairs to their secret fort. Lincoln couldn't get enough of my attention while Alex squirmed under it. It seemed that Alex didn't have needs, Lincoln had too many, and Rachael only focused on mine. Though I felt inadequate, I knew no one could replace a kids' mom, mentally ill or not.

Mitch spent hours researching bipolar disorder. I could tell he felt nervous about having me home. While doctors had brought us this far, our confidence in the mental health field was shaken.

When reading about bipolar disorder, the words "avoid antidepressants" came up several times. The very antidepressants doctors had been giving me for years made bipolar worse; many even trigger manic episodes. At the time, we thought my sudden mood switches were a positive sign when they were actually bringing out a different side of the illness. My thoughts about the past, the present, and the future were tangled together like a big, messy ball of yarn. All I knew was my bipolar disorder, marriage, and kids all had to figure out a way to coexist.

Despite my discomfort with my diagnosis, Mitch was glad doctors had located the problem. Our plan was for me to diligently take medication and go to therapy. For now, we hoped that would be enough.

CHAPTER 16

The Routine

Baton Rouge, Louisiana, 2007

Who am I? Just released from the psych ward and now I'm a walking display case of gold bracelets. I ran my fingers across my armor. Jewelry was my obsession. *How many gold bracelets will it take to get me through church today?* I walked over to my dresser, repurposed as a jewelry box, and opened the drawers to inspect my collection and piled more gold bracelets onto each wrist until I felt better. I looked in the mirror, not connecting to the person who stood in the reflection.

Our little crew walked into church that morning and huddled together on a bench as though nothing had happened. I was glad Mitch and I could come to church and uphold the appearance of being a normal family. It felt nice to fit in. I couldn't believe I had been to a psych ward and back without any friends—in fact, without anybody in the whole congregation except my family members on this very bench—knowing about it. I sat quietly, poised in our church's pew with my three children and husband as the congregation sang: *"Where can I turn for peace? Where is my solace? When other sources cease to make me whole..."*

Dressed in my Sunday best, my hair tied in a bun with every strand combed into place, listening to the lyrics, crumbling inside, I vowed to keep this part of me, the bipolar disorder, so deeply hidden that it would feel like a dirty secret.

—m—

That Monday the kids and I stepped out of the car and walked through the humid Louisiana greenery onto cracked tennis courts. The boys set down their red water jugs and jogged out to the middle of the court for warmups. My daily routine was slathering on sunscreen and putting on my big hat for safe measure. We were always half an hour early so the boys could practice serving to targets. I researched how much time kids needed to practice to become professionals and built a homeschooling schedule around those hours. They had a private tennis coach and practiced five to six hours a day, six days a week.

Their coach, Vincent, arrived, and I dumped tennis balls into the ball machine while the boys hit. Normally, Vincent would have his students pick up after a drill, but if they spent twenty percent of their time retrieving balls, they were wasting practice time. Rachael and I took turns picking up the balls they hit and refilling the ball machine so Vincent could coach them the entire time. When it was my turn to pick up, Rachael sat in a wobbly plastic chair doing homework under the shade of the lone tree leaning over the court.

Aside from Vincent's coaching, the only sounds were the *pop* of tennis balls hitting thick racket strings or a tennis grunt when the boys hit the ball with all their might. Yellow fuzz flew over my head and rattled against the metal fence before falling into a bounce on the green concrete. Rachael and I tried dodging as many as we could, but it was impossible to leave practice without a few hits in the back, arm, or leg.

Hard work, excellence, and overcoming failure were important family values. Mitch working on his grandpa's farm in the summer taught him the value of hard work, and tennis was the boys' version of a farm. Mitch saw the hard work as its own end, whether our sons became professional tennis players or not, but I told Mitch and Vincent *many* times all this effort was only worth it if the boys went pro. It was all black-and-white in my mind: either they become pro tennis players or we stop lessons. There was no middle path where the boys did tennis just to have fun, make friends, and learn sportsmanship. It was either a career or a waste of time. I appreciated that the boys were learning hard work, but I needed a bigger payoff in exchange for the toll tennis took on me, personally and financially.

The investment we made was substantial, spending over $30,000 a year in tennis lessons, shoes, rackets, and tournaments. Each loss on the court was emotionally catastrophic for me, and each win was redemptive and addictive. With bipolar disorder, it had to be all or nothing, win or lose—a dichotomy that gave me indescribable highs and cataclysmic lows.

A problematic part of mania was even though it gave me superhuman strength to achieve the impossible, some things were still out of my control. The boys got injuries, games were rained out, and at times, coaches gave lousy advice. Mania could not solve everything, but its emotional force still ran through me like a freight train. My laser-focus mindset put an enormous amount of pressure on the boys.

"Read your books," I told my sweaty kids as we got in the car. I had them read while I drove to and from tennis. Time was precious, and I wanted every minute to further their development. I was such a stickler about not wasting time that one of our tutors called me a slave driver behind my back.

As soon as we got home, the kids piled bottles of dish soap into their arms and ran under the carport for their thirty-minute break. They loved filling storage bins with water and soap to make their own tiny swimming pools. While the kids played, I read a romance novel. My mind moved at such a fast pace I could complete two or three books in a day. We had three fifty-gallon storage bins in the garage for all the romance novels I'd finished reading, since there was no place for them on the bookshelves. I put my book down and looked out the back door. Alex had his shirt off and sat in an old bucket, chin-high in bubbles. I opened the screen door and walked out. He turned to look at me through a pair of fogged-up goggles.

"We're snorkeling," he said. Water dumped over the rim as he looked under water.

I took a step back from the puddle and saw empty Dawn bottles strewn on the wet driveway and smiled. *They're having a good childhood. I'm providing them moments of happiness. That's all that really matters.*

"Mom, look at mine!" Lincoln said, squeezing the last bit of dish soap into his bucket. Rachael sprayed the hose at it, turning all his blue soap into foam.

I couldn't help but laugh as he strapped on his own set of goggles and dove in, struggling to get more than half of his face underwater since his bucket was so shallow. He came up for air and wiped off the bubbles around his mouth.

"You can play for five more minutes. The reading tutors will be here soon," I said, setting a pile of towels on a patch of dry cement.

I went inside and pulled a heavy Stouffer's lasagna out of the oven and set out plates. If we weren't having frozen lasagna, we were having Taco Bell. Or Hot Pockets. The kids came running in and scarfed down their food as Amy and Charlotte's little red car pulled into the driveway.

"Hi, Sonja!" they greeted, sidestepping the soapy water.

"The kids are ready to start; just take them upstairs," I said.

Usually, I helped the tutors with the kids' reading, but today, I had to deep clean. I sprayed each bookshelf with lemon-scented wood polish. The spray looked like heavy mist in the sunlight. As I reached for my cloth, an unexpected surge of panic grabbed me by the throat. I dropped the dusting cloth and wrapped my hand around my neck. I struggled to breathe, and my heart rattled inside me. No matter how deeply I breathed, I couldn't get air in fast enough. *A heart attack?* That had to be it. My ears rang. I sat on the carpet, struggling to breathe, and dialed Mitch's number.

"Mitch, I can't breathe!" I gasped.

"What? Seriously? Should I come get you? You need to get to the hospital," Mitch said.

"I'll have one of the tutors take me," I wheezed.

I stumbled to the playroom and leaned against the wall. "Can one of you take me to the ER?" I whispered.

"Are you okay?" Amy asked, getting a better look at me.

"I think…I think I'm having a heart attack." That got her attention.

She dropped me off at the emergency room where Mitch was waiting for me. He took me by the hand, and when we approached the front desk, the receptionist did a double take. It's not every day the CEO comes to the emergency room for anything other than business. The receptionist picked up a phone to make a call, and within minutes we were in a room with several nurses.

"Sonja, you need to take deep breaths. You're hyperventilating," one nurse coached while other nurses put warm blankets over me.

The doctor opened the door and came to my bedside. "I'm Dr. Griffin, and I'll be taking care of you today. Mr. Wasden." He nodded, shaking Mitch's hand.

"Deep breaths, Mrs. Wasden," the nurse reminded me.

I nodded and tried breathing slower, but my whole body was shaking. I rasped, "Something's not right."

"I want to run some tests before we do anything," Dr. Griffin said.

After the tests, Dr. Griffin returned to my room. "I want you to know your vitals and the ECG came back normal. You're going to be just fine."

Mitch gripped my hand. "You're going to be okay."

I didn't believe them. All I could feel was the burning in my chest and the lack of air going to my head. My body was in distress. I needed medicine, surgery—something more than a pat on the back.

"However, you are having an acute panic attack," Dr. Griffin continued. "I'm going to have the nurses start an IV that will calm you down."

I'd had panic attacks before—this was different. My body was shutting down.

"You'll need to go see your psychiatrist and set up a plan to deal with these attacks in the future," the doctor said.

The medicine ran through my veins, flushing away the pain. My breathing regulated and I felt the oxygen in my lungs. I drank a cup of apple juice and snuggled into the warm blankets while we waited for the IV to finish. Once I was full of drugs, Mitch and I left the hospital.

"Is Charlotte still with the kids?" I asked, looking at the sky, realizing it was night.

"Don't worry. I called and said we'd be home a little late. Rachael's got it covered." Mitch held my hand. "How are you feeling?"

"Better, but honestly, I don't want to make another plan with my psychiatrist and get more meds. I want to medicate myself."

"And how would you medicate yourself?"

I buckled myself in and thought about it. "Chocolate," I finally answered.

"What?" Mitch laughed.

"I would medicate myself with chocolate."

Mitch turned out of the parking garage and looked at me. "And you think that could help your anxiety?"

"Yeah?" I looked back at him and shrugged.

Mitch got quiet and turned on the radio. I looked out the passenger window at all the navy clouds and taillights reflecting in the rain on the street. I couldn't stop thinking about the panic attack; it felt like a near-death experience. That night, I felt a lot like the puddles we were splashing through—cold and unsure if I'd be there the next day. Mitch parked the car. I did a double take before getting out. "Why are we at Target?" I creased my brows at the glowing red letters. Of all nights to stop and run an errand, tonight was not the one.

"Well, Dr. Wasden, I think it's time you try your new prescription." Mitch smirked.

I sat staring at him. "How much chocolate can I buy? That was a very serious question," I cut Mitch off before he could laugh.

"As much as it takes. In your professional opinion, that is," he said. The bright-red sign didn't seem as obnoxious now.

We stood in front of all my closest friends—Godiva, Ghirardelli, Lindt, and all things dark chocolate. I filled my cart with every version those brands offered. As any doctor will tell you, there are multiple medications to try, and I planned on trying them all.

"Do you think we got enough?" Mitch asked, placing chocolate bags on the conveyor belt.

"I think we got every chocolate pill they offer." I pressed my lips against his. "Thank you," I whispered.

When we pulled into our driveway, I realized I had to find a place for all this chocolate. I walked into the kitchen and emptied a cabinet that famously became known as my "Chocolate Cupboard." Like a medicine cabinet, but better.

"You're home!" The kids ran into the kitchen.

"Hey, stinkers!" Mitch set down his briefcase and hugged them. Mitch excelled at compartmentalizing his life. His religion, family, career, and my illness all lived in separate boxes that he could shut and open at will. Suppressing his thoughts and emotions was as automatic for him as breathing, and it seemed to me he developed that skill as a defense mechanism.

The kids told him about tennis and Rachael's near miss to the face by Alex's tennis ball. He tried his best to follow their poor job at trading off storytelling.

"Well, you guys must be too tired for a Cowboy Johnny story after how crazy your day has been. You probably want to go straight to bed," he said.

"No!" The kids panicked.

Years ago, he created a story about a boy named Cowboy Johnny, and the idea stuck. Mitch's improvisational skills had gotten good, and he could create a twenty-minute story within a few seconds.

"All right, maybe a short one!" He smiled.

Mitch changed out of his suit and led the kids upstairs. Even though they all had their own bedrooms, they preferred sleeping together in Lincoln's room. The boys crawled under the covers of the queen bed, and Rachael curled up in her designated spot at the foot of the bed. It didn't look comfortable, but we didn't stop them.

"Do you all know what you want in the story?" Mitch asked. It was tradition they each got to pick something to make an appearance in the story.

"A green cheetah!" Alex called out.

"A parakeet!" Rachael added.

"Lincoln, what do you want?" Alex asked.

"I want an egg," Lincoln replied.

"An egg?" Alex raised his eyebrows.

"All right, a cheetah, a parakeet, and an egg," Mitch said, scooting in between the boys. "There once was a boy named Cowboy Johnny," was his opening line.

The kids listened intently for when each of their additions were going to enter the story. I sat on the edge of the bed until it was over, and Mitch and I tucked them in.

"I want a trophy," Rachael said, looking at the boys' dresser crowded with tennis awards. They had so many we started storing them in the closet. After going to countless tennis tournaments where Alex and Lincoln came home with trophies, Rachael had been talking for months about wanting one to put on her dresser.

"We can buy you one that says, 'World's Best Daughter,'" Mitch said.

"But I want to earn it." She sighed.

"You have." Mitch kissed her forehead and turned out the light.

"Good night, kids. We love you," I said, shutting the door.

Mitch and I went downstairs to get ready for bed. I shook my pill bottle into the palm of my hand and looked at the blue-and-white pills. *These are part of my life now.* I swallowed them down with tap water.

"You forgot one," Mitch said, holding out a small chocolate in his hand.

I snatched the chocolate and peeled off the wrapper. "I love you."

CHAPTER 17

Let's Not Talk about It

Baton Rouge, Louisiana, 2007

As a recovering psych patient, I continued my visits with a psychiatrist named Dr. Pope. He was much younger than Dr. Barry, and from my first impression, I could tell he would smile more. He had brown hair, blue eyes, and a few freckles. His office had the requisite framed diplomas with the thin, golden sticker proving their legitimacy, but my attention was pulled toward the colorful artwork done by his children. Next to the watercolor paintings were pictures of his wife and kids at the beach. It brought positive energy into the small, brown office.

"Sit down, sit down," Dr. Pope insisted. He walked back to his desk and sat down. "So, Sonja, you recently got out of the hospital. How're you holding up?" He folded his hands and gave me a good look over.

"I'm not sure why, but I had a bad panic attack yesterday. I had to go to the ER."

"I can get you a prescription that helps with severe panic attacks," he offered.

"Thanks." My eyes moved over to his pad of paper as he jotted down a medication.

"You also recently got diagnosed." He shifted in his seat, preparing himself for a long conversation.

"Yes, I have bipolar, but we don't need to talk about it."

"Sonja," he leaned forward with a small smile, "you're actually paying me to talk about it." He had me there.

"Well, all right, but only in this room," I said. I hoped he'd have answers for me but doubted he would. "How do I know what's the disease and what's me?" I asked.

"That's the big question now, isn't it?" He folded his arms. "If you continue taking your medicine and go to therapy, things will become clearer."

"Are you telling me, while I was unmedicated, most of my behavior and thoughts were because of the disease?"

"A lot of it, yes, but now that you're medicated, you'll start feeling more yourself," he assured me.

How was I supposed to identify my real personality? I hadn't been medicated my whole life! According to Dr. Pope, that meant I hadn't even met myself yet. So how was I supposed to *recognize* myself? The thought scared me. *Who was I? Can I trust myself, my judgment, my choices? And how will I coexist with this all-encompassing disease?*

"Let's talk about your childhood." He leaned back in his black office chair.

"It was great. I had a perfect childhood."

"So there's nothing in your childhood you have issues with?" he asked.

"Nope."

"Because it was perfect," he clarified.

"Right."

"You really believe your childhood was perfect?"

"You keep asking the same question. My childhood and family are perfect. There's nothing more to investigate," I insisted.

"Bullshit."

I jerked my head back. "Excuse me?" I widened my eyes. He had my full attention.

"Bullshit," he said, calmer this time. "No one has a perfect family or childhood."

"Well, I did and still do. There are exceptions to everything," I said.

"Your grandfather physically and verbally abused his ex-wives and children."

"He changed. Did you know three weeks before he died, he visited his oldest daughter and asked her to forgive him for all the times he hit her, and she asked him to forgive her for praying he would die? My grandpa sat there in his wheelchair and told her, 'Don't forget! You and I are clean!' He wanted to repent. The grandpa I knew would line up his grandkids and ask for hugs and kisses in exchange for dollar bills—"

"But Sonja, " Dr. Pope tried interrupting.

"Then my cousins and I would sit around and play poker with the money we got from him. He was a fun grandpa."

"What about the fact that he was married seven times, or that he held your grandmother at gunpoint, forcing her to marry him a second time?" Dr. Pope challenged.

"Yes, but he *changed*," I reiterated. "My grandpa took my sister and me to Goodwill and bought us real wedding dresses for dress-up. He even took us on his garbage runs. We'd get in dumpsters and fish out all the good stuff stores had thrown away. Then you know what we'd do with that stuff? Take it to the poor! He did a lot of good."

"But he also threatened to kill his wife."

"Why do you keep bringing that up? What's your point?" I snapped.

"That mental illness has an ugly side you seem set on blocking out. I'm not saying your grandpa was all bad. I know he changed for the good later in life. But you're not acknowledging the things he did when he was sick."

"That's not true."

"Sonja, I'm not just talking about oddities."

I held up my hand. "Let me finish. When I was sixteen, he prophesied that I would die in a car wreck and he'd take my body up a mountain and bring me back to life. Believe it or not, Doctor, even a woman straight out of a mental hospital knows an old man's belief that he can resurrect his granddaughter is bizarre."

"That's a start, but we've got a long way to go. You see things in black and white. You think things are perfect or horrible, when most of the time it's probably somewhere in the middle."

I didn't want him to see how much he had shaken me. It was jarring to have Dr. Pope poke holes in my childhood. "Maybe that's true." I shrugged.

CHAPTER 18

Damaged Goods

I would rather be ashes than dust!
I would rather that my spark
should burn out in a brilliant blaze
than it should be stifled by dry-rot.

I would rather be a superb meteor
every atom of me in magnificent glow
than a sleepy and permanent planet.

The function of man is to live,
not to exist.
I shall not waste my days trying to prolong them.
I shall use my time.

—Jack London's "Credo," 1916

Baton Rouge, Louisiana, 2007

"Why are we writing all this?" Rachael asked, holding up the sheets of printed poems from the back seat.

"Because one day you might need some encouragement, and these poems could say things how you need to hear them," I said.

"Do we have to write all these poems today?" Alex asked.

"No, you'll copy two that stand out to you each day."

I played Disney's *Tarzan* soundtrack while I drove to Walmart, occasionally checking the kids in the rearview mirror to see if they were still working. It was Saturday, and Mitch stayed home to work on his doctorate from George Washington University. He had a love of learning and read books on business leadership and neuroscience for fun. For him, learning was something he could do when I couldn't leave the house because I was too depressed. Learning provided him relief and escape. So when his older brother Chris approached him about a doctoral program he was applying to, I saw Mitch feel a flash of excitement and I encouraged him to do it.

I pulled into Walmart and the kids grabbed a grocery cart. They followed behind me through the rows of cereal boxes and trail mix. I stared at all the options, unsure why I was even at the store. I put two boxes of Raisin Bran into the cart and moved to the chip aisle.

"Let's get these!" Alex said, putting two bags of salt and vinegar chips into the cart.

"What did we need again?" I blanked.

"Tortilla chips are good, too," Alex suggested.

I looked at the racks of tortilla chips and knew we needed them. I just didn't know which ones to get. So many choices; I felt overwhelmed. I put five bags into the cart and hovered over my options for a sixth bag: Tostitos Hint of Lime, On the Border, yellow corn, blue corn, organic black bean, Tostitos Cantina Thin & Crispy, Santitas.

"Which one?" I desperately asked, holding up two bags to my kids.

"Um, On the Border," Rachael replied.

I looked at the two bags. "Why not Thin & Crispy?"

"I don't know; I've never tried that," she said.

I put two bags of On the Border chips into the cart. "Should I get another bag, or is this enough?"

"Mom, this is plenty! I'd put some back," Rachael said, reaching into the cart.

"No, leave it! I think we need more." I couldn't grasp what amount of chips would last us through the week. "How fast will you guys eat these?" I asked, putting another bag into the cart.

"Not fast enough," Rachael said under her breath.

"Just tell me a number. Do we need four bags or five?" I felt confused, like I was stuck on a math problem so long none of the numbers looked familiar anymore.

"Two," Rachael said firmly. "We only need two bags of chips."

"Two? But I have seven!" The thought of removing bags felt more complicated than adding them. "I'm going to put one more in." I reached for another.

"Mom, no." Rachael took the chips out of my hand.

"Seven isn't enough!" Even in my confusion, I felt that had to be true.

"Okay, let's get three then," Rachael said softly.

"Just one more than two? No, we need more than that!" I dumped three more bags into the cart.

"You're right. Let's get another one for safe measure." She looked at me. "I think ten bags is good." She pushed the cart out of the chip aisle before I could second-guess the number.

We strolled through the cheese aisle, and I stacked five blocks of medium cheddar into the cart without hesitation. Rachael looked back with a raised eyebrow, but didn't say anything, probably afraid it would only escalate the situation to ten blocks of cheese. We checked out of Walmart and headed to the bookstore.

Our car tires splashed through the rain in the Barnes & Noble parking lot. I parked the car and the kids ran to the front doors. The aroma of coffee beans and vanilla seemed to be the ever-present welcome of the bookstore. The scent never lingered between the covers of any book, though. Each page still smelled of raw paper and ink, one of Barnes & Noble's best qualities.

"Mom, let's start in the kids' section!" Lincoln tugged my hand, leading me to the area with fake trees and a green frog in overalls perpetually climbing onto the second step of a ladder. Lincoln ran to the stuffed animals, and I waited for him at one of the benches by the wooden train set.

A little blonde girl set Thomas the Tank Engine's wheels into the grooves of the worn tracks after her brother crashed it off the table. She clipped magnetic train cars together, but only got to car four before her little brother swiped Thomas off the track again.

"Come over here," said a blonde woman. She gently picked them up. "Let's read a book." The two kids sat in their mom's lap in front of the open book.

I looked at the seemingly perfect family, thinking back to Dr. Barry's comment about all parents damaging their kids. I wondered if that young mom—spending her afternoon in the children's section of Barnes & Noble watching her kids play with trains—also scarred her kids. I wondered if all parents really did unintentionally harm their children. If so, what was a normal threshold of harm? Or at least the average damage done? I clenched my fist under my chin and stared with what I'm sure was a little too much intensity at the toddlers in her lap. They looked safe and happy. As much as I wanted to believe I harmed my kids no differently than the cute mom in blue jeans, I knew I had undoubtedly done so in ways she never had. I slammed the brakes at these thoughts before they destroyed me and decided to see myself in that young mom. I, like her, was also at Barnes & Noble with my kids, whom I fiercely loved. At least for today, we were the same.

"Mom, can I get this one?" Lincoln held up a fluffy puppy with a brown patch over one eye.

"Sure, but you still need to find a book. We're going to take turns reading to Dad when we get home."

Lincoln's eyes lit up. "This dog comes with a book!" He ran to where he found the stuffed animal and brought back a book with a cartoon version of the dog on the cover.

I thumbed through the pages. "Sure, that'll work." I closed the book and tucked it under my arm. My eyelids grew heavy and my arms felt weak. A family bustled past me toward the books on sale, and I leaned against a bookshelf for stability. These horrible meds were wreaking havoc on my life. Everyone around me seemed to be enjoying themselves; I envied that. I was in the same place they were, looking through the same books, yet I felt like I was the only one unable to take it in. I wanted to be them. I wanted normalcy. My eyelids closed without my permission, and I knew I needed to get home before I fell asleep. Otherwise, my kids would be trapped at Barnes & Noble until I woke up. I dumped our stack of books on a random table and screamed to the kids we were leaving. I pushed my way past people on our way out. Hobbling through the parking lot, I held my eyes open with my fingers.

"Mom, what's wrong?" Rachael asked, squinting at me.

"My medicine's making me fall asleep."

I sped home, driving with one hand on the wheel and one hand holding my eyes open. Parked under the carport, I sighed with relief. I opened the door and yelled for Mitch.

"What is it?" He came running.

"Help! I'm falling asleep!" I fell to my knees.

"You shouldn't be driving like this. Come on, let's lie you down." Mitch took my hands and led me to the bedroom.

"No! I don't want to sleep. Do you understand me? It's not fair!" I sobbed. "Mitch, I have things to do; I can't live like this. What kind of life is this?" I asked, my eyes shutting.

I hated it. I hated having no say when I fell asleep. I constantly had to leave stores, movies, and friends, all because my medication knocked me out right as I was in the stride of my day.

Mitch sat on the bed and held out his hand. "Come here. Want me to brush your hair?"

Usually, that would help calm me down, but not this time. I ignored him and paced the length of the bedroom, trying to hold back tears.

I breathed in through my nose, and it stung the same way chlorine did when it got up my nose.

This lifelong illness affected my weekdays, weekends, and every moment in between. I couldn't get away from the symptoms of bipolar disorder. I wanted to treat it like a painful part-time job where a doctor told me when to clock in and when to clock out. I'd work hard and deal with all the bad customers filling my head, but in return, I wanted days off. My doctor said bipolar disorder was a lifelong illness, but even lifelong careers got holidays. I had to prove to myself *lifelong* did not mean *life sentence*.

—m—

My eyes slowly opened. *How did I get into bed? Mitch.* I took a deep breath. Heavy blankets from all over the house were sprawled over me. In a sweaty blur, I flung my foot around until I managed to kick a few blankets off the bed. The side of my neck felt warm; something furry was tucked under my chin. I picked it up and squinted at the little yellow and brown dog. It was Lincoln's toy from the bookstore. *I survived.* I heard the shuffle of plastic bags and the kids laughing.

"Wow, this is a lot of chips! I guess we're having nachos for dinner… again." Mitch's voice echoed. I walked into the kitchen. "Feel better?" he asked.

"How'd I get in bed?"

"Dad carried you like a bride." Rachael clasped her hands together.

"A dead bride," Alex laughed.

"No, Mom looked like Sleeping Beauty," Mitch corrected, ruffling Alex's hair.

"We went back to Barnes & Noble and got the books," Lincoln said.

"The kids took good care of you while you were sleeping. They each picked out a blanket for you."

"And I put my dog, Spot, in the blankets to keep you company," Lincoln added.

"Thanks, Lincoln." I hugged him.

"Tomorrow's your first day of the intensive outpatient program." Mitch nudged me with his elbow. "It's like your first day of school. Do you need any lunch money?"

I shot him a glare. "No."

I liked the idea of group therapy purely for the fact that the therapist wouldn't be focused on me the whole time. I hoped it would be like a classroom where the therapist lectured and I could melt into the background, unseen, and—just maybe—never be called on to share my story.

CHAPTER 19

You Get Me

Baton Rouge, Louisiana, 2007

"Will you *stop* that?" I heard a woman say as I entered the intensive outpatient program. Since I was early, there were only two people in the room: a tall blonde woman and a man no older than thirty holding a thick stack of printer paper. I took a seat next to them, and the man started shuffling his papers front to back. Every single sheet was blank. "Seriously, stop! It's so annoying." The woman stomped her foot.

"Sorry," he mumbled, tucking the papers under his chair. Two minutes into the silence, he fidgeted in his chair. His fingers trembled nervously as he reached for the papers then stopped himself three times. It was painful watching him restrain himself. Eventually, he rescued the stack under his chair and placed it back in his lap. His shoulders dropped as he relaxed into another noisy paper shuffling episode, shuffling with no foreseeable end in sight. I wondered how he went grocery shopping or ate dinner with his unusual compulsion.

More people came into the room and filled the empty seats. A man wearing the equivalent of a Halloween lumberjack costume sat next to me. He kept his head down, and his eyes didn't shift once from his steel-toed boots.

A woman in a light-blue suit shut the white door and walked across the carpet to find a seat. "Okay, I believe everyone is here. Let's get started." She crossed her legs and leaned over her knees, appearing friendlier than I expected. "Say your name and something you want to improve." She pointed to Mr. Lumberjack next to me.

"I'm Kent. I like to set stumps on fire. So I'd like to find more tree stumps to burn 'cause I'm runnin' out." His beard moved over the collar of his flannel shirt as he talked.

The blonde woman went next. "I'm Sherri." She smiled and waved to the class. "I want to cut my anxiety meds down to three times a day instead of six, so I can hold down a job."

It was my turn. "Hi, I'm Sonja. I haven't showered in ten days, so my goal is to shower twice a week."

Sherri jumped to her feet. "Oh my god, me too!" She slapped her hands on her thighs, laughing. "I'm not the only one!"

"No. You're definitely not. Showering's really hard for me. My husband can't understand it," I said.

Sherri sat back down. "You get me." She pointed to me.

We waited for the paper shuffler to speak, but he continued fumbling through his pages.

"Brad, it's your turn," the blue-suit woman prompted. His eyes widened as he looked around the room and shook his head no. "Okay, maybe next time." She smiled, motioning for the next person to go.

"I'm Karen. I suffer from depression. I just want to feel joy again. That's my goal."

"Karen, you'll get through this dark time. You won't always feel this way. It will go away," blue-suit reassured her.

My head perked up. "It will?" I blurted.

"Now, let's not compare ourselves with each other. Everyone here has different struggles. There are environmental and biological illnesses. I know from Karen's diagnosis hers is environmental, so hers will pass; but Sonja, yours is biological, so it won't," she said.

I sank back in the chair. The whole class stared at me with looks I assumed were pity.

Most problems like ex-boyfriends or broken bones aren't permanent. There are hard things you grow up knowing won't stay a part of you. Puberty, friend drama, college exams, pregnancy. But this, my bipolar disorder, was my hardest problem, and my entire soul rejected the idea of its permanence. *How am I supposed to accept this? If I do, my life is over.* Hope keeps people going, and hope is what I needed right then. What the therapist said couldn't be true. My thoughts continued to circle as I left the session to pick up my kids from their friend's house.

The car's engine hummed in Evelyn Henry's driveway. The yard looked like a page out of an *I Spy* book. It was a child's playground, and mine loved it. Evelyn's house was one of Rachael's favorite places to play. Bicycle tires, tree stumps, and chicken wire took over the small yard. Rabbits hopped in the backyard with their small, white poodle. Rachael and Laura, Evelyn's daughter, played on a swing they made from the seat of an office chair and some rope. I pulled the key out of the ignition and knocked on the door.

"Come in!" I heard Evelyn call from inside.

She sat barefoot on the couch, dressed in one of her floral-print dresses. She was so short her legs didn't touch the floor. She pushed up her glasses to her nose. "Hi, Sonja. Come sit down!" she said.

Her husband, Don, was sitting in a big La-Z-Boy. He acknowledged me with a nod of his head. Rachael and Laura ran in, chasing the rabbits around the family room. I walked toward the couch, avoiding the critters hopping around. I was no stranger to a disorderly house, despite what many of my friends thought. At times, my house was so dirty Social Services could've deemed it unlivable, and other times the house was so sterile, you could eat off the floors. Currently, I was in my sterile phase, but I knew it wouldn't last forever. As eccentric as the Henrys appeared, I found myself comfortable with them.

Evelyn was friendly and loved to chat, but I was tuned out for most of the conversation. My medication caused me to zone out, but unlike the movie *The Secret Life of Walter Mitty*, I didn't go to cool places. Everything just went silent. In the middle of conversations, my kids would wave their hands past my eyes to check if I was still conscious. When people tried to get my attention, I woke up slightly, but still felt disconnected. Luckily, Evelyn didn't need much of a response to continue talking, so my silence didn't seem to strike her as odd.

"I got honorably discharged from the military." Don said, as he looked at Evelyn.

"Wait, what?" Shock drove me back into the conversation. "Why'd you get discharged?"

"Because he has schizophrenia," Evelyn answered as if she'd said it five times. In fairness, she probably had. "He thought the CIA was sending him secret messages, which wasn't true."

I looked steadily over at Don. "But you're still not sure the CIA wasn't sending you messages, are you?" I asked.

He glanced up at me and shook his head no. I understood the fuzzy line separating reality from fiction. Stepping away from what you *think* is real and into what others tell you is *actually* real is the ultimate trust fall. I think everyone wants to believe they can trust their own senses and mind, but that luxury was not afforded to Don or me.

Listening to Evelyn and Don talk openly about his diagnosis felt foreign. No one outside my family and therapy group knew I was bipolar. Their honesty not only struck me as brave, but also showed me a level of acceptance and trust of others I had not experienced. I admired their courage but didn't want to make myself that vulnerable. I didn't want to be talked about or judged. The stigma of mental illness made me vow I would keep my mental illness a lifelong secret.

CHAPTER 20

Calm in the Storm

Baton Rouge, Louisiana, 2008

All of Louisiana was preparing for Hurricane Gustav to hit in two weeks—except the Wasden family. Looking back, I can't believe we didn't take the warnings more seriously, but we had never prepared for a hurricane. We found ourselves in a postapocalyptic Walmart three days before the storm. Our cart rattled down the canned-food section, which didn't have a single can of food left save for a couple of dented Chef Boyardee ravioli that had rolled under a shelf. I leaned down and put them into our cart.

"Do you have any more canned food in the back?" I asked one of the employees in the store.

"Nope, everything's been cleared out, honey," the employee said.

The kids found it all very exciting. They had never seen a major grocery store empty before. We checked the cereal, trail mix, frozen food, and candy sections, each with the same underwhelming conclusion. Rachael thought this was the coolest place to play *Survivor*. Alex and Lincoln followed her down the aisles, pretending there was a war outside and they had to live in the store for the next month.

"We'll sleep on these shelves and use grocery bags as blankets!" Rachael told the boys.

"And we can hide in the freezers when bad guys come," Alex said.

"Come on, little scavengers," I yelled behind me on my way to check out.

The cashier scanned my five items. The cans of Chef Boyardee, a single box of mandarin fruit cups, a box of Grape-Nuts, and a can of Easy Cheese. I wasn't too worried since Mitch kept food stored for emergencies. We had oats, pancake mix, powdered eggs, as well as a barrel of water.

The day of the hurricane, we set to our schoolwork routine like any typical day. Mitch remained at the hospital, sleeping there to make sure the generators continued to work and that patients were able to receive the care they needed. The hurricane would be hitting within hours. I looked outside our playroom windows, but nothing seemed out of the ordinary. It was the calm before the storm.

I was on the phone with my mom when it started. Rain, wind, and twigs bounced off the windows. Then the call suddenly dropped. The kids and I sat huddled on the couch as we watched pieces of our roof fly past the windows. The lights flickered on and off.

"Power's out," Alex said, flicking the light switch.

We froze, then returned to watching the wind rip leaves off trees. The house creaked, and branches from our huge oak tree snapped to the ground. Rain whipped the windows, making it hard to see what was going on outside. We did see a tree fall through our neighbor's house, cutting it in half. Oddly, I was unafraid. The destruction felt almost calming to me.

Even though the news discouraged being near windows, we sat by the windows to play Five Crowns in the dim light. It didn't take long for the whole house to feel like a sauna. Louisiana was humid enough, but add a tropical storm and no AC and the air became warm mist.

"It's so hot." Rachael squirmed on the floor.

"Go change into some shorts," I said, sliding the cards into their purple cardboard box.

By the time the storm had passed, several more trees had fallen into houses. Neighbors walked the streets, discussing the disaster and the mess surrounding us, but when I looked around, I didn't see what they saw. I felt like I was in a modern-art museum. I saw original shapes and designs all around me. Hundred-year-old oak trees torn up from the ground, exposing mazes of roots designing intertwined strokes. Downed power lines looked like Jackson Pollock had dripped lines of paint across the streets. Branches, leaves, flowers, and roof shingles covered the ground, creating patterns that my hands itched to recreate. But I no longer owned paint, canvases, or brushes—I gave that up long ago—so I designed in my head.

When the sun set that day, the house was completely dark. I hadn't realized how much I relied on the lights until they were gone, but it didn't bother me. I was familiar with darkness, and now it entered the real world, which I liked. We ate Chef Boyardee straight from the can in the dark, brushed our teeth in the dark, and walked to bed in the dark. The electricity didn't come back on for another thirteen days.

The kids and I saw Mitch only after the roads had been cleared of power lines and debris.

People were going crazy, but not me. In an odd way, seeing all my neighbors share in this epic misfortune made me feel at ease, like we were all finally in something *together*. We were all trapped in our houses, but unlike the temporary storm, the storm trapped inside my body was going nowhere. It was my unwavering companion. So for this short while, I actually felt normal. For once, my outside world matched my inside world: complete chaos and darkness.

CHAPTER 21

Two Steps Back

Baton Rouge, Louisiana, 2010

The pressure to educate my children weighed heavily on me. I homeschooled for four years so the boys could practice more tennis. I thought I couldn't do enough to educate them, so I had them do homework on weekends and during family vacations. In the summer, I took an extra suitcase filled with homeschooling materials, so the kids didn't fall behind. I had my kids enrolled in Baton Rouge Fine Arts Academy—an incredible two-year art program—as one of their electives. We changed up our school routine from using tutors to attending a school run by an elderly couple from New York. They rented out a trailer where they taught K–12 to around fifteen kids.

The school was one big room with long tables and roller office chairs. The elderly couple, Mr. and Mrs. Johnson, had hired an elementary school teacher and a math teacher to work alongside them. Mrs. Johnson's specialty was English, and Mr. Johnson—bless his heart—was so old and frail, he mostly walked around the room with his cane until Mrs. Johnson demanded he sit back down. Unlike her husband, Mrs. Johnson was an energetic, four-foot-tall woman who led the loudest and proudest Bible hour I'd ever seen. Her political tangents were legendary and often quoted in our house.

I parked the car in a patch of loose gravel outside Mrs. Johnson's school. "Go on in, kids."

The boys slipped out of the back seat and ran inside. Rachael put her hand over mine. "You okay?"

"Yes. I just need a minute." Rachael didn't move. She watched and waited with me.

We walked in, hand in hand, and sat listening to the closing message of Mrs. Johnson's Bible lesson.

"Sometimes life is like a puzzle: all you see is a bunch of pieces that don't look like anything, but slowly, one by one, as you put it together, you see the beautiful picture God created in your life." Mrs. Johnson rested both hands on the desk. This was one of her favorite ideas she shared often, but I couldn't see how my life's puzzle could become a beautiful picture. My puzzle pieces were more like glass shards, cutting me every time I touched them. And I was running out of bandages.

That evening I called my dad while tidying up the kids' playroom. Waiting for him to pick up, I pulled a few stuffed animals the kids wouldn't miss from the toy chest and added them to my personal collection. I had started carrying stuffed animals with me on errands and sleeping with them. These portable comforts made me feel safe in this new, scary bipolar world I was living in.

"Sonja! It's so good to hear from you!" my dad yelled over the phone.

"How have you and Mom been?" I asked, trying to meet his gusto.

"Great! Did your mom tell you about Brandon Curtis?"

"No, who's that?"

"Brandon Curtis was a football player who died doing donuts in the Springville High School parking lot with his friends. The car flipped."

"That's terrible. I'm sorry to hear that." Death clung to my thoughts daily as a hopeful release, yet so many people died who had a life worth living.

"Brandon donated seven major organs, which saved many people's lives! Sonja, organ donation is a divine cause. It's such a selfless gift of love." My dad started a passionate rant.

"Wow!" I leaned the phone against my ear. "That's—"

"Imagine if everyone was an organ donor, how many lives we'd save!"

Organ donation became my dad's fixation. He wasn't *interested* in organ donation; he was consumed by it. He started the Quest for the Gift of Life Foundation beginning his dream of creating a monument for those who donated their organs. Working with Intermountain Donor Services, he raised money to help build a tall, glass wall engraved with donors' names at Library Square in Salt Lake City. In the end, he ended up paying for most of the memorial himself. While it was an amazing tribute, I still have mixed feelings about it. I felt this cause was what brought out my dad's mania in full force.

I heard the kids run up the stairs.

"Mom! I need help heating the oven. I'm making pizza," Lincoln said.

"Hey, Dad, I—"

"The state of Utah could save four thousand people!"

"Dad, I—"

"We're going to start campaigning tomorrow! T-shirts, wristbands, all in the name of Brandon Curtis!"

I knew my dad well enough to recognize when he was on autopilot. He could monologue for hours. I set the phone on a bookshelf and headed downstairs to help Lincoln put the pizza in the oven. When I came back up, he was still talking.

"August 28 is going to be Brandon Curtis Make a Difference Day. We teamed up with the Utah Organ Donor Coalition, and a group of his friends will be helping to organize the fundraiser. We're going to have a Brandon Curtis scholarship break the *Guinness Book of World Records* with the most people signed up for organ donation in a day."

"That's a lot of work, Dad. I'm sure Brandon Curtis's parents appreciate it."

"Yeah, I've been going over to their house every day, counseling and emotionally supporting them."

I wondered if he was smothering them. They were grieving for their son, and I hoped he was giving them the space they needed.

"It's a heavenly cause! Saving lives!" he shouted through the phone. Mitch tried calling me while my dad was at his peak. "Suzanne's going to help me see this through, and we're going to have a celebration with food and a bouncy castle for the kids—"

"Dad, I have to go. Mitch is calling. I'll call you back." I hung up and accepted Mitch's call. "Hey, Mitter, what's up?"

"I have some big news for you when I get home." I could hear him trying to keep his excitement measured.

"What is it?" I asked. I hated suspense.

"I want to tell you in person. I'll be home in twenty minutes."

"I hate surprises," I said.

"I'll be home soon."

I couldn't think about anything except the adrenaline in my body. I sat staring at the patterns in the wood table for so long I could've drawn them from memory. Then I heard Mitch's car pulling in the carport. I ran to him. "So?" I said, opening his car door for him.

He stepped out of the car and straightened his tie. "I got a call from a recruiter today. They want me to apply for a chief operating officer position at Covenant Healthcare in Lubbock, Texas."

A set of paradoxical needs existed in Mitch: one to create stability for me and the kids and the other was an unquenchable need to climb his career ladder. Unfortunately, the two rarely coexisted well. The word *Texas* had me jumping up and down inside. The kids loved living in Texas. But the thought of moving our entire lives made my anxiety rise.

"Whoa," was all that fell out of my mouth.

"It'd be a great career opportunity. Also, that's where I graduated from high school, and you loved Texas when we lived in Sugar Land. Obviously, we'll pray about it, but what do you think?"

The importance of being a supportive wife was drilled into me not only from my religious leaders, but my family culture, so I stayed positive.

"Mitch, we could live there for twenty years. You could move up and become the CEO when the current one retires, and we could finally settle somewhere!" It seemed too good to be true.

Mitch grabbed my hand and shared all the ways this new job blew his current position out of the water. The pay, benefits, and title were an obvious step up. But the fact he could get more promotions within the health system without having to move us is what got me excited.

"But who knows, I probably won't get it. The recruiter said there are already more than twenty candidates." The challenge sealed the deal for me. We needed this job.

"You always make it to the final two," I reminded him. And for better or for worse, it was true. We'd done this process countless times, and every time Mitch made it to the final round of interviews—making us hold our breath until the last second.

The possibility of moving consumed us. We looked at houses in Lubbock "just for fun," and our hearts jumped whenever we talked about the salary increase and potential future promotion of him moving from COO to CEO. We got nervous before interviews and got nervous after interviews. When we weren't waiting for Mitch's phone to ring, we were mentally preparing ourselves for the long road ahead, because moving would be a feat with three kids and four cats.

Months passed, and Mitch made it past the third round of interviews. Now we were waiting for a phone call to see if he had made it to the final two. I dropped off the kids at school and stopped at Walmart on the way home to pick up more medication—the chocolate kind. My coat pocket vibrated, and my hand fumbled around to pull the phone out and answer it. I hoped it was Mitch with news.

"My name is Nancy," a woman's voice said. False alarm. Letting out a nervous breath, I leaned my ear against my shoulder. "I know your house is off the market, but I have someone who wants to buy it."

"Seriously?" I yelled louder than intended.

Scooting my cart down the candy aisle, I focused in on the details Nancy gave me. I threw a few chocolate bags into the cart and called Mitch.

"I was just about to call you." He laughed. "I made it to the final two for the Lubbock job!" he announced.

"Mitch, you'll never believe it: a realtor called me and said someone wants to buy our house!"

"Seriously?" Mitch's shock sounded just like mine.

"Mitch, this job in Lubbock is meant to be! God is paving the way for us." I felt God owed me blessings after all I'd gone through. And our house selling right when we're about to get a job offer was the blessing I had in mind.

"The recruiter said they want us to fly out for the on-site interview."

"Mitch," I sighed in relief. "I'm so ready for this!" I could've cried. The hope that life would hand me victories without me having to claw my way to them felt refreshing. I needed a break. I needed a moment I could enjoy without wondering if the sacrifices I made along the way were worth it. I was so used to overworking myself for small wins, I couldn't imagine big wins coming to me with minimal effort.

When the plane landed, Lubbock was as hot and sunny as the Texas I remembered. I loved it. A realtor took me around to look at houses while Mitch interviewed all day. I found the perfect house. It was cream with dark wood, and I couldn't help but fall in love because the striking color scheme reminded me of my childhood home. As I walked through the bedrooms, I knew this would be our future home. It was too gorgeous to pass up. I wanted to put an offer on it right then but restrained myself, knowing we needed the official job offer first.

Dinner with the team that night felt natural, and the conversation flowed easily. The recruiter told Mitch to prepare himself for an offer.

We flew home on cloud nine. We sold our house, which Mitch felt was a risky decision, whereas I felt confident it was an obvious one. We moved into a two-bedroom, five-hundred-square-foot apartment, with most of our belongings in storage. Rachael and Lincoln slept in bunk beds, and Alex slept on a couch. Our family camped out in the small apartment, waiting to hear when we'd be moving to Texas.

I had an insatiable desire to have the best. Whether it was Mitch applying to the number one grad school, my sons having the best tennis coach, Rachael having the best art classes, or buying the right brand of tortilla chips—when it came to making decisions, I got lost trying to avoid the mediocre. When Mitch informed me there was a better job opportunity, it didn't matter how I felt about my current situation in the beginning, I would become ready to abandon camp and go hunting until we came back victorious.

Maybe my dad and I weren't so different after all; he lived for the battle, and in some ways, I did too. But hunting success came at a price; while new job opportunities began with excitement, the uncertainty of the process left me unhinged. Every time. It often seemed we were doomed to repeat the same cycle of self-sabotage.

"I'm in so much pain! I'm going to kill myself!" I screamed. "Being married to you makes me absolutely *miserable!*"

"Stop! You're going to wake up the kids," Mitch tried to whisper.

"It's you! You've made my life hell! I need to divorce you!" I raged, slamming my hands on the kitchen table.

"I think you're in pain. You're not getting better." He dropped his head. I was certain it had nothing to do with the diagnosis—the problem was him.

"No shit I'm in pain! All the decisions *you* make put *me* in pain!" I cried. "It's our life, your career. You've been working insane hours!"

"My decisions? *You* put us eighty thousand dollars in debt. That's why I've been working insane hours for years to get those raises, promotions, and bonuses to pay that debt off!" He fought back.

"You paid that off years ago! You decided to leave your job at the Ochsner Hospital to go work with your brother on a startup in Texas. Then we moved to Albuquerque and only lived there for six months before moving back to Louisiana for another big step up in your career! Let's not forget, more money, more prestige! Instability is all you've given me and the kids. You have a need to move up the career ladder at the expense of your family!"

What started as a way to get out of debt turned into an addictive ego boost. Each promotion, bonus, and endless praise soothed Mitch. He craved what fed his ego, and work was the one place that did. When he arrived at Ochsner Medical Center in Baton Rouge, they were losing money and had the worst patient and employee satisfaction in the hospital system. During his time there, he focused relentlessly on improving the culture of the hospital, and after four years, the hospital was not only profitable, but had the highest employee engagement and patient satisfaction in the whole system. Their quality scores even tied for first with the flagship hospital. While Mitch's career aspirations started out of money insecurity, they developed into something so much more. He did more than get us out of debt, he made us wealthy.

"I've sacrificed for you, for the kids!" he yelled.

"And the kids have sacrificed for you! Do you think moving is easy on them? They leave friends in every state only to have to start all over again. They have nowhere to call home. When they're older and people ask them where they're from, what state will they say, Mitch?"

"Sonja, you've told me many times you felt spiritually we were supposed to move."

"You use God against me every time. Stop! This is spiritual manipulation."

"What I mean is, you've been fine with moving many times."

"That's because I was fine with it in the beginning! But then I become not fine with all the moving," I crossed my arms.

"I can pull out of the job search. Our family is more important."

"No! I want you to stay in it. We're already this close, and you might get it."

"I can't hit a moving target!" He raised his hands in the air. Even I had no way of knowing what I really wanted versus what my illness demanded.

"All I know is these job searches make me sicker," I cried.

"Let's have faith the right thing will happen."

Would he give up his career ambitions for my stability? I hoped, but the evidence showed otherwise. Mitch did what he always did—say he would pull out of the search once my mental decline got drastic, but he never did. He would stay in the search no matter how much pain it caused me and use God to justify it. He sacrificed many things for me, yet his career would never be one of them.

"Sometimes your behavior can be completely abnormal. You have to see that," he said.

"Maybe I'm perfectly normal and any person would be miserable in this situation."

"This situation? We're in the top one percent of the planet's population. We have a house, food, a wonderful family; we love each other. I'm not getting why our situation equals misery for you."

"I can't do this *anymore*! I just want to die!" I slumped in defeat.

"Sonja, you need therapy."

"No! *You* need therapy!" I pointed at him.

"We *both* need professional help," Mitch acknowledged. He didn't know how to handle my suicidal thoughts. They scared him. But whenever he took me to a doctor, I told them I didn't have a plan to take my life, so they'd let me go home.

"It's been years, and nothing is changing. Do you know what the definition of insanity is? It's doing the same thing over and over again, expecting different results. We are living in *insanity*!" Mitch yelled in frustration.

"*Fine!*" I screamed back. "*You* call the therapist, a *marriage* therapist. It's the only therapist I'm willing to see. Because you're part of the problem, too!"

—m—

The marriage therapist pulled his hands into a ball around his chest, pretending to hide a box. "All of us have a tender and vulnerable feelings box inside of us." He opened his skinny fingers as he looked at us. "Inside this box are the emotions we don't want to reveal. I'm ashamed. I'm jealous. I'm insecure. I don't feel valued. When we hide these feelings, we usually express anger in its place." The therapist relaxed in his seat and looked at me. "What are the vulnerable feelings you're experiencing right now?" he asked, tipping his gaze over his glasses.

"I feel weak," I cried.

"And Mitch?" The therapist tilted his head.

Mitch took a breath. "I feel sad and empty." He paused and turned to me. "I feel like you need me, but you don't want me."

"Are you kidding?"

"I know you value the kids. They're your everything. But when it comes to me, I feel more like a means to an end—someone you need things from—but you don't think needs anything in return," he said.

"You think I don't care about you? *Seriously?*" I became unhinged. "I love you; why do you think I'm still here?" I stomped my feet. "It will never be enough!" I slapped my hands on my legs. "I can't take having another thing to work on! So *don't* even go there." I pushed a stiff finger in his face. Mitch and the therapist remained silent as my anger melted into violent tears.

"Sonja, maybe I should work with you one-on-one," the therapist tried to say over my sobbing.

I wiped away my tears, trying to calm down. "What? No. This is an *us* problem, not a *me* problem."

"That is true, but we won't be able to get to the 'us' problems until we address the underlying issues you are having. I would like to do a Mood Disorder Questionnaire," the therapist advised.

"I think we're done here," I said coldly. I stood, suddenly composing myself. "Mitch, let's go."

I already had a thousand knives in me, and bringing up more pain points was another blade I didn't have room to fit. We tried many marriage therapists as we moved around, each time with the same result—the therapist recommended working alone with me before doing any couple's therapy and I'd walk out.

One therapist forcefully told me my big emotions were one of the underlying issues in my marriage. That was the last time I agreed to therapy. I fought against the indication I was the broken one. My personal stigmas around mental illness kept me from getting the help I desperately needed. I thought I would be viewed as broken and not capable of being a good mom if I was mentally ill. To me, mental illness equated failure. So Mitch and I were left to deal with our issues on our own.

Marriage therapists say, "It takes two to tango." But when a severe mental illness is involved, it really only takes one—the illness. Mitch and I thought we were fighting each other, when in reality we were both fighting the illness. Moving around so much meant there was never enough time for me to develop trust with my doctors. I didn't open up, which made it hard for them to find the underlying pain and help me. Starting at square one each time we moved was one of the many detriments to my mental health.

CHAPTER 22

Role Reversal

Mental illness laced its way through my family tree like an unpredictable virus. My dad had unofficially "adopted" a Hispanic family he met in a parking lot. He tried to throw a random party for them but got so agitated and demanding at the party store, a cashier got scared and called 911.

He was becoming delusional. One night, he was at the cemetery talking to his dead father, who he claimed was instructing him how to solve the organ donation crisis. Someone called the police, and my dad was taken down to the station.

Even though he was sick, his psychiatrist refused to send him to the psych ward against his will. My dad was so convincing and charming that duping even well-trained psychiatrists wasn't difficult for him. Many of my brothers and sisters tried to hospitalize him with no success. His friends even wrote his doctor multiple letters begging, "Please hospitalize him. This is not the David we know." But the doctor continued to believe my dad and would only admit him if a family member insisted he was at risk of hurting himself or others. I flew to

Utah, determined to get my dad hospitalized. The irony of our role reversal was not lost on me.

When I was growing up, no one knew my dad had bipolar disorder. My siblings and I just thought our dad was unique and eccentric. It was our normal. And like any child, we loved him with our whole hearts. It wasn't until he attempted suicide by asphyxiation, in his late sixties, that he got diagnosed with bipolar disorder. It was a diagnosis he did not accept. Instead, he believed he had hypomania and that was the reason he had unusual energy, enthusiasm, and creativity. He thought it gave him an upper hand in life.

Mitch parked the car at the airport passenger drop-off and handed me my bag.

"Call me when you land." He pulled me in for a hug.

"I will," I said into his shoulder. "Pray for me."

"You're very brave, Sonja." He squeezed my hand.

"I don't feel brave."

"You're one of the bravest people I know," he insisted. "Don't worry about us. I'll take care of the kids and hold down the fort."

When my mom picked me up from the airport, she was silent. I kept my gaze forward as she drove.

"So, where's Dad?" I asked, hoping the lack of eye contact would help her answer.

She shifted in her seat and regripped the steering wheel. "I don't know."

"Is it true he got banned from Springville High School?" My siblings told me he threw packs of gum onto the football field during the game and advised the coach which players to put in. The cops escorted him off school property after he started dancing on the field with the cheerleaders.

After a long pause, my mom replied, "Well, there's no sense in talking about it."

I never could get the full truth from her. Growing up she talked a lot about her family being refugees in World War II. She shared details about their poverty and how her mother struggled to find places to live or food to eat, and her baby brother dying from starvation. But my mom left gaps in the story. As an adult looking through a photo album of my grandparents' wedding, I was stunned to see lines of men wearing Nazi armbands as they held up their hands for a Seig Heil as my grandparents walked under it. I didn't know my grandfather had been part of the Nazi party. There were many layers to my mom and her life that she didn't share with me.

We drove up the long, steep driveway to my childhood home. As much as I didn't look forward to this visit, it did feel good to be here. I walked down the dark-green-carpeted hallway glancing at the famous art lining the walls and remembered my dad making fun of how clumsy I was. He would say, "Whenever Sonja walks down that hall, paintings just fall behind her."

I wondered if my dad was in his usual spot: upstairs in his room, on the phone, holding his yellow notepad. My mom and I climbed the stairs up to the wooden doors leading into my parents' bedroom. I peeked in, but he wasn't there.

"I moved him to the guesthouse," she informed me.

"That's sad."

"But necessary. You can put your bag in here and sleep with me."

Before we went to sleep that night, my mom locked the bedroom door. She turned the clock toward her as she climbed into bed. Being home and under that same blanket with my mother tricked me into a sense of parental safety that didn't exist. We lay awake not talking, waiting for my dad to come home.

The lights outside flipped on, and we heard my dad come into the house. My mom looked at the time and scribbled down "3:30 a.m." on a piece of paper. I assumed the doctors had asked her to keep track of his nighttime habits. I fell asleep with nerves in my stomach, knowing that tomorrow was the day my mom and I would take him to see his psychiatrist. I was going to hospitalize him.

The next morning, I jumped out of bed before my dad had the chance to start his scattered day. His psychiatry appointment wasn't until 3 p.m., so I planned on spending the day with him to ensure he got there. When I came down the stairs, I found him sleeping on the couch in the main house with a newspaper over his belly. I ate breakfast and texted Mitch while continually checking if my dad was still asleep. After an hour, I heard the newspaper fold, and my dad sat up. One suspender strap hung off his shoulder, and his wispy, gray comb-over was ruffled. He stood in his slippers and rubbed his eyes, which endeared him to me.

"Hi, Dad." I walked over to the couch and hugged him. I tried to take in the warm embrace he tiredly offered back, knowing soon he would hate me. "I'm going to spend the day with you. Do you have anywhere you need to be?"

"You need to meet the family I adopted. But first, I have to go grocery shopping." He put a pen into his shirt pocket and patted his pants for his wallet.

"It's on the counter." I pointed. "So, you adopted a family?"

"You'll love them." He shuffled his slippers across the floor as he headed toward the car. I followed and got into the passenger side. He made several urgent phone calls to people about his organ donation program as we drove. "I'm ordering five thousand wristbands!" he yelled into the phone with a toothpick jumping around in his mouth. His forehead wrinkled as his eyes widened. "Well, heck, let's do it!" He laughed.

He called the kidney transplant center, every hospital in town, and any person in the state of Utah he could convince to become a donor. When he wasn't on the phone, he was telling me about the donating process.

"I'm going to solve this crisis by getting every person in the United States to be a donor! Every single person!" He pounded the steering wheel. "The party I sponsored was a hit! I called it Celebrate Brandon Curtis Day. There was a bounce house, tons of balloons, and food. We invited all the kids from his high school and signed them up to be donors. We broke the *Guinness World Record* for the number of donors signed up in a single day!" His excitement erupted in the car.

I listened in forced silence since he left no room for commentary. On his way out of the car, he continued talking about saving lives as he marched toward the store. I picked up the car keys he hadn't noticed he dropped and grabbed a grocery cart.

"Okay, Dad, what do you need?" I asked.

"It's not about what *I* need. It's about what *they* need!" he shouted.

"Okay." I followed him toward the refrigerated section as he looked over the milk. A man walked past us, barely brushing my dad's shoulder.

"Hey, hey, hey! Don't touch me!" my dad screamed.

I patted him on the back. "It's okay." I put a gallon of milk into the cart and tried to direct him to an aisle that wasn't as crowded—a difficult task to accomplish when it only took one person to freak him out. Whenever people shared a narrow aisle with him or came too close, he screamed. Right alongside his powerful mania, which was taking over his life, were exhaustion and frustration. In these moments I saw the frustration in him dying to get out. He acted like a caged animal. He bumped his way into other aisles of the store and added bread, eggs, and cheese to the cart.

"Don't touch me!" he yelled at a woman reaching for a box of rice next to him.

"Sorry," she said.

"All right, Dad, let's go." I put my arm through his and walked him toward the checkout. I didn't think he would last much longer in a crowded space, so we quickly paid and left.

"We need to drop these off to my adopted family," he said, tossing bags of groceries into the car.

"Okay, I'd love to meet them." I buckled my seat belt.

We drove until we reached a small apartment building; he pulled over on the side of the road and pointed to the door on the right. "That's the one." Three new bicycles lay on the front lawn.

"David!" The mother of three kids came out smiling and waving for us to come in.

"This is my daughter, Sonja," he introduced me.

She smiled wider and shook my hand. "Carmen," she said, placing her free hand on her chest.

"Nice to meet you, Carmen." I smiled back.

"These are for you!" my dad said, stepping inside and setting grocery bags on the counter.

"Oh! *Gracias! Gracias!*" She set down two cups and poured us some juice.

My dad finished his juice in one gulp and slammed the cup on the counter. "That's it! I've decided to pay for all three of your kids to go to college!" he yelled. "Don't say anything!" He held up his hand to Carmen. "It's happening!"

I choked on my small sip of juice.

"And cars for everyone!" His eyes glowed.

"Dad, you can't afford that," I whispered.

"Shh!" He elbowed me. "You're just jealous."

Carmen seemed very nice, but there was no way he could afford all of this. My dad was completely broke and in mounds of debt. I silently watched him make big plans with Carmen for her boys. It was clear the Gomez family viewed my dad as their hero and an answer to many prayers—and maybe he was, in some ways—but he was making promises he couldn't keep; he just didn't know it. On our way out, I stopped him before getting into the car.

"Dad, you're not thinking straight. You have to know your behavior's been a little off."

"Stop right there; I've given this a lot of thought. Am *I* crazy, or are *you all* crazy? Because I know I'm not crazy, so it's gotta be all of you!"

His blue eyes were like marbles, leading to a hollow core. My dad was gone. The illness had taken him to a place I couldn't go. Was everything catching up to him? He dealt with an abusive childhood, legal battles, financial stress, fatherhood, marriage, and his own illness and obsessions. He had so many cracks—how could he possibly keep repairing them? How soon until the dam was permanently breached? He was bleeding out.

I took a close look at my dad's face, knowing he had to be somewhere in there. But all I saw was illness, and it scared me. The thought that our disease was strong enough to do that struck me with a new fear: I could disappear and not know it. As I looked at my dad, I wondered if I was looking at my own future. I felt nothing but compassion for him. I had to get him out of this.

I hopped into the driver's seat before he could. "Dad, get in the car." I started the engine, and he quickly scampered to the passenger seat.

"Where're you taking us?" he asked, popping a new toothpick into his mouth.

"To pick up Mom and then to your psychiatrist appointment," I answered once the car was in motion.

We picked up my mom, and three minutes into the drive, my dad started pretending to sleep. It was painfully clear he was faking, but he thought he had me fooled, like a child hiding a cookie behind his back.

"I don't think I can make it." He reclined his seat and started to cough. "I don't feel well," he added, peeping one eye open to see if I was watching him. My mom stayed quiet.

"Dad, you're going," I said.

I parked the car, and he stumbled his way out, keeping up the sick act. I'm not sure what sudden sickness would cause a grown man to lose his ability to walk, but apparently, he had it. I put my arm around him and helped him into the waiting room. He slumped in one of the chairs, pretending to snore until his name was called. I was forced to get him on his feet and into the room, as my mom stayed seated in the waiting room.

"Hello, David," the psychiatrist greeted us. "So, who's this, another daughter?"

Since most of my siblings had already tried to admit him, this psychiatrist had seen a lot of us lately. My dad kept his eyes closed and hung his head to the side, pretending to be sick or asleep; it was becoming unclear which one.

"I'm assuming you, like the rest of your family, want to admit him to the hospital. But I'm not convinced he's a danger to himself." The psychiatrist shrugged.

I bit my lip in a fury. "The very fact that all the people closest to him have been asking you to hospitalize him should be convincing enough, but if you're going to need me to spell it out, then read my lips." I raised my voice. "He *is* a danger to himself!"

"Fine. We can admit him and see if that changes anything, but I wouldn't bank on it."

"No! You can't do that!" My dad jumped up, miraculously healed.

"Yes, we can," the psychiatrist assured him.

My dad frantically dug around in his pocket for his phone, and in no time at all, he was talking to his lawyer.

"They're trying to lock me up. They can't do that!" he shouted as we escorted him to the emergency room, where doctors and a security guard waited for us. We entered a room, and the doctors asked my dad some questions. He wasn't honest when answering, so I'd talk over him to clarify; but whenever I talked, he loudly hushed me. It was hard to know what the doctor was hearing between the two of us.

The last doctor left, and my dad and I were alone in the room with a security guard.

"Don't turn on me. Just go with what I say," my dad whispered. I ignored his comment and pulled out a bag of caramel popcorn I'd brought as a peace offering.

"Here." I handed him the popcorn. He held the small bag in his lap and popped a few pieces into his mouth.

"What's your name?" he shouted to the security guard as he munched. "Hey! What's your name?" he shouted louder. The guard ignored him.

"You got a family?" He threw popcorn at him. "Hello?" The popcorn bounced off the guard's stiff uniform and rolled onto the floor. "Hell-loooooo?" He threw another piece of popcorn at the guard.

The doctor came back in. "David, we're hospitalizing you."

"Look, I'll go to the psych ward if you give me a little corner with a desk, a phone, and pad of paper, so that I can get on with my work," my dad informed the doctor.

"We can't give you that," the doctor said.

"I'm saving lives through organ donation, and the work can't stop." He stood. "I don't have time for this!"

"We'll see what we can do." The doctor tried to calm him down.

"Let's go," the security guard spoke to my dad as another joined him.

"Don't touch me!" My dad yanked his arms away from the guards.

The guards dropped their hands but walked tightly next to him down the hospital hallway.

My dad's eyes turned sharp as they cut into me. "What type of daughter turns on her own father?" He spat. "Everyone hear that?" he looked at the nurses and doctors he passed. "My daughter turned on her own father!"

"I love you, Dad," I insisted.

He flailed around, trying to turn and yell at me, but the guards kept him tightly facing forward as they walked.

"I will never forgive you for this, Sonja."

At seventy-three years old, my dad was a wounded person falling apart. Deep down, I knew he had fought the fight of a lifetime; he had battled this illness—unmedicated for decades.

"I hate you!" His scream echoed down the hall.

As tears slipped down my cheeks, I screamed back, "I love you, Dad!" and patiently waited for him to turn back and say what he always said to his children, *I love you more*. But the words never came, and he left without even turning to look at me. That was the last time I ever saw him in person. The look on his face and his words inflicted permanent wounds on my soul that to this day still bleed.

CHAPTER 23

Shattered Faith

Baton Rouge, Louisiana, 2010

Forty-eight hours later, I woke up to a phone call.

"He's out. He's out of the hospital," my brother's voice rang through the line.

"What? How? He just got admitted!"

"It didn't matter. Dad talked himself out of the hospital. Mom is as mad as a hornet."

"So I hospitalized him for nothing." I clenched my jaw.

"No, Sonja. You did your best."

I hung up the phone and locked myself in the only bathroom in our apartment. I pounded the walls, wanting to let out the loudest scream, but ended up crying instead. The pain of hospitalizing my dad and not knowing where this illness would take him crushed me. I couldn't get the image of his vacant eyes out of my mind. They were like hard stones, empty of any light. He was gone, and I wondered if I would ever get him back. This illness took so much.

My dad was the strongest person I knew; if he couldn't survive his bipolar disorder, how in the world could I? I put my head against the wall as the pain raged on. I squeezed my eyes shut, trying to hold back tears, but they escaped anyway. I let out my breath with a moan. I started to hit my forehead against the wall. Times like this I wished I could pay someone to beat me up—hit me, throw me, and inflict physical pain upon me. After a quick reality check, I knew that wasn't really an option. But it didn't make it any less of a temptation. My life became white noise as I stayed in bed the rest of the day.

That night when Mitch came home, he found me in the safety net of my bed reading a romance novel. "Hey, Sonja." Mitch sighed. He sat on the edge of the bed to unlace his shoes.

I put down my book. "My dad's out of the hospital. I hospitalized him for nothing." My voice cracked.

"Oh, I'm sorry, Sonja." He reached out and touched my cheek. I looked up into his eyes. His mind was somewhere else.

"What's wrong? Something's wrong. What is it?" I asked.

"The recruiter called. I didn't get the job."

"What?" I sat up, seeing our apartment for what it was, cat litter caked into the carpet and dirty clothes scattered throughout the room. This two-bedroom, one-bathroom apartment wasn't a temporary launching pad, but a crash landing. In that moment, I felt God was cruel. I was mad at God for leading me on like this. *What about the house we found in Lubbock? What about our house suddenly selling right as we get asked to interview? Wasn't that a sign?*

Next, I was mad at the recruiter. *He said to prepare for an offer! Why would he lie to us and get our hopes up? How unprofessional!* I considered calling him to tell him he was in the wrong profession and detail how his unprofessional encouragement led me into this mess. But then I was mad at Mitch. *Why did he need to move up in his career? Why couldn't we just settle for once? Why did Mitch keep doing this to me?*

"God must hate us." I swallowed.

"No, Sonja. The other candidate is God's child, too. The job was meant for him and his family. Also remember when you had a spiritual impression we'd move in two years? That was seven months ago, so it hasn't been two years yet."

I think Mitch knew this disappointment might deepen my faith crisis. My God questions were often targeted at Mitch, but he felt like an inadequate spokesman for God. His answers were no wiser or more profound than what he learned as a child in Sunday school. God loves us. We are his children. God's ways are not our ways. And none of those answers brought me comfort. The idea that God's will might include intolerable, emotional pain was unfathomable to me.

"Have some faith, Sonja," Mitch said.

"Mom, I love you." Rachael stroked my head.

I hadn't noticed her come in, but there she was sitting next to me, listening to everything. She often appeared at my side instantly. At sixteen, she still felt the need to hide steak knives and monitor how I was handling life. Her instincts seemed heightened; like a trained animal, she was capable of sensing the smallest change in my moods.

"I know this is hard, but hard doesn't always mean bad," Rachael said.

"I've already had hard things in my life. When will enough be enough? Rachael, help me. Tell me why God's doing this to me? Have I not suffered enough?" I cried.

"The hotter the fire, the more bendable the steel. Maybe God's shaping you for something greater." She gently rubbed my back.

"I don't want to be shaped. I want to be stable," I sobbed.

"I know this is really painful. But everything's going to be okay." She looked at my red eyes with such confidence that I wanted to believe her, but I couldn't shake my doubts.

"I don't think I'm going to make it, Rachael. God is pushing me beyond my capacity. He keeps putting me in these dangerous situations. He must want me dead," I concluded.

"You're safe, whether you feel it or not. You're safe," she said, running her finger over my nose as I closed my eyes crying.

"We're here for you, Sonja. You're not doing this alone. Just have faith." Mitch grabbed my hand.

No matter how encouraging Mitch or Rachael's words were, I didn't feel them for myself. *Do I feel betrayed or forgotten by God?* I wasn't sure which I'd prefer. Mitch said to have faith, but it was *faith* that failed me—faith the doctors would help my dad, faith we'd get Lubbock after selling our house. Because of faith, we ended up crammed into a two-bedroom apartment with no prospect of moving, and my dad was out of the hospital roaming the streets. My faith was dried up, and in my spiritual drought, I did not want to pray for rain.

CHAPTER 24

A Step Toward Temptation

Baton Rouge, Louisiana, 2010

"When were you going to do it?" Rachael stared at me.

"Do what?" I set my phone on the kitchen counter.

"Kill yourself. Today, tomorrow, next week?"

Shit, she found my suicide notes. I had typed heartfelt letters the night before to each of my children saying goodbye.

"Rachael—" I reached my hand out to comfort her.

She pushed my hand away. "When?" she asked again.

"I don't know," I answered honestly.

"You really want to leave us?" Tears welled in her eyes.

"I—"

"Does Dad know?" She sat on the floor with her arms over her knees.

"Not about the letters." Mitch took my medicine to work with him every day. *Suicide* was an unspoken word in our home, though my desires were no secret, so Mitch tried his best to prevent me from purposely overdosing.

"You didn't even write him one," she said, offended on his behalf.

"I was going to. Rachael, look at me." I waited, but she stayed focused on the cat next to her. "Look at me."

"What?" she snapped.

"Rachael, they're just letters. I don't have a plan. I don't want to leave you, your brothers, or Dad. Ever. I'm still here because of how much I love you. It just gets so painful I think I can't do another moment. I wrote them in one of those moments. But I'm still here."

"For now." She cried into her arms, gripping the sides of her sleeves.

"Rachael, I love you." I sat next to her.

"Then don't leave! If you really loved us, you'd stay!"

"I'm fighting to stay with you guys." I hugged her.

Although my suicidal feelings were no secret to my family, Rachael finding my suicide letters made it real. I talked about taking my own life, but never acted on it—never turned those thoughts into something tangible. I took a step toward my greatest temptation, and that scared me.

CHAPTER 25

Merry Christmas, Dad

Baton Rouge, Louisiana, December 2010

Our small apartment didn't require much to look adorned with Christmas decorations. We put up a three-foot plastic tree and taped three stockings on a wall. I kept up my tradition of wrapping the kids' favorite cereals and a big box of Capri Suns as presents. Those gifts were all I could fit under the tree without gifts spilling into the hallway.

On Christmas morning, I called my dad.

"Merry Christmas!"

He didn't respond.

"Dad? Are you there?"

"Yeah," he sighed.

He felt far away, but the distance was more than the space separating our two states. I knew even if I were sitting next to him in Utah, I would still feel all 1,223 miles between us. Allyson told me he spent his days sitting in his La-Z-Boy staring at the wall, detached from everyone and everything. The Opa that adored his grandkids wasn't present enough to greet them when they came to visit.

"Dad, you don't seem happy. What's going on?" I asked. I was met with more silence. "Please just tell me what you're thinking."

"You all think I need medicine because I'm crazy," he said.

"Do *you* think your behavior has been a little off?" I asked.

"It doesn't matter what I think at this point. I embraced who I thought I was, but you all rejected me." My dad's passion was an essential element to his personality, and he was lost without it.

"No, Dad, we're not rejecting you. We just want you to be healthy and happy."

"That's not a choice anymore. Being on medicine makes me hate my existence. I'm not myself. I can't experience anything. I'm doing this for your mother. I'm a model citizen now. I can't feel anything—no passion, no energy. All I feel is flat. I don't even know who I am anymore."

"You need to get a new doctor, Dad. You might be overmedicated," I said.

He didn't respond. He seemed resigned to the idea there were only two extremes he could live within: his manic side that turned his zest for life into an unmanned forest fire, or a medicated life snuffed out and vacuumed of any light.

"I love you, Dad."

He stayed silent, and I wished I could see his face. He still hadn't forgiven me for hospitalizing him. I could still see the fury in his eyes as he screamed, *I hate you.* I wanted to patch up our last encounter, but I couldn't do it over the phone, not like this.

"Dad?"

"Merry Christmas, Sonja." He hung up.

CHAPTER 26

The Phone Call

On February 8, 2011, I sat with my kids at the dinner table, staring at a warmed-up Stouffer's lasagna. Mitch's conversation with the kids turned to white noise as Mitch's phone rang.

"Hey, Heidi," he said, then got quiet. "It's your sister." He handed me the phone.

"Hello?" I said.

"Sonja, Dad died."

"What?!" I said, adrenaline rushing through me.

"He shot himself."

My hands went limp. I dropped the phone. I fell to the ground and let out a terrifying scream. *"No, no, no, nooooo!"*

Mitch swooped in and picked the phone off the floor. "Heidi, we'll call you later," he said.

"What's wrong?" Rachael asked, frightened.

"He shot himself!!" I cried out.

"Who?" Alex asked.

"Opa! Opa shot himself." I was too shocked to say it more delicately for my children.

The kids went silent. Their superhuman, horse-loving partner in crime was gone. He had created a magical world for them and then completely shattered it. Rachael cried with me while the boys watched silently. I curled up in a tight ball on the floor and frantically began rocking back and forth, howling in pain. Rachael sat next to me, mirroring my grief.

"Come here, Rachy," Mitch said, gathering all the kids in his arms. He worried what insecurities this would put into their minds. I was very open about my suicidal thoughts, and he feared the kids would think I was dying next.

No one tells you about the gruesome details of suicide—the specifics all those involved are left with after the death. Like how my dad told a family friend he needed to borrow his gun to go rabbit hunting with his grandkids—a gun he instead used to end his life. Or how when my mom called him on her way home, he asked her to stop and pick up some food first so he'd have enough time to carry out his plan before she arrived. How he took off his watch and placed it on the kitchen counter alongside his wallet with a note that read, "Time to go home." Or how when my mom saw the note, she searched the house looking for him, only to find him in the garage in the back seat of his car, dead, and the receipt for the bullets in the front seat.

What about my mom's bloody handprints that covered the phone while she called 911 after checking for my dad's pulse? Or how my brothers handled the police and my dad's body and the cleanup? We never talk about these things, but I wonder, how does someone let go of those moments before sleeping at night?

His death that day affected seven children, twenty-seven grandchildren, and his wife. For the first time in forty-nine years, my mom sat in a house without her husband, with those images burned inside her. I don't know about her private moments, but I never saw her crack, not once.

In the collision of tragic events, I was sure my injured heart wouldn't beat another day. But somehow, I found myself dressed in black, sitting in a window seat on a flight to my childhood home. Mitch and the kids would fly out a day later. Two girls in front of me laughed and chatted before takeoff. I couldn't help but wonder if I'd ever laugh again.

My haunting reality boarded the plane and took a seat next to me, and it was in a chatty mood. I sat while that nagging little devil filled my head with the facts. My father was dead. He would never call me again to take two hours of my time or hug me in that belly-scrunching type of way only he knew how. In the summers, I'd no longer spend time outside watching him study hummingbirds, and I'd never hear his voice reassure me I was loved and understood. I'd no longer see him wearing his Settlers hat and T-shirt during night games of Settlers of Catan.

Why couldn't there be phones in heaven? I wanted to call and make sure he was okay. I wanted to tell him I loved him, and maybe this time I could hear him say it back. I sat with my book up to my face during the whole flight to Utah, trying to hide from the people sitting next to me. I could feel a deep throat-sob surfacing as tears hit the page.

"Must be a good book." The woman beside me leaned over, trying to peer at the cover.

I ignored her and slid my window cover open to view the tall, beautiful mountains. I silently prayed in my head. *Dear God, this is Sonja. Please help! Will my life ever get better?* The plane rumbled as the wheels touched the runway. Holding my bag in a line full of people about to exit the plane, I felt a hand touch my shoulder. I turned and saw an older gentleman.

"It will get better," he gently said to me.

"Thank you." I nodded, acknowledging his kindness. God had answered my prayer through a complete stranger.

Heidi was waiting at baggage claim with her arms wide open. When my mom was pregnant with me, Heidi told everyone she was getting a baby sister for her birthday. People just laughed, thinking she was a silly four-year-old, but she was right. On her birthday, March 15, I was born. She told me I was the best birthday gift she ever received.

The second I saw her, I sprinted into her arms and broke down all over again.

"I'm so sorry, Sonja." Heidi hugged me.

She had just lost her father, too, but here she was comforting me. Heidi was the oldest daughter and the glue of our family—the strong, rational, stable one. I knew it was a heavy load to carry. Even though she seemed to have it together, in my opinion, she is the most sensitive of us all.

She pulled away from me and looked me straight in my eyes. "We can do this." This was going to be one of the hardest moments in our lives, and I was glad I didn't have to go through it alone.

All my siblings were at the house sitting on the couch together, comforting my mom, who cried but didn't say much. I hugged my mom and wondered how she was holding it together. I looked around and saw somebody had flipped every picture of my dad facedown except for one. It was a photo of his hands, a hummingbird perched on his finger. I was positive my mom had flipped the photographs over because seeing his face brought back the images of finding him in the back seat of his car.

"I'm going to bring my bags up. You want to come?" Allyson asked. Without saying anything, I picked up my bag and followed her. We hiked up the expansive staircase we had walked as children. As we passed our parents' bedroom, the pain hit me hard, like the house itself was causing it. I turned and walked into my parents' room.

"Allyson." I stopped. "I can't do this."

"Yes, you can." She hugged me, but I stepped away from her into my parents' bedroom.

"No. I really can't!" I collapsed on my parents' bed and pounded the mattress.

I should have flown out again and gotten him more help. I should have helped him find a new psychiatrist. I should have done more.

I felt a big responsibility because I knew what it felt like to be dangerously suicidal. Everyone downstairs could hear me screaming and they quickly came up. Allyson went through my bags and got my medicine.

"Take this." She handed me my pills with a glass of water, then got on the bed and held me tight.

"Get the horse bracelet!" I cried.

The horse bracelet was a beautiful gold bracelet my dad designed. Seven wild horses ran off its sides with the word *Freedom* engraved on the inside. I felt like he wanted the same freedom his horses always seemed to reflect. He wanted freedom from his illness, just like I did. My family knew gold bracelets were one of my strongest comforts, and tonight the horse bracelet housed the comfort I needed. Allyson put the bracelet on my wrist, and my siblings knelt around the bed for a prayer as I continued to cry.

The next morning, I woke up to chilly winter weather pressing against the window. Mitch and the kids had flown in, but I might as well have been on the moon. I didn't interact with them; I wasn't able to be present. Mitch took care of the kids and allowed me to mourn in silent distance.

Downstairs, I found Heidi at work on the funeral program: planning the casket, flowers, and obituary. Allyson, my mom, and I went to the morgue to take the clothes they'd dress him in. The short car ride felt like a quick heart attack. I was winded at the thought of seeing my dad. *What would he look like?*

"If you'd follow me this way." The morgue worker motioned us down the hall to a small sitting room where my dad's body lay on a metal cart. My mom immediately broke into tears. Allyson wrapped her arms around our fragile mom like she was ready to absorb all her pain. His face was wrapped tight like a mummy but looked deformed underneath the gauze. "I'll give you a moment alone." The morgue worker nodded reverently and left the room.

I sat frozen, feeling like this was a strange hospital visit. Like we were witnessing the aftermath of a near fatal car wreck. But there were no IVs or nurses, and my dad didn't move. Still, as I looked at his bare body laid out on the metal cart with only a sheet draped over him, I thought, *He must be cold.* I looked back and forth between my sobbing mother and dead father and reached out to take his hand. His hand had all the same freckles and age spots as before, but his skin was white. His cool, heavy hand felt like putty filled with sand. I noticed his wedding ring was still on.

"Mom, do you want to take his wedding ring?" I asked.

"He wanted to be buried with it on. He said it a thousand times," she responded through her tears.

"Mom, if you want his ring, you should take it," Allyson agreed.

"He has never removed that ring, not once, in forty-nine years, since our wedding day when I put it on him," my mom said.

"It meant so much to him. It can comfort you," I said.

"You're right. I'll take it," she nodded.

"Can you remove his wedding ring?" I asked the morgue worker once he returned.

"Of course," he said. The morgue worker handed my mom the ring, and she slipped it on her middle finger.

—⟋⟍—

The day of the funeral, I tugged my feet into black heels. The cool February air filled my lungs, and I gripped Allyson's hand for support. The long line of people came up to give my family their condolences—people I've known my whole life—but I felt frozen. I stood like a statue as close family friends hugged me.

Large rose arrangements filled the front of the chapel. Two hearts looped together in red and white roses with a banner that read, "Double Double Sweetheart." As I walked up to the podium to share a few words about my dad, I passed my dad's casket. I looked out at the black velvets and silks filling the benches in an overwhelming mass of ruffled fabric. Like the audience, his casket was still and quiet—the very two things my dad was not. I bent the microphone down and let out a shaky breath.

"One of my favorite stories about my dad is when his brother, Roger, applied to join the Operation Engineer Union, so he could do construction work and feed his family. Roger was denied because he didn't have a high school diploma. However, if he passed the GED, he could get in. Uncle Roger knew he couldn't pass since he dropped out of high school, so my dad took the GED test for him. Roger's score ended up being in the top one percent in the nation. A short time later, Roger was surprised when he received a letter from the University of Utah offering him an academic scholarship. Roger kept that letter as a reminder of my dad's love for him." All seven of us children spoke and paid tribute to our father, a father we loved and adored.

After a suicide the guilt of what more you could have done to save your loved one haunts you. The "what if" questions become almost a mental maze you can't seem to find yourself out of. The memory I have sitting in the emergency room with my father for hours when the doctors and I decided to admit him to the psychiatric hospital against his will still stings. His words, *I hate you, Sonja! I will never forgive you for this!* Still plays in my mind. To this day, unrealistic as it may be, I wonder if changing even one small interaction could have stopped the falling dominos leading to his death.

My father's death caused a clash of emotions in me. When a person dies from natural causes, people tend to think in terms of "it was their time" or "it was God's will," and are able to find peace. Or when a person dies of homicide, the survivors fight for justice and direct their anger at the perpetrator. The difficulty with a suicide is the person who is the victim is also the perpetrator. I felt my father was a victim of his mental illness, but I also felt a sense of anger and abandonment. What I knew for sure was God and I were making a pact that before I ever tried to take my own life, He would take me out first. He couldn't let me do something like this to my family. I believed with my whole soul God would protect me from it—He had to.

CHAPTER 27

Haunting Memories

I was back in Utah several months after the funeral to help my mom move out. Moving trucks filled the driveway, and I shielded my eyes from the sun as I looked up at the brownstone mansion from my childhood. I stepped over the pavement to her garden, where the flowers sulked as their dry roots waited for water. Many things had been put on pause after my dad's death, and gardening was one of them. Since he was gone, I felt it was unfair for the house to still exist, reminding us of him in such vivid detail. He used to sit for hours in the big field where the home now stood, sketching his dream; everything about it reflected him.

One of my high school classmates and her mother pulled up the driveway. "We're here to see the baby grand piano," she called out the window of the car.

"Park, and I'll show it to you," I said, walking away from the dying roses.

My mom was selling almost everything as she got ready to move into a smaller home. I walked them to the white room, where, like its name, all the furniture and decorations were white except for the shiny, black baby grand piano. This room was my dad's shrine to his family. Oil paintings of every child and their spouse covered the walls. My parents' portrait hung above the fireplace presiding over their children.

My dad had a predictable routine for visitors. Before the usual house tour, he began in the white room. Now, instead of hearing my classmate playing Chopin on the piano, all I could hear was my dad's booming voice reciting the résumé and accomplishments of each child and their spouse. He liked to share details like their GPA and salary. It was boasting in its most shameless form, but that was Dad. "These kids are my pride and joy!" he'd say.

"We'll think about it," she said, interrupting my thoughts.

"Sounds good," I said, with my dad's voice still ringing in my ears.

I slept with my mom in her bedroom that night, on my dad's side, and kept thinking he should be there instead of me. My mom silently cried. Maybe when I woke up, he'd be sleeping on the couch, newspaper over his belly and hair ruffled from staying up too late. The balcony's sliding door was open, and I could feel the mountain breeze swirl into the room. Memories trailed in of family barbecues out on the patio and water gun fights on the lawn. I closed my eyes and thought of the racquetball court downstairs where, as a teenager, I practiced my ballet routine for hours. Voices and memories haunted me in this place, and I couldn't wait to leave.

I flew home several days later; only this time, there were no fumes left to propel me forward. I collapsed in my bedroom closet with a steak knife gripped in my hand. I hadn't cut in years. I knew I shouldn't, but I needed it. Emotions hit me like a hurricane—flooding, drowning, and damaging my soul. Watching suicide rip through my entire family made my own suicidal feelings harder to accept. *I will not do that to my kids!* But the truth was, my dad's death didn't relieve me of my suicidal tendencies and, now that I understood suicide's toll, I felt a new urgency: my illness wanted me dead. I tried hard to stop the suicidal urges and thoughts, push them away, or at least postpone their arrival, but I couldn't control the pollution in my mind.

I hit my head against the wall and tried to let go of the knife. Pain ran through my entire body like electricity. A current of pain beneath my skin. *Stop!* I screamed in my head. I stood, ripped off my sweats, and sat against the wall. I took the knife and cut a long, straight line down my thigh. The physical pain registered immediately, and I could take a breath. Relief—it felt so good, too good. A small line of blood ran down my leg. I didn't care. The emotions started back up, and I cut again. And again, and again, and again.

"Mom? Mom, where are you?" Rachael called down the hall.

I froze. The closet light flicked on. My swollen, cried-out eyes looked up at Rachael. Alex stood a few feet behind her. His stare sent a dagger through my heart.

"Please go," I whispered.

"But Mom!" Rachael cried.

"Call Dad!" Alex said. It was a phrase the kids became accustomed to repeating. Mitch was the kids' 911 responder when things were in crisis.

"Just go!" I looked down at my legs, my hands, the knife. "You shouldn't see this." I grabbed my sweatpants and covered my legs.

"Here." Rachael held out a brown marker. "Use this. Give me the knife."

I looked up and met her eyes. Guilt and shame washed over me. *I am a horrible mom. No child should see their mother cutting.* I peered around the corner and saw Alex on his knees, praying. I felt beyond even God's help, yet there Alex knelt, praying for his mother. I was sure I was going to hell for this.

It took everything in me to hand Rachael the knife, but I did. She handed me the marker and left. I had wanted to cut along my arms, too, so I removed the cap and traced the veins from my arms to my hands.

Neither my kids nor my husband ever discussed the marker lines that continued to decorate my arms. In a defiant move, I wore short sleeves, not caring who saw them. I had always cut in places no one would see, but these lines were out on display. People stared, but it didn't stop me. I didn't know what caused this newfound defiance, but it brought me comfort. The pain continued; the suffering continued; but I made a promise that my children would never see me cut again. And for them, I kept that promise.

—⟋m⟍—

Mitch worked later hours to escape the chaos of our home life, leaving the kids and me to fend for ourselves. I was grieving my father's death and suicidal myself, yet I was the one expected to parent the children out of the two of us. Even though he knew I was in no state to make sure the kids were okay, he left them in my care. The reality was they were growing up in a dysfunctional home and Mitch had emotionally checked out.

I lay in bed and dialed my dad's number, knowing he wouldn't pick up but ready to be shocked if he did. The phone rang and rang and rang until it went to his voicemail.

"Hi, you've reached David Nemelka. I'm not at the phone right now, so leave a message, and I'll get back to you."

His voice felt so real, like maybe in that moment he really was too busy to pick up. I let myself believe he was out with the horses or getting a Diet Coke at the local gas station, but when his message ended, the illusion vanished. I closed my eyes, remaining hopeful that some peace might penetrate my sick body.

"It's okay, I understand," I told God. "You let illnesses carry their course in people's lives. But don't forget we made our pact!"

Mitch came into the bedroom and tried to tug me out of bed. "Sonja, come on. Let's go to a movie."

"I'm not going." My cheek lay deep into my tear-stained pillow.

Mitch sighed. "Sonja, it's becoming unhealthy for the kids to see all this. Please just come." I felt he was only willing to acknowledge these facts or do anything about it when the solution was to do something fun. When it came to the hard work of prioritizing family and having difficult, vulnerable conversations, he was offline. I worked hard to fill in that gap as good as any grieving mother could. So when it came time for fun, I let him take over.

"Go without me." I pulled a blanket over my shoulders and continued looking at a picture of my dad. "Go be happy without me."

I knew I sounded dramatic, but I meant it. My family didn't need my somber mood hanging over them 24/7. I felt they'd have more fun without me. I couldn't stand being around myself, so how could they? Incessant crying seemed to be my new routine. I knew Mitch wouldn't go without me because I was too unstable to leave home alone. Leaving me meant risking I'd harm myself in some way; and even if I didn't, he knew I'd hate him for leaving me. Mitch was often in a lose-lose situation. He came back into the room, and instead of lying down next to me like he usually did, he stood by the bed, not touching me.

"Something has to change," he said to the floor.

"What do you mean?" I asked, lifting my face up to him.

He remained standing. "We've got to get out of this two-bedroom apartment and move on. We just lost your dad; we can't lose you, too." He exhaled. He was breaking, but I was already broken. "The kids can't keep living this way." But I knew he really meant him. Mitch turned and walked out. I heard the front door close behind him and the kids.

The challenge with mental illness and marriage is that people wrongly assume one person is healthy and one is ill. I assumed because Mitch wasn't bipolar, he was always functioning at 100 percent and should be able to make up my emotional deficits. But in truth, when I was depressed, he was depressed. When I was anxious, he was anxious. When I didn't sleep, he didn't sleep. When I was manic, he lived in a world spinning out of control. In bipolar support groups, they call this "compassion fatigue," and I had seen Mitch suffering from it. The worse I got, the worse he got; we were linked that way.

The kids needed to feel some semblance of normalcy. I couldn't expect them to stay in bed with me all day as I cried and worked through months of grief.

"God, I'm losing my family. I have nothing left inside to give. You have to help me. I can't do this alone."

I started burying my grief deep, deep in the abyss of my soul, never to be found. I wrapped my arms tightly around myself and closed my eyes as God gave me strength. I felt pieces of my soul coming apart; for now, I would use these broken fragments to provide me with just enough strength to save my family, not knowing if I would ever be whole again. I slowly stood and tucked my dad's picture away in a book to start the process of turning my ship around.

CHAPTER 28

Private School

I found a realtor and we bought an adorable townhouse in a planned neighborhood with walking trails, a community swimming pool, and workout facility. We had finally moved out of the two-bedroom apartment, and I unpacked in record time. Tennis came to a halt; I decided it didn't feel right anymore. Our tennis community was shocked. Everyone knew my boys put in insane hours hoping to go pro, and they couldn't believe we quit at the drop of a hat. Without my mania and now being in a depressive episode, Wimbledon seemed unreachable. The boys were confused but trusted my intuition without question.

I started focusing on private schools. The kids were thrilled to be attending school where there would be more kids, and have facilities, like a gym, library, and football field. The kids wrote application essays and got letters of recommendation. The schools we looked at were harder to get into than many colleges. My kids were accepted to a private Baptist school, and we paid $10,000 per kid to attend for one year.

Every Tuesday, their school had chapel, which they loved. They sang upbeat Christian rock songs with a live student band featuring a drummer and electric guitarist. The students and teachers danced in the aisles, praising the Lord. My kids introduced me to all the gospel songs, and we fell in love with K-Love radio.

After school, the kids would drop their backpacks on either side of my bed and hop on top of the comforter. My bedroom was our family room. We ate snacks, talked about their day, worked on homework, and watched movies there. It was the first place we all gathered. I was very present in their lives, even though I didn't want to leave my room. My bed was my safe place, and it became theirs.

Rachael's English teacher told me she was a gifted writer. Her teacher's praise made me proud that her creativity was finally able to shine through her dyslexia.

Alex's reading scores came back at college levels. I was in complete shock. In second grade, he had been the only student who couldn't read their Mother's Day card. In fact, back then, Alex wasn't just bad at reading, he hated it. After two years of having him read out loud books he chose from Barnes & Noble, I found him sitting in the playroom reading *Eragon* on his own. He finished the 400-page book in a few days. I knew he had progressed as a reader but hadn't realized he had become advanced.

I had just received an email from Alex's history teacher telling me how polite he was and how much he contributed to class discussions. In the past, his teachers and principal wanted to meet with me constantly to talk about his disruptive behavior and poor test scores. He'd have his classmates time him running around the room whenever the teacher left, and he pulled the fire alarm. I wished I could go back in time and tell my younger self not to stress so much about Alex and that things would turn out just fine.

Lincoln got straight As and was gifted at math, which I hadn't known. He received the Extra 10 Percent Award, which was given to one student who gave more than 100 percent in their schoolwork. Lincoln even branched out and joined the football team.

My kids were thriving, despite our families' traumatic events and chaos. They had become professionals when it came to swimming in rough waters. Private school relieved me that all my efforts to educate them were paying off, and I felt like there was a little more air to breathe. But not enough air to stop me from holding my breath.

I continued pretending I was fixed. I put on a brave front: showering, changing my clothes, taking my meds, attending my therapy sessions, and keeping an immaculate house. When the kids were at school and Mitch was at work, I spent hours sitting on our couch, staring at the wall. While I blocked out most of my grief, the one thing I couldn't stop were my dreams. In them, my dad and I would talk on the couch as he read his newspaper. I told him about my kids, and he told me about his horses. Toward the end, I'd beg him to stay, but the dream always ended the same. I'd get the phone call from Heidi saying he'd died. I secretly continued to call his phone, even though it'd been disconnected. I called hoping he might answer. It was a fantasy I wasn't willing to give up.

CHAPTER 29

Unresolved Grief

"I have to tell you, I'm in a somber mood today," Dr. Pope said, starting our psych appointment. "I'm a little more on the sadder side than I tend to be."

"Okay?" I was confused why he was sharing that information.

"Right before you came, I was feeling really sad. I started thinking about you, and I don't know if I've ever seen your sadness—in terms of like tears and grief. I've seen a lot of your tiredness and exhaustion but no grief, especially around your dad's passing. Do you feel like you inhibit your grief?"

"No, I'm fine." I fidgeted in the chair.

"Sonja, grief isn't something you can skip over like a song on your playlist. We call that inhibited grieving. You have to go through it. You can't shove it and put it away. It will bubble back up and demand you deal with it."

"I believe that if I bury it deep enough, I'll forget it's there," I said.

"It doesn't work that way. Sonja, you need to start your grieving process."

"I can't deal with it right now. It's not a good time."

"Grief isn't something you can put off. You lost a loved one, your father, in a very dramatic way. I want to help you process this traumatic event, but you have slammed the doors and bolted them, so no one can even get near the event. Can you open the doors?"

"No. No, I can't," I stated.

"Sonja, it won't work. It will burst through and cause more wreckage than if you would open those doors willingly."

I refused to answer. There had to be another way.

When I got home, I set a bag of Taco Bell on the counter and called the kids for dinner. The kids grabbed the paper-wrapped tacos out of the bag and sat at the table.

"Sonja, can I talk to you?" Mitch asked, getting up from his chair.

"Yeah, what?" I looked at him as we moved into the living room.

"I made it to the final two for a job in Columbia, Missouri."

"What? When did you apply? Why didn't you tell me?"

"I applied six months ago. I didn't tell you I was interviewing because I knew the uncertainty would affect your mental health. I waited to tell you until the very last interview. They want us to fly out next week to meet the team. The job is a COO position of a bigger health system."

"Wow!" I was shocked and stunned, but in a good way for once. So many traumas had happened while living in Louisiana that I welcomed the idea of moving. I wanted a redo.

The hospital put us in an adorable bed and breakfast with welcome goodie baskets on our bed. Stepping out of the hotel into Columbia's beautiful weather put a smile on my face. I was so used to Louisiana humidity that this crisp air felt like a fresh start. I needed Mitch to get the job. Luckily, this time, we did. I believed this move would allow me to leave my pain behind, not realizing my problems were not housed within the state of Louisiana or my neighborhood, but within me, as I would soon learn.

CHAPTER 30

Moving

Columbia, Missouri, 2012

We moved into our house under the June sun and comfortably sank into our new Missouri lifestyle. Every day, our family had lots of reasons to believe the Midwest was a hidden gem.

The man who stained our deck brought us blackberries from his garden. They were such a small gift, yet it felt like he gave me something so much more than fruit. The neighbors made their rounds to welcome us into the community, and it wasn't long before my boys had an army of friends.

That summer, Mitch took Rachael to Europe for two weeks before she left for college. While they explored Rome's Colosseum and the Louvre in Paris, I was surrounded by a troop of teenage boys. Our place became the party house. The basement was consistently loud while they played games and I provided a seemingly unending supply of pizza and soda.

During the two weeks Mitch was gone, I began eating less each day until I stopped eating completely. It was like my body lost its will to live if he wasn't here. I realized if Mitch died before me, I'd be gone three months later. Soulmates don't do well without each other. Even though it felt like an eternity, Mitch did come back, and I sat snuggled in his arms while he and Rachael flipped through their slideshow of pictures.

"Rachael, a friend told me there was a woman named Sarah at church who has some learning disabilities and a mental illness. I told him we'd go visit her tomorrow. Are you okay coming?" I asked in the middle of her showing me a picture of her and Mitch in Venice.

"Sure, I'm fine with that." She nodded, going to the next picture.

We soon knew Sarah better than anyone. I had many people come up to me at church and tell me how good I was to be her friend. I simply responded, "No, I'm lucky that she is my friend."

They would just stare, not knowing what to say. I felt people often dismissed those with mental illness instead of looking deeper to the person inside. Most weeks, Rachael and I read the children's version of the scriptures with her and took her to get groceries at the local Hy-Vee. She'd walk me down aisles of food, showing me the products like I'd never been to a grocery store before. We became so regular that whenever I went to the store without her, the cashiers asked where my friend Sarah was.

On Sundays, I drove Sarah to church, and we'd make our way to a chapel bench together. While the prayer was said, the whole congregation sat reverently waiting for the sacrament—except Sarah.

"So I brought some of my hair in a Ziploc bag to the doctor, and he said I'm *not* going bald, but I don't believe him." Her voice filled everyone's ears.

"You can tell me after," I whispered.

"You believe me, right?"

"Of course."

Mitch looked at me, uncomfortable that our pew was drawing unwanted attention. No matter how many times I explained to her this was a quiet time, Sarah talked throughout the whole church meeting.

I related to Sarah's inability to stay quiet and conform. Often while having dinner with friends or people from Mitch's work, I'd stare at the person across the table from me. No matter how many times Mitch kicked my leg to get me to stop, I couldn't. When I talked, I tended to repeat myself, saying the same thing four or five different ways. I had this compulsion to make a point and hammer it home, even if everyone already agreed with me.

Sometimes, Mitch smiled and said, "Sweetheart, take yes for an answer." Other times, he'd cut me off and say, "Sonja, you're repeating yourself."

It got to a point where I asked him to give me a cue if I started repeating myself in public. We agreed on the phrase, "Did the kids call?" When Mitch said this, I could modify my behavior.

Maybe Sarah needed a phrase, too. Or maybe she just needed someone who understood her. Either way, who was I to admonish her for something I did myself?

Our mismatched family grew as I invited two new people to join us in our church pew. Bob—a quirky old man with a comb-over—spent all his time on the computer at the library. Every week, I invited Bob to sit with us at church, but he refused. He sat in the very back of the church all alone. After three months, he finally started sitting with us and never stopped.

Carol was a frail, little old woman who told the most elaborate stories about her life. One was about her son, a police officer, losing his hand in the line of duty. Another was about her other son, a missionary in some remote place, living off the land with his wife and three children. She told me about the letters he sent her from their island, explaining their latest adventures. I came to find out none of the stories were true. I don't like to say she lied; I believe she told the stories she could live with. The reality was she had no contact with her sons and hadn't for years. I'm not sure of all the ins and outs of their lives, but they had essentially disowned her.

I made the rounds to gather all my passengers, and we piled into my car for church.

"What if I drove us all to Mexico right now? We just go without telling anyone," I announced out of the blue. One of my fantasies was to up and leave and see where life took me—no plan, no responsibilities, no illnesses.

"I can go," Sarah said.

"Can we stop back at my apartment so I can get my swimsuit?" Bob asked.

"I don't have anywhere I have to be. I can go," Carol added.

I laughed. "I love you guys. You'd be willing to go on an adventure without notice? That's rare, my friends, very rare indeed. I can't today, but maybe someday.

We made quite the scene walking into the quiet chapel. I'd help Carol get into her seat with her walker while Sarah and Bob bickered the whole way to our seats.

During the service, several people shared stories of unexplainable blessings happening because of their obedience. As I sat and listened to how God swooped in to help the people who were staying devoted to His laws and commandments, I wondered if I was the only one God left hanging despite living what I thought was a faithful life.

A woman in a purple dress raised her hand in front of me. "My dad lost his job. They couldn't find a way to pay rent, and so they went to the church leader and told him they couldn't pay tithing that month. He told them they needed to have faith and pay their tithing anyway. So they paid their tithing. There was no magic check in the mail. They ended up having to go on welfare. Sometimes that's the true test of faith. Going through it and trusting God even when things don't work out the way you thought they should." She paused. "That's the hard part of life. That's real faith."

I looked at her; she seemed familiar. Then I remembered we had met at her house on the Fourth of July; she lived on a hill and had invited people over to watch the fireworks. Her name was Lorie.

After church was over, I approached her and suggested we go to lunch sometime.

"I don't do lunch," Lorie said.

Her honesty caught me off guard, and I liked her even more. She was going to be my best friend; she just didn't know it yet.

Later that day, I kept thinking back to Lorie's story in church about how sometimes things don't work out, but God wants us to exercise faith anyway. I felt like she was someone I could relate to, like she had wisdom I'd benefit from. I knew she was going to be an important person in my life, so I was determined to win her over.

I made a floral arrangement and dropped it off at her house. She wasn't home, so I left it on the doorstep. She called me that same day.

"I don't do lunch, but would you want to go to dinner with our husbands?" she asked.

That weekend, Mitch and I went with Lorie and her husband, Dean, to a local restaurant, Chris McD's. Candles lit the middle of each table. I looked over the menu and ordered an appetizer before the waters were passed out.

"I've got a joke for you," Dean announced. "Why was King Arthur's army too tired to fight?"

"Why?" Mitch asked.

"They had too many sleepless knights." Dean barely waited for a reaction before telling the next joke. "I couldn't figure out why the baseball kept getting larger. Then it hit me."

Lorie rolled her eyes. "Dean collects G-rated jokes."

When our entrées came, I boxed my meal and asked to see the dessert menu. After briefly skimming over the menu, I told the waitress I would take one of each.

"You ordered all six desserts?" Lorie laughed.

"That way we can all try a bite of each." I shrugged. "Desserts are kind of my thing."

"It's true. She has a chocolate cupboard at home filled with chocolate," Mitch added.

"Some people drink coffee in the morning, but when I wake up, the first thing I eat is a piece of chocolate," I said.

"I love that! I want a chocolate cupboard," Lorie said.

Food is what instantly bonded us. I went out and bought tons of mini chocolates and gave them to Lorie with a note: "Now you can start your own chocolate cupboard."

She and I became fast friends. Lorie had a beautiful voice and had been the lead singer in a band. Art and interior design were some of our favorite topics to debate. She raised four sons and supported her husband through medical school. I either talked to her or saw her every day.

Getting out of the house was a constant struggle for me, so it was great when Lorie and I ran errands together. When we went grocery shopping, we'd do yoga poses as we put our food on the checkout conveyor belt. Lorie and I had many traditions, like regular pedicures at Walmart or going to restaurants where I'd make things up about myself to tell the waiter. When my stories got too far-fetched, Lorie would kick me under the table. We went to the local frozen custard shop and got kids' cones before watching *The Real Housewives of New York City* each week. We discussed the show in-depth, as if we were watching some type of mind-bending documentary.

It became clear Lorie was an answer to years of prayers. She not only strengthened me but helped me in a million little ways to survive my days. Yet I still wasn't ready to share my secrets with her.

CHAPTER 31

My Kids' Greatest Trial

Columbia, Missouri, 2012

I cried my eyes out when Rachael left to start her freshman year of college at Brigham Young University–Idaho (BYUI). She graduated from high school a year early, and though I advocated for her to do so, it was harder than I expected to watch her go. I kept her bedroom door closed because whenever I saw her room, I'd start to cry all over again. Rachael was an essential part of my everyday life. We did everything together: grocery shopping, house cleaning, and discussing how to raise the boys. She kept me laughing until my stomach hurt. Her zest for life brought me a sense of joy in my tortured existence. Going through the weeks without her presence felt strange. We talked on the phone every day, and I was happy to keep her in my life that way.

Alex soon followed Rachael in graduating from high school a year early and left for BYU Provo. The house felt emptier and emptier. Alex was the responsible one. He was the man of the house when Mitch was gone. He made sure doors were locked, prayers were said, and no inappropriate jokes were told. He was the enforcer of order in our chaotic life. Although we could be a handful at times, his steady presence was a comfort to me.

With them both gone, I started organizing their bedrooms and found copies of their college admission essays. The prompt from the admissions committee was, "Tell us about your most difficult trial."

Rachael Wasden's College Essay: "My Most Difficult Trial"

My most difficult trial has been having a bipolar mother. One night, when everyone was asleep, I turned the computer screen on, letting a soft glow illuminate the dark room. The first thing that popped up on the computer was a Word document. Out of curiosity, I read the short paragraphs. Barely comprehending the first sentence, I quickly reread it after I realized my mom had written it. It was a suicide note.

All the years of my mother's disease came back to me. The nights in the emergency room, the weeks in the psych ward, the fighting and depressive states when she would spend months in bed. Feelings of anger filled my heart faster than any feelings of sorrow could. While desperately praying that night to my Heavenly Father for help, I felt this overwhelming love, compassion, and understanding for my mother that I had never felt before. I learned that God hears heartfelt prayers. Although God has not taken this difficult trial away, I have gained a testimony that the Savior will comfort and sustain me through any of life's trials I will face.

Alex Wasden's College Essay: "My Most Difficult Trial"

The hardest thing I have faced in my life is having a mother with severe bipolar disorder. I didn't fully understand the impact of this trial on my life until I had the following experience. I had just gotten home from school when I found my siblings in Mom's room. The expression on their faces signaled that something was terribly wrong. My mother looked at me with an eerie calm and said, "What do you want of mine? I am going to die tomorrow and want to leave you something." This time it felt as though her illness had broken her. This time she said it with a chilling acceptance that shook my soul.

That night we prayed fervently, like we always did, that God would help her one more time through this trial. She didn't take her life that night and is still alive today. I am grateful for having this challenge in my life. I have learned from having a bipolar mother that God gives us tender mercies just as we feel that the very gates of hell will consume the ones we love. I have also learned that I will never give up on family no matter how hard my life or my relationship with them seems.

I held the essays to my heart and wondered what business I had being a mother. Unwanted memories flooded my mind. How many times had Mitch been at a work dinner while Alex held my hand as I cried for hours? He would patiently listen to all my nonsense with only a simple reply: "I love you." Alex would coax me into taking my meds and tuck me into bed.

What type of mother makes her daughter sit and write her will every time she thinks she couldn't live another hour? I didn't want to believe that when my children were asked, "What has been your hardest trial?" their answer was me, their mother.

CHAPTER 32

Cause and Effect

Columbia, Missouri, Fall 2014

As a junior and sophomore in college, Rachael and Alex both decided to put their studies on hold while they participated in church service missions. They would teach others about Jesus Christ and help with community service projects. Rachael went to Berlin, Germany, while Alex went to Philadelphia.

Although I was used to them not being home, having them farther away, and one in a foreign country, made the house feel emptier. Luckily for me, Lincoln was my most social child and filled all the empty spaces of the house with crowds of friends. He was also my most sensitive child. That week I became aware of how being raised by a sick mother was affecting him when one of his teachers called me and requested I meet with her.

"Mrs. Wasden," she greeted me. "I have to tell you Lincoln is a very unusual teenager. I called you in today because my students were gossiping about our Spanish teacher on Friday."

"Oh, I'm so sorry—"

"Except Lincoln," she cut in. "Despite being the youngest in the class, he stood up for a teacher he had no obligation to defend."

"I'm glad to hear that," I said.

"One of our students lost his brother and mom in a car accident," she continued, reaching into her desk drawer and handing me a wristband. It was blue and said "Rock Bridge Cares" across it. "Lincoln and a bunch of students organized a fundraiser to have a memorial bench put at the little brother's elementary school by selling these."

I looked at the wristband. "I had no idea."

Her eyes never left mine. "Lincoln is so aware of other people's suffering."

She waited for a response I wasn't willing to give.

"It's very unusual for someone his age," she pressed.

I had no answer to give other than that it was because I, his mother, suffered, and I didn't want to admit that to her. I started to panic as I realized she wasn't going to let this go.

"I'm sorry. I have an appointment. I have to go." I picked up my purse and ran out of her classroom.

I knew Lincoln wouldn't tell her our family secret. Not one of my kids had told their friends about my illness. It was our family rule to keep it quiet. We never let people in, ever.

That weekend, Mitch and I watched one of Lincoln's tennis matches. He made varsity doubles as a freshman and felt in his element. It was easy for him to fall back into a sport he excelled at. While we waited for the game to start, a woman in a white Nike hat walked up to us.

"Hi, I'm Connor's mom." She put her hand on her chest. "I just wanted to thank you for what Lincoln did yesterday. It meant a lot to us."

"Sorry, what did he do?" I asked.

"My son plays on the junior varsity team, and the top varsity players usually bully him. Yesterday on the bus ride to the tournament, the ringleader of the bullying started throwing food at him and had the rest of the varsity players call him names and throw food at him, too. But when they handed Lincoln food and demanded he participate, Lincoln told all of them to knock it off and then proceeded to walk to the front of the bus and sit with Connor." Tears filled her eyes. "Sorry, it's just the bullying has been really hard on him, and because of your son, they've left him alone."

"Thanks for telling us." I hugged her.

"Enjoy the game," she said, patting my shoulder.

I looked at Mitch. "Did you know about that?"

"No," he said with wide eyes.

For years, I sat paralyzed by the thought that my outward suffering scarred my children in ways they'd never recover. I'd never considered that any good could come from all those raw moments until now.

CHAPTER 33

Say it Out Loud

Columbia, Missouri, 2014

Since our church consisted of a lay ministry, we had no paid clergy. Each member took their turn in church assignments as volunteers. One of the group's assignments included speaking. It was my turn, and I prepared a talk on trials, since I felt that was my specialty.

As the congregation sang the opening hymn, a strong feeling came over me that I needed to share about my dad dying from suicide. Everything in me rebelled against that thought. I didn't talk about those types of things, especially to a group of 250 people. I assured myself that nobody needed to hear it, and I, for one, did not want to share it.

I got halfway through my talk and the thought, *You need to tell the truth about your father,* hit me so powerfully that the words, "My father died from suicide," slipped right out of my mouth. I looked out at the audience and saw I had everyone's attention. "I have many questions and fears. But I have hope Christ will one day help me come to peace with it."

After my talk, I hurried out of the building as if it were crumbling. I pushed open the double doors and was stopped by a woman chasing after me.

"Wait! Wait!" she yelled.

I let go of the door handle and slowly turned around. "Yes?" I asked.

There stood a young woman in tears, holding her two-year-old daughter. "My mother took her life three months ago, and I haven't known how to handle it or how that type of a trial fits in church. Your talk was such a comfort to me to let me know I'm not the only one struggling with this type of tragedy." She pulled me in for a hug. "You were an answer to my prayers today. Thank you!"

I was stunned. I never wanted people to find out about my demons or that suicide was part of my family history. I thought if people knew, they'd judge me. The idea that opening up to people about my life could be helpful was new to me.

On my way home, I stopped at Lorie's house.

"I need to tell you something—something that until today no one outside my family knew," I started.

"Okay," she said hesitantly. She seemed nervous, knowing I had come here with a clear assignment. We walked over to the couch and sat.

"My dad died by suicide. He was bipolar. And so am I."

"Oh, wow."

"I've struggled with suicidal feelings most of my life," I said.

"I'm so sorry." Lorie put her arm around me. "Thanks for trusting me with that information."

"It's all right. I just wanted to tell you."

"Well, I'm glad you did. Just so you know, I struggle with depression."

"You do?"

"I'm on antidepressants, and I don't like to leave the house because of my social anxiety."

A light bulb went off. "Oh, the 'I don't do lunch' thing."

"Yep!"

"I used to be fat." I shrugged.

"You were fat?" She laughed.

"Yeah, I have pictures."

"I need to see these. I don't believe you."

"I'll show you."

"You know what's funny? The first time we went out to dinner, you barely ate any food, and I thought to myself, 'Ugh, another skinny girl who doesn't eat.' But then you ordered so many desserts!"

"Don't worry. I only took one bite of each dessert. My bingeing days are long over," I assured her.

As scary as it was, I let her into my fortress and allowed her a glimpse into my world. Some days I was shocked she loved me despite it all. I believed I had to hide my illness from people, but Lorie gave me confidence that one day I might be strong enough to share myself freely. She became like a sister to me.

—⁄⁄⁄—

When Lorie's mother was dying of cancer, people took turns sitting with her in her bedroom. She was on hospice. I sat next to her mother's bed during one of my shifts and listened as she talked.

"Another thing: I don't want anyone taking my Christmas ornaments. I really like those," she said.

"Don't worry. Those ornaments won't hang on any tree other than your own," I assured her.

"Can you bring me my box of chocolates?" She sat up. "They're in the fridge."

I got up and put the small box on her lap. We each took a piece and sat together, eating the small squares of chocolate.

"I don't usually have a second piece, but Lorie told me my doctor said I'm not able to gain weight. So I guess I'll indulge," she said, reaching for a second.

I bit my lip and tried not to laugh. It was clever of Lorie to tell her mom she was unable to gain weight. I stayed at her bedside while she slept.

"Are you still here?" Lorie's mom yawned, waking up.

"Of course. I'm not leaving anytime soon." I held her hand. "Can you do one thing for me?"

She smiled. "Sure."

"I don't know what happens when you die, but if it's possible, could you go find a David Nemelka? He's my dad. If you find him, tell him I love him."

"Yes, I'll do that." Her eyes slowly closed as she went back to sleep. "David Nemelka. David Nemelka," she repeated.

Lorie's mother wanted to live as long as possible—she was always saying she still had so much she wanted to do. I watched her sleep, confused. Here I sat a few inches away from death, but death was taking the wrong person. She wanted to stay; I wanted to go. Yet I remained, and she left. There was a time when I looked at death with sympathy instead of envy, but that was years ago.

When I was a freshman in college my grandpa was dying of cancer. I surprised him one day by covering his hospital door in dozens of paper hearts. As I left his room, I heard a man in the next room wailing in pain. I looked around. *Did anyone else hear it?* The nurses were chatting around the front desk. I peeked inside the door and saw an old man lying in his hospital bed, crying in pain. I slipped into the room and leaned over his bed.

"It will be okay. You won't always feel this way," I whispered, taking his hand in mine. He kept crying. I started to sing to him. I sang one of the songs I knew by heart: "Abide with Me; 'Tis Eventide."

"Beautiful," he whispered, still crying in pain.

I kissed his hand, feeling connected to this man's suffering. I didn't understand the connection at the time, but later I realized my own life would be full of pain. Somewhere deep down, I think I always knew it was coming for me.

CHAPTER 34

The Need for Control

Fall 2015

I flew to Utah to visit my mom for a week, and she took me on a drive down memory lane. We drove past my old elementary school, my old high school, and our old homes. It should have been a pleasant experience, but I hated the drive. I hated seeing all the places of my past. I couldn't handle the memories that would pop up with each stop to an old neighborhood or street. My dad was part of them all, and it hurt. My mom talked as she drove around and reminisced, but my throat was closed off. I looked out the window and wondered how she could revisit these memories and not feel the torture I did.

"One last stop," my mom said, cranking the steering wheel to the left. We pulled into the cemetery, and I clenched my jaw. We pulled right up to my dad's grave.

"Come out and say hi to your father." My mom got out of the car.

I glanced at his gravestone and then looked away. I couldn't do it; I could not stand at his grave knowing he was buried underneath me. I still hadn't let myself accept he was gone. I wanted to stay hidden in the car where he couldn't find me.

I rolled down the window. "I'll just say hi from here," I said, watching her fill the vase of flowers with water. The grief I had buried started pushing back up, and the feelings I had toward my dad's death were crushing me.

—⚬—

"I can't visit my mom in Utah anymore. I'm never going back to that state again, ever," I told my new therapist, Dr. Randall.

"*Never* is a strong word." He raised his eyebrows.

"I don't feel safe there."

"Sonja, most people feel the safest and most comfortable in their childhood neighborhoods and homes. There is a reason you're feeling this way. Could it be your father's suicide?"

"I just can't. I can't talk about it. If I open that box, I'll shatter, and what would that do to my husband and kids? It's too risky. I'll never go back to Utah; that'll be my solution."

"That doesn't seem like a good solution to me."

"My father killed himself. What if I killed myself? Can you promise me I won't do it? Can you?"

"No, I can't," he admitted.

"So don't tell me my solution isn't good. I have to protect myself and my family at all costs."

"Just because your dad's life ended that way doesn't mean yours has to," he said. My therapist clearly had no idea what he was talking about or what was at stake.

The next morning I woke up and my brain greeted me by screaming, *You're a horrible person! You don't deserve Mitch or your kids! You're worthless! You're so pathetic.* I rolled over and put my hands over my ears as if that would stop the voices in my head.

Stop! Just stop! I haven't even done anything wrong today. Let me start the day before you start yelling at me! I fought back, but the feelings of worthlessness stayed.

I felt grief start to seep in, and I jumped out of bed as if it were on fire. "No!" I yelled out. I immediately called Allyson. "What are you doing?" I asked.

"Making homemade bread and my strawberry-rhubarb jam. What about you?"

"I'm just at home. I feel like I can't do this another minute. My life's impossible."

"Sonja, you have Mitch, the kids, and *me*! You're important to all of us. I believe in you."

"At least someone does."

"Hang in there. It will get better," she said.

"But when? It's been over twenty years, and things haven't gotten better. Do you have a date you can give me?"

"I don't know when, but one day things will get better. You have to believe that, too."

"I don't understand what God's purpose is for me. Is it to stay in bed all day? I'm accomplishing nothing. All I do is endure. Is God trying to teach me something I haven't learned? Or am I just suffering for suffering's sake?"

"Those are some big questions you'll have to take up with God."

"Well, I want to know where the customer service desk for God is located because I have a lot of complaints. I will not be giving them five stars on my review, I can tell you that!"

Allyson laughed. "I've got to run some errands. I'll talk to you later today. Have faith, Sonja. I love you."

Lincoln walked in from school and sat at the kitchen table. "Mom, I want to graduate early like Rachael and Alex did, and I want to make varsity singles instead of doubles."

"You can do those things," I told him. "We'll just need to make a plan."

"Can we do that now?"

"Sure." I got a piece of paper and wrote out the days of the week and highlighted the free hours he had in the day. "During these hours, you can do extra homework and practice tennis. I'll call your counselor to talk about graduating early."

I lived on the phone for the next three days. I called Lincoln's school counselors to finalize a graduation date. I signed Lincoln up for an online math class on top of his current classes. Then I hired a tutor to help him study for the ACT; he needed to take it now because he was graduating early.

I called the very best tennis coaches and players to practice with him. Falling into full tennis mode felt like second nature to me.

Looking into the tightest of corners for something that resembled consistency and control, I typed out every hour of Lincoln's day. I left no time for breaks and made sure no hour was wasted. The Word document was measurable proof that for all my faults, I was a great mother. I hit print, and my masterpiece came out of the printer. Everything about this felt right. I let out a sigh of relief and slapped the pages on the fridge with magnets.

"What do you think?" I asked him.

"There's no down time." He seemed worried.

"I know," I smiled. "Hard work pays off, and if you follow this schedule, you'll reach all your goals by the time school ends."

"Okay, then I'll do it," he said.

"You'll be glad you did." I hugged him.

That evening, the painters I hired showed up. Mitch walked around their ladder, his shoes crinkling on the plastic drop cloths. "What's going on?" he asked.

"I'm having the whole house repainted," I said.

"I thought you liked the color of the walls." He watched the painters, confused.

"Oh, I love them. The paint color is staying the same, but I saw a few scuffs, so we're repainting the house."

"This is a brand-new house! Sonja, you don't even let people touch the walls. They're in perfect condition."

I gave Mitch a piercing look. If he wanted to go head-to-head with me in front of the painters, he would lose.

"Whatever." He sighed and went into the bedroom.

After the painters were done, I looked at all the paintings I needed to hang back on the freshly painted walls. I felt a strong desire for everything to be perfect, so I could find some peace. While inspecting which pictures should hang where, I noticed the frames had some scratches and just like that, the framing section of Michaels craft store became my second home.

I marched through the automatic doors of Michaels for the fifth time that week, carrying a large painting. The counter at the framing department was starting to feel like my office. I even had a regular seat, the barstool on the right.

"Is Mark here?" I asked an employee.

"Yeah, he's in the back. I'll go get him."

"Tell him Sonja's here," I shouted as she walked away.

I didn't have time to start all over with a new employee. Mark and I had already spent ten-plus hours talking about this piece; plus, he'd gained my trust, a feat that was hard for most to accomplish. While I waited for Mark to come out, I pulled out the frame samples we'd been deciding between.

"Which one do you think is more gorgeous?" I stopped an older woman with a puffy hairdo.

She hesitated, looking over the gold and silver corner pieces I was holding up to the painting. "Um, I like gold frames. So I'd say that one?"

"But which one is more stunning?" I pressed.

"I don't know…maybe the silver?" She switched, thinking her first answer was ill-received.

"If you had to rate them one to ten, what would they be?" I kept my eyes locked on the samples.

"The gold would be an eight and the silver a five," she said more confidently.

"Okay." I quickly turned to the next person. "Excuse me, which one do you think is prettier?" The young mom jolted to a stop then gripped her cart handle as she narrowed her eyes at the frames. "Definitely the gold. Hands down."

Her confidence got me excited. She sounded like she knew which one I should pick.

"Why's that?" I asked, holding the painting closer to her.

"The gold makes the painting pop and adds some class. The silver's nice, too."

"But which one is more stunning?"

Mark sighed and walked up behind me. "Good morning, what're we looking at today?"

I immediately got back into my regular spot and laid down the painting in front of him. "I'm still deciding between the silver and gold. Which one do you think looks best?"

"My answer is still the same: the gold."

I looked at the gold sample piece, studying it next to the painting as if for the first time. I turned to the new employee.

"Which frame is more gorgeous?" I saw Mark roll his eyes, but I felt we had to get to the bottom of this.

"I like the silver," she said.

"Really?" I leaned in, intrigued. "Because Mark thinks the gold is better."

"Which one do you like better?" she asked.

"Oh, I don't know." I stared at the two samples. "I can't decide."

"Ma'am, I need to help another customer," Mark said, leaning to the side, where a man was waiting.

"Mark, why do you like the gold better?" I asked.

"Just because I think it looks better," he answered, exasperated.

"But *why* does it look better? You see paintings all day, I need your expertise."

"It just does," he said, leaving me at the counter.

I sat staring at the silver and gold frames agonizing over which was more stunning, gorgeous, and unique. With my large painting in hand, I approached more shoppers for their opinion: six hours passed. Mark was fed up and got the manager involved.

The manager stood in front of me. "Ma'am, you need to leave. You've been here all day. You're disturbing the customers and making it hard for Mark and the other employees to do their job. And this isn't the first time."

"Okay, okay," I said, hands up in surrender. "Just real quick, which frame is more gorgeous?" I slid the gold and silver samples to her.

"Is there someone we can call to come get you, so we don't have to call the police?"

"You can call my husband," I suggested.

"Okay, let's do that."

I lit up. "And maybe he can pick the frame."

The manager explained the situation to Mitch over the phone, and he assured them he was on his way. When he got there, he tugged my arm toward the exit.

"C'mon, Sonja, let's go," he urged.

"No, not yet. You need to see something first." I pointed to the frames. "Gold or silver?"

"We can worry about this tomorrow, because today you need to leave the store." Mitch turned to the manager. "I'm sorry."

The next day, I was back at Michaels as soon as it opened. Painting in hand, I marched to the framing section. Mark tensed up when he saw me and refused to talk to me. I called Lorie to meet me at the store, but like everyone else's opinions, nothing satisfied me. Mark went and got the manager again.

"We're going to have to ask you to leave," the manager said.

"How will I frame my painting then?" I asked, frustrated. "You're losing business! I have five more paintings to frame after this."

"Please take her out of here." The manager turned to Lorie.

"Let me frame my painting first, and then I'll be gone, promise!" I frantically looked at the frames, wishing I could choose one. "Just give me one second!"

"I'm not asking you to leave. I'm telling you that you can no longer shop here," the manager corrected.

"What? Wait—what about my painting?" I gasped.

"Take your painting *somewhere* else. We refuse to frame it."

I slid down onto the floor and sat in confusion. "No, this can't be happening. You don't understand. I can't leave until a frame is picked out." I slid my hands over my head. "This can't be happening."

"Please get off the floor," the manager said.

"I can't," I whimpered.

"Don't worry, we'll get your painting framed." Lorie pulled me off the ground. "Sorry again." She waved to the manager.

A week later, I opened the front door of my home to find two of my favorite things: Lorie and my painting. Framed. The painting looked beautiful. She had gone with a light-silver frame and a white mat. "It's done." She smiled.

People often wonder how I couldn't see my obsessive behavior. My only answer: slipping into insanity is easy; it's coming out of it that's hard.

CHAPTER 35

Searching for Solace

Columbia, Missouri, 2015

"Your ACT tutor is coming in thirty minutes," I reminded Lincoln. He'd been living out my rigid schedule for months without complaint and seeing success because of it.

"Can I have a thirty-minute break then?" he asked.

"No." I shook my head, shocked he was even asking. "You have to finish your homework for tomorrow. When else will you do that?"

"Mom, nobody else is doing this."

"Good. That's how you get ahead in life. Outworking everybody else."

"You're being crazy! I can't do any more studying!" He hit his fist on the table.

"Well, we all have to do things we don't want to." I unzipped his backpack and dropped the books onto the table.

"You're not listening! I'm exhausted! I'm done!" He screamed until my ears hurt.

My need to control something—anything—in my unraveling world was so intense that I didn't notice he was cracking.

"You have to follow the schedule. These are *your* goals! *You* want to make the varsity singles tennis team. You want to graduate early, and this is what it takes. We aren't quitters in this family."

"You don't get it!" He clenched his fists with tears in his eyes.

"I do get it. Now start your homework," I said.

Lincoln picked up his phone and chucked it against the wall, shattering the screen and chipping my freshly painted wall.

"Lincoln! You're going to pay for that! Now sit down and get back to work. You have twenty minutes to calm down before the ACT tutor gets here!"

Lincoln sobbed for those twenty minutes as he picked up the pieces to his phone. When the ACT tutor came, Lincoln sat at the table.

Conducting Lincoln's daily schedule gave me some sort of grip on my life that I otherwise didn't have. Even though Lincoln and I repeatedly fought about his schedule, I held on to it as if my very own life depended on it.

Confused and depressed, I lay in bed with my laptop. I was watching dozens of jewelry items on eBay and kept a constant tab open for each of them. Today four of the items were ending, and like a bad gambler with nothing to lose, I bid high and won them all. A storm was brewing in me, and it dripped one eBay package at a time.

"This came for you." Mitch handed me a box.

I grabbed it. "Thanks."

"What is it?" he asked, tossing junk mail in the trash.

"Oh, just a little something I got off eBay on a deal. It's nothing." I took the box into the bedroom.

EBay boxes started arriving daily, making them impossible to ignore.

"What is all this?" Mitch carried six boxes of gold bracelets into the bedroom.

I looked up from my computer and froze. Mitch had opened the boxes.

"I'm taking them back." I tensed up.

"What about the other seven boxes from last week?" he asked.

"I can't have you get mad at me today! Seriously, Mitchell, do you want me to lose it? Just don't go there!" I held up a firm hand to him.

"I'm not getting mad; I'm asking what this is." He pointed to the gold bracelets. "The receipts say they're each over two thousand dollars. Where are you getting the money from?"

"You know what—no. You are not going to send me spiraling. I don't have to tell you. I'm taking them all back, so don't worry about it." I looked back at my laptop.

"You're returning *all* of it?" he asked for clarification.

"Yes!"

As I dropped deeper into a full-blown mania, my jewelry addiction climaxed, as did my standard of perfection. Each piece of jewelry required weeks of mental deliberation. It felt like a piece of me would die if I didn't have them. A piece of jewelry arrived at least every two days. We had so many packages that the mail carrier would bring a bin stuffed full to my front door. One day she asked if I ran an eBay business, to which I replied, "No," and shut the door.

I spent hundreds of hours over several months on eBay; there was little time for anything else. My mind was a punishing taskmaster and it felt like I was being dragged by its need for exactness. I bought a pair of Brian Gavin diamond-stud earrings, one carat each. They were immaculate, but shortly after getting them, I wondered if one carat in each ear was too small. My mind would not rest until I came to a conclusion. Brian Gavin was one of the best diamond experts in the world. I called his staff to seek their reassurance about my earrings' size, brilliance, and quality. I couldn't hear their answers enough times, so I called with fake names to re-ask my questions.

"This is Hannah from Brian Gavin. How may I help you?"

"Hi, this is Margie. How would I know if my diamonds are too small?" I inquired.

"Isn't this Susan? I recognize your voice. You've already called several times."

I hung up and called back, hoping to get a different sales representative.

Although the diamonds were beautiful, the recurring thought that they were too small remained. I returned them and began a new and more challenging hunt to match my own set of three-carat earrings. I spent days scrolling through eBay from morning till night. It didn't matter if the Gemological Institute of America (GIA) diamond report thought they were an excellent cut or if the seller thought the two stones' roundness was close enough to be a match. I needed perfection. Toward the end of the third month, the stars aligned, and I found two GIA-certified diamonds from different sellers on eBay.

One was a diamond in a wedding band, and the other was a loose diamond. I bought the wedding ring and had the diamond removed. My only problem was the other diamond's crown angle was 41 when it should be under 40.9. *Was it actually 41?* I knew the GIA rounded up or down if it was a close call. I needed to know if the GIA had rounded up.

I called GIA headquarters and asked to speak to a representative from the department in charge of measuring diamonds. They pulled up the certificate on the diamond I wanted to buy, and thankfully, they *had* rounded up. I could now purchase the diamond in confidence. This addiction was a cycle of momentary relief followed by constant craving. No purchase, no matter how challenging, satisfied me in the end. A week later, I walked into the kitchen with gold bracelets lining my wrists.

"I thought you returned those," Mitch said.

"I will!" I snapped. "Now, real quick, which is prettier?" I held my arms out to him.

"Seriously?" He shook his head in disbelief.

"This one is the prettiest, isn't it?" I pointed to a thin, gold bangle engraved with scrolling vines and flowers.

"I'm not doing this." He walked out of the kitchen and I followed him.

"I just need to know which one is the most unique, the most stunning."

"If you're really returning them, why does it matter!?" he shouted.

"I'm researching!" I shouted back.

"No, you're still shopping." He glared.

"I'm returning all of it," I said, but our credit card statements rolled in with numbers that disagreed.

The next month, I spent $35,000 on jewelry, and there was no indication of anything being returned. Mitch threw the credit card statements onto the kitchen table and unclasped the gold bracelets off my wrist.

"What are you doing?" I batted his hands away.

"I'm returning all the bracelets. Where are the rest?" he barked.

"I returned them." I yanked my arms from him.

"You're lying." He picked up my purse and took out my wallet.

He removed every credit card and put them into his pocket. "This isn't over." He stormed out and headed to our bedroom.

Mitch searched my drawers and under the bed, where he excavated several pieces of jewelry. In the bedroom closet, he cleared off every shelf, letting stacks of clothes fall around him, finding diamond bracelets tucked between sweaters. Mitch lifted the mattress and found a pile of credit cards with their statements. He glanced through them and saw many statements with his name on them. He stood there like a statue. I thought he was going to vomit.

"Why is my name on these?" He held the bills in front of my face. "I didn't open these!"

"I know," I said. My eyes were looking anywhere but into his.

"Explain *now*."

"I opened them in your name," I said.

"Sonja, you're in a manic episode."

"I can't stop," I cried out. "Please, help me!"

"Help? Help how?" He threw his arms in the air. "You're bankrupting us."

"I can't control it! I've tried, and I can't! I returned a bracelet, and my OCD had to find another one just like it. I spent two days on the computer looking for an identical match. It's driving me crazy!" I screamed.

"Credit card companies don't care—charges are charges. They have to be paid. Return the bracelets and cancel the credit cards," he said, exhausted.

Mitch took my name off the house, the cars, his bank account, all his credit cards, and anything that would provide me a way to access money. He bought a safe and locked away his checks, credit cards, and wallet. He didn't trust me, and I had to accept he had reasons not to.

—m—

In my desperation, I met with my psychiatrist. I didn't give him the chance to sit before declaring, "Help me! I'm on a runaway train. Not one of the medicines you've given me is working."

"Sonja, sit down," he said, trying to gain some control.

"I've tried six different medicines. They either don't work, or the side effects are worse than the illness. I need real help!"

"Sonja, breathe," he said. "It can take years to find the right medication. Don't worry."

"I feel like I'm in the passenger seat of a car with my illness at the wheel, and I have no say where we're going." I panicked, feeling he wasn't seeing the same sense of urgency I was. "I spent sixty-eight thousand dollars in two weeks, and that's just on one of my ten credit cards!" I looked at him, waiting for him to wake up and see the dire situation.

"People with bipolar disorder often have impulsive spending when in mania and are more at risk for being debt-ridden than the average population," he told me, as if he were conducting a lecture to a bunch of students. I didn't engage with his classroom facts. In silence, I stared at him, demanding he see past my illness to the person—*me*—in this body, who needed serious help, not a debriefing on bipolar symptoms. He said nothing and looked away. I felt I had no other option.

"Lock me up," I demanded.

CHAPTER 36

Roommate

I was back in the psych ward, only this time, it was by choice. Late into the night, a nurse and patient barged into my room. "This is your new roommate, Amber."

I looked over at the flailing woman to whom the nurse was referring.

"Stop that!" The nurse yanked my roommate's arms back. She was shaking and tried to use the zipper of her jeans to cut into her wrist. I sat silently on my bed, watching the scene play out.

"I know it's there," she mumbled. "I know it's there." She dug the zipper deeper into her wrist. She and the nurse got into a tug-of-war over the jeans.

"You need to stop this!" The nurse sat her on the bed and held her wrists tight.

"I want it out!" she screamed.

"For the last time"—the nurse gritted her teeth and yanked the jeans from her hands—"we did *not* put a tracking device in you." She slammed the door on her way out.

Amber fell into the fetal position, threw her arms over her knees, and began to rock back and forth sobbing. The resemblance was all too familiar to the thousands of meltdowns I had experienced.

That night was the first time I'd ever seen someone behave like me up close. I cringed as she shook and moaned. *Is this the same type of broken that Mitch cuddles and attempts to comfort daily? Is that what my children saw?* My eyes burned. My children—*my children*—had seen me like that. It must have scared them. How could I ever accept that *this* was part of the person my kids called *Mom*? I wanted to tell her to stop, to sit up, to get a grip, and to be an adult, but I knew better than anyone that those things were not going to happen. I couldn't watch any longer. I got up and walked out to the nurse's station.

"I need to be moved to another room," I stated, firmly gripping the corner of the desk.

"You can't just change rooms, Sonja," the nurse scoffed.

"You have to move me to another room. I can't sleep with her. I can't be around her." I was starting to hyperventilate.

"Calm down. Why don't we see how it goes?"

I stood in the hallway next to my room, unable to go in. Nurses were coming in and out, administering meds to calm Amber. I was still shaking. I couldn't move. My feet stayed planted in the hallway as I leaned against the wall with my eyes closed. I didn't want more meds, so I resorted to deep breathing, although my breaths were fast and shallow.

I talked to my Savior as I always did, pleading. "This is Your daughter, Sonja. Please help!" I wondered if He ever got tired of my prayers.

I don't know how much time passed, but slowly my heart calmed down. I carefully opened my eyes and gathered all my strength. I quietly walked toward my room, afraid of being surrounded by the reminder that my roommate was my mirror. When I peeked behind the door, she was no longer in a state of panic. Instead, Amber sat cross-legged on the floor, wiping our bedroom walls with a T-shirt.

I watched for a minute before I asked, "What are you doing?"

"I'm getting the blood off the walls." She didn't look at me and continued wiping.

I looked at the white wall and saw there was no blood. It was her reality, and I wasn't going to tell her it was nonsense.

"Do you want any help?" I asked.

"No," she replied.

I walked inside and lay in my bed, listening to the cotton drag against the concrete walls until it went silent and she got into her bed.

"Did you get most of it?" I asked.

"Yeah, you can turn off the lights now."

I got up to flip the light switch off. "Goodnight," I said into the dark.

—⟋⟋⟍—

The next morning, I found myself in a rather lengthy session with a psychiatrist.

"Sonja, you need to stop fighting your illness," he said.

"I can't," I answered, frustrated. I couldn't even get massages without the massage therapist constantly asking me to relax because I was so tense.

"What is keeping you from—"

"It's not safe."

"Can't you stop fighting it even for a moment?" he asked.

"No. I feel like I'm going to explode—blow into a million pieces. So I keep holding myself together as tightly as I can. If I let go, I'll make worse decisions."

He looked at me and leaned forward. "You have to let some of it go. You need to pull yourself out of this episode, Sonja."

"I'm fully aware I have to pull myself out of this, but I don't see how relaxing into this deep pit I've dug for myself is going to help me get out of it. I'll have to claw my way out inch by inch and stay in control."

"What do you think will happen if you take a break from fighting your illness?"

"I don't know for sure."

"Exactly. So why not try?" he asked.

"But what if I lose it?" I looked up at him, wide-eyed.

"But what if you don't?"

"It's just safer to resist it."

"Is it?"

"It seems so." I shrugged.

"From where I'm sitting, it doesn't look like that's worked out for you."

"Well, I'm still alive, aren't I?"

"Can't you let go for just a second? We can try the experiment right now."

"You don't know what you are asking me to do!"

"Yes, I do," he said.

"Oh, really? To end up dead like my father? To go completely *crazy*? I'm already somewhat crazy, but I refuse to be utterly *gone!*"

"You don't know that will happen."

Even though the doctor was the one with the degree, it was hard not to feel like he had no idea what I needed or what was at stake. It felt like he was asking me to give into the illness, the very thing I was fighting to avoid every day.

"I don't need to relax into this illness to know it's going to kill me. I've already seen what getting lost in this illness looks like through my dad's life, and that's not a scenario I'm going to watch play out in mine."

"What you're doing is making your pain worse."

"Do you have any clue how scary it is to have some days when the thought of going out like my dad paralyzes me and other days when it sounds seducing? And on those days, I'm scared of myself because of how much I want it."

"Have you heard the story of the bear?" he asked.

"Yes. He grabs hold of a burning kettle, and instead of letting go, he holds tighter, trying to get rid of the pain," I mumbled.

"Exactly, when all he had to do was let go of the kettle and the pain would stop."

"So if I let go, my illness will be separate from me?" I forced a small laugh. "The problem is it's in me, and there is not a doctor on this planet that can cure me. Do you hear me? *Incurable!*" I was so angry I got up to leave.

He stopped me. "But not untreatable. We'll put you back on your old antipsychotic. That medicine helped get you out of a manic episode last time."

I needed to calm down. I walked out and saw everyone going to activity time. The tables were filled with magazines and glue sticks. I sat at a table and picked up a magazine.

"What's the activity?" I asked my neighbor.

"We're making collages of things we like," he responded.

I thumbed through the magazine and saw lots of vacation spots I wanted to put in my collage.

"Can you pass the scissors?" I asked.

"We can't have any. The nurse said to tear them out."

Attempting to tear out a small picture of Bora-Bora, the paper tore in the wrong direction, leaving me with half a grass hut on the beach. I rolled my eyes and threw away the picture. Everyone around me seemed to be enjoying themselves, gluing poorly ripped photos of puppies and sports cars onto their papers. Luckily, I loved reading magazines, and they had my favorite: *People*. I grabbed two and read outdated celebrity news for the rest of activity time.

"Everyone, line up for meds!" the nurse shouted.

I got in line behind Amber. She looked at me like she saw a ghost. She always looked terrified, so I wasn't offended. She backed away and stood a few feet outside the line. She started shaking and trembling, and I knew she was on the verge of a panic attack. I looked at the nurse administering medicine.

"Can Amber get her meds next? She needs them."

The nurse looked up at me and then at Amber. "No, she needs to wait her turn. There are a lot of people in front of her."

Frustrated, I turned to the other patients in line. "Do any of you mind if Amber cuts the line, so she can get her meds?"

"No," a few people around us said. People moved out of the way for Amber to go ahead of them.

"All right, Amber, come on up." The nurse waved to her.

Amber returned to our room after getting her meds, and I followed after I got mine.

"You okay?" I asked.

"Yeah. Thanks for that," she said, lying in her bed, facing the wall.

"No big deal."

"I'm in here because I see people bleeding from bullet holes. My life is like a horror movie."

"Have you ever seen me like that?" I asked.

"Yes. Everyone looks like they're injured and bloody to me. I never know what's real and what's not," she said.

"That must be really scary. I'm sorry, Amber."

"When I was admitted to the ER, I tried so hard to escape; I heard voices telling me if I didn't leave immediately, they'd blow up the hospital. I didn't want anyone to die. I was trying to save them."

"It was kind of you to try and save everyone. You're brave," I said.

She turned and looked up at me. "No one has ever called me brave before. People usually say I'm strange."

"Um, anyone who saw what you're seeing would act strange. I'd be more concerned if you saw bullet holes in people and weren't terrified. So you're actually very normal."

"Ha, I've never thought about it like that. But you're right." She smiled.

"If you could trade your illness with someone, would you?" I asked her.

"No, I don't want anyone to have this." She shook her head.

"Really? You wouldn't be tempted to get rid of it, even a little?"

"No, no, no. I wouldn't be able to live with myself if someone else had this because of me. I've been in and out of psych wards since I was ten, so I've gotten good at handling this."

"You're better than I am." I sighed. "If I could trade my mental illness away, I would. I'm not as kind as you are. God is proud of you."

"I don't know much about God, but you think He would be proud of me?"

I reached my hand out, and she took it. "I know for sure God is not only proud of you, but He loves you and is aware of you."

Tears started to fall onto her pillow. "Thank you."

—⟫⟪—

Coming home from the hospital four days later, I was still in terrible shape. I was now well aware that hospitals don't cure mental illness in the same way they cure a broken hip or heart failure. Once you've been diagnosed, the hospital is where you go if you're a threat to yourself or others. Sometimes they tweak your medications, but often it's just a holding room, and after three to four days, you go home with the same problems you went in with.

People often told me, "You need to get help, Sonja." But I'd tried dozens of medications, seen countless therapists, was hospitalized more than once, and had a strong support network. So what was the additional help they were referring to?

CHAPTER 37

Flowers

Columbia, Missouri, 2015

"I want to resign and give my family my two-week notice. I need to die," I told Dr. Randall.

"Sonja, suicide is very selfish," he said.

"Do you even see my pain? No, I don't think you do. I think it's selfish of you and my family to insist I stay when I'm in this much pain. Plus, they'd be better off without me."

"That's distorted thinking. They need you. Things will get better."

"When? No one can tell me *when*! I hate my life."

"Think of one thing you like about life besides your family."

"I like flowers."

"Then your homework this week is to buy some flowers and enjoy them. Can you try that?"

"I'm really good at trying. Just know that if you want success, you're not going to see it with me. Failure, that's more my style."

"I'll take trying. Go buy flowers and *try* to enjoy them."

Flowers. That was what my therapist thought could save me—thin petals and long stems. I wanted to believe it'd work, but I was doubtful.

Mitch drove Lincoln and me to Home Depot to buy flowers.

"When is Chase coming over?" Lincoln asked.

"We need to pick him up after Home Depot," I said, my forehead pressed against the window.

"We're tight on time. Can't his dad bring him?" Mitch asked, a bit irritated. I ignored him, lost in my thoughts.

Jump out of the car! my brain screamed at me. *Open the door and throw yourself out.* I pressed my head harder against the window, trying to smash the thoughts away.

"Hello? Sonja?" Mitch said.

"Just roll with it," was all I could mutter back. I didn't have the energy to explain. I told Chase's mom I'd pick him up because she was working, and her husband would've had to pack all their little kids into the car just to bring him over. We didn't have small children; it'd be easier for us.

In the Home Depot nursery, Mitch and I each pushed a flatbed cart as I placed cartons of roses, marigolds, and mums on it. I bought enough flowers to fill our entire front yard; I hoped my therapist was right about this.

I spent a week outside in my big hat with my hands in the dirt planting the bounty of flowers. I became a landscaping expert overnight, and many of my neighbors wanted to know who I hired to landscape the yard. I was proud of my creation and all the attention it was getting, but the next week, when I reached out to touch my roses, hoping to feel the beauty of my favorite flower, I felt nothing. My fingers snapped the stem in half. *Why did I go outside? Did I really think I could break the glass walls my mind built around me?* I dropped the rose on the ground and turned my back on the beautiful day.

I felt so uncomfortable inside: like wearing clothes that were too tight, but I couldn't take them off. The truth was, I didn't know how many more days I had left in me. It scared me. I wanted to plead with doctors, researchers, medicine companies, and investors to help save us—the mentally ill. I wanted to tell them to keep working hard, that we were counting on them to save our lives. Yet I wondered, do they see us? Do they hear our cries? Our screams? I hoped so, because time was running out for me.

CHAPTER 38

Losing Control

Columbia, Missouri, 2015

M itch and I had been living under the same roof, sleeping in the same bed, but we might as well have been living in different countries with how little we communicated. The tension in our marriage increased, and Mitch realized that paying off my credit cards was not a permanent fix. The next statement rolled in at a dangerously high number, and Mitch pushed it back to me.

"Sonja, I'm not going to pay off the credit cards," he said. "You have to take responsibility for your debt."

"But how will I pay it off? I have no job, no money," I said.

"We've talked about this enough for you to know my answer to that: return the jewelry." He clenched his jaw. It was becoming hard for him to remain even-tempered on the subject.

"You know I can't do that." I teared up. For him, the solution was obvious: return the jewelry and pay off the credit cards. But my obsession with each item ran too deep.

"I've enabled you. I shouldn't have paid off your spending for so many years. I can't have you bankrupt the family because you want to buy jewelry," he said.

"Fine. Whatever. I have bigger problems to worry about." I walked back to the bed and climbed under the covers. "If I was in a wheelchair, you wouldn't expect me to get up and walk. Just because you can't see my illness doesn't mean it's not there," I said.

In the beginning, Mitch wanted me to see how sick I was and accept I was bipolar; now it seemed he wanted me to pretend I wasn't.

"This debt is yours to figure out," he said.

All at once, I felt the weight of my spending as if every dollar of my $150,000 had fallen on me in pennies.

For months the bills arrived, and I shoved the unopened envelopes into my dresser drawer. Even though the interest was compounding, I avoided every aspect of my spending. The credit card companies called nonstop, but I never answered. So the banks sent debt collectors after me. I told myself I wasn't going to answer until I had a plan.

I filed for bankruptcy, but once Mitch found out, he told me I didn't qualify and had it dismissed. I was stuck. I didn't know how to solve this problem. It only added to the already massive burden I walked around with and created more anxiety. I couldn't believe Mitch wouldn't help me. It felt unjust for him to leave a mentally ill person on their own like that; I was in no condition to take this on.

My phone rang so frequently with calls from debt collectors I had gotten good at ignoring my ringtone. One day I almost missed a call until I realized it was Allyson.

"Sonja, I have to tell you something." Her voice was stern.

"What?"

"I have stage-four melanoma cancer in my lungs and brain."

I covered my mouth with my hand. "Is there a treatment for it?"

"The doctor said there's no cure. There's a trial drug, Keytruda, I can try, but there's no guarantee it'll help. I'm dying."

Everything in my whole being fought that word. *Dying.* I refused to accept it. My anger burned so fiercely I caught fire. *WHY IS THIS HAPPENING?!* My insides screamed. I understood trials could be refining, but now God was just getting sloppy.

"Mom's flying out, and we're driving to Minnesota so I can get my treatments at Mayo Clinic."

"I'll meet you guys there. I love you, Allyson." The words seemed hollow; they didn't even begin to describe my feelings toward my sister.

In my heartbreak, I felt explicit distrust in God's "bigger plan" and "loving hand." How could anything this bitter come out of love, and how would her death be for anyone's greater good? Allyson had five children, and her youngest was three. *Will he remember her?* My heart screamed at God: *How could You? How could You take her from me?* I pounded the carpet harder and harder, like a child purging a tantrum. My whole life, I believed God gave me Allyson as a tender mercy, and now He was taking my gift away. I was furious.

Even though she had children who depended on her more than I did, I felt just as needy as her three-year-old. She was the person who reached into my illness and pulled Sonja out. Allyson had access to my sanity. Why would God want to take her away when He knew I couldn't survive without her?

A few days later, I tossed my duffel bag into the airplane's overhead storage. The setting sun glared through the window. I violently yanked the visor down, immediately silencing the sun. All my anger melted into bottomless sadness. I did my best to stop the tears before arriving at Mayo Clinic.

The place was gorgeous, with high ceilings and well-dressed patients. It was easy to forget we were in a hospital. I ran to Allyson and my mom. We hugged before entering the doctor's office, where a man in a nice suit waited for us. All the doctors wore suits instead of lab coats.

"I'm Dr. Harris." He shook our hands and turned to Allyson. "Your diagnosis is terminal."

We all sat in shock hearing the words out loud. My mom broke down crying.

Dr. Harris continued, "Keytruda is a newly approved drug, but not for your diagnosis. We'll try it anyway to give you more time. I won't lie to you: this is going to be a nasty fight, but you can decide when you're done."

I could not believe what I was hearing, and to be honest, I was jealous. No one had ever told me I got to decide when I'd had enough of *my* illness. I couldn't imagine what it'd feel like to have an out like that—a doctor's note allowing me to say when I was done fighting for my life.

Yet Allyson did fight. She had the gamma knife take out two tumors in her brain. She had radiation on a tumor as big as a tennis ball in her lung. She had nine tumors cut out of her small intestines. Then the experimental drug Keytruda filled her veins every three weeks. The question of how long we had left with Allyson weighed heavily on me. *What will my world look like without her? Who will make the peace once the peacemaker is gone?*

———ɷ———

I flew home, and Lincoln told me he got a B on his biology test. He was a straight-A student, and with all the tutoring he was doing, I was surprised. We met with his biology teacher after school to get to the bottom of it.

"Lincoln did very well. He didn't miss any questions on the multiple-choice section." His teacher pulled out his test and pointed to the essay portion. "His essay responses were just a little short."

They didn't seem short to me, but I was willing to go with it.

"Okay." I nodded. "Lincoln, why don't you meet with your teacher before the next test and go over the study essay portion."

"I can do that," Lincoln said.

On the next test, he got another B. The rage simmering in me since Allyson's diagnosis now unleashed a manic episode of epic proportions.

Before school started, I drove to Lincoln's school and walked straight into his teacher's classroom.

"Show me the test," I demanded. His teacher looked shocked I'd come to her room unannounced. "Show me what he got wrong."

She got out Lincoln's test and flipped to the back. "He didn't have enough on his essay questions."

I looked down at the lengthy paragraphs. "Okay, so what information is missing?"

"I don't know; he just needs more," she said.

"What more could he have written?" I challenged.

"Just more."

"More what? Are you grading this on length or content?"

She had no answer.

"You're just taking points off for no reason! Give him the points back!"

Her eyes got big.

"I'm not joking." I narrowed in on her. "Give him all three points back on each essay question." I pushed my finger into his test.

"I've never done that before."

"Well, you're going to do it now."

She froze.

"This is how it's going to happen. I'll file a complaint against you to the principal. Then I'll rally all the other parents, and we'll put a story about you in the newspaper." I leaned over her desk. "Trust me. It's in your best interest to give him the points back."

She got out a pen and gave Lincoln full credit on the essay questions. The bell rang for school to start, and students lined up at her door.

A male teacher poked his head in. "Are you okay?" he asked her. The look of fear on her face was hard to miss. She didn't say anything.

"You need to leave. School's started," he told me.

"That's fine. I got what I needed." I pushed past him.

Although I'd never behaved this intensely with my kids' teachers before, I felt justified. Being in a manic episode felt so good, no one else's perspective mattered. Mania created an intoxicating feeling that my perception was truth. I felt I had the power to make anything happen. I could buy a lottery ticket every day, and every day I'd fully expect it to be the winner.

A week later, a letter came from the school district, banning me from school property. Not being permitted on school property was something that happened to my dad. One would think after seeing my dad go through the experience, I'd logically say, *Wait, this is a manic episode just like Dad went through. I should reconsider my feelings and make a better choice,* or some internal narrative like that. But when in a manic state, there is no reflection or learning from the past, because everything inside is shouting that your feelings are completely real and true.

Mania was the ugly bullying side of the illness I wasn't willing to address, mostly because it was an amazing and addictive high. So I took the letter, shoved it into my dresser drawer along with the credit card bills, and proceeded with my pain-ridden day without another thought about the incident.

I continued to push Lincoln's schedule with clocklike precision, as if he were a cog in a Swiss watch. I needed him to keep up with my pace so he'd achieve all of our goals. But I wasn't working with cogs and springs. I was working with a human, my child. I pushed him beyond any human's natural limit until I broke him.

"Mom, please cancel the tennis match tonight!" Lincoln pleaded.

"No, I'm not doing that!"

"Move it back just one hour. I need one short break today. Just one," he said.

"An hour is not a short break, Lincoln. You need to learn how to sacrifice for your goals. That's what truly successful people do." He was already dressed in his tennis clothes and there was no reason to cancel my reservation for an indoor court.

"I'm done." He stood to leave.

"Lincoln! You're only hurting yourself! My life stays the same whether you become better at tennis or not. Your choices affect your life! *Your* dreams are on the line!"

He cried. I knew he felt conflicted. He didn't want to be a quitter, and I hoped that family value would push him to the finish line.

"You need to own your life," I preached.

"I just need thirty minutes to sit and do nothing," he pled.

"You know that's not an option. Your goals demand your attention. We don't have time for breaks."

"Ah!" Lincoln pulled at his hair.

"It's hard to work for goals, but if you want to be successful, hard is what it takes." I started a new lecture. Without missing a beat Lincoln bolted out of the house. He didn't put on shoes or a coat. He just ran, leaving the front door wide open. A frigid wind blew through the house.

"Lincoln! Stop!" I screamed out the door. It was early December, and our house was at the bottom of a snowy hill. I quickly put my shoes and coat on and chased after him. The roads were icy, but I saw his yellow tennis shirt sprinting up the hill without stopping.

"Lincoln, come back!" My lungs burned in the freezing air as I chased him, but he continued to run until he disappeared into the falling snow. I blinked through the snowflakes melting on my face and peered through the darkness. I lost him.

I frantically called Mitch. "Lincoln ran away, I can't find him."

Mitch came home immediately and drove the neighborhood looking for him. We called friends and neighbors, but he wasn't with any of them. Mitch knew what made Lincoln run. He had been telling me for weeks, "A bow constantly strung will lose its spring." He asked me to give Lincoln space to be a kid, but I felt I was. I just wanted him to be a successful kid.

Two hours later, we heard the front door open. Lincoln's hair was white with snow and his skin was raw. His face, hands, and feet were bright red. He'd been outside the whole time. Mitch walked Lincoln into the living room and turned on the fireplace. Lincoln lay in front of the fire, ignoring me. Mitch wrapped a blanket around him and sat beside Lincoln with his arm around him.

"I'm so sorry, Lincoln. Help me understand what you're feeling," Mitch said.

Lincoln nodded, and they stayed on the floor in silence until he was ready to talk. I sat on the couch watching but not daring to interrupt. *This is my fault.* Shame filled me, but I didn't know how to change.

CHAPTER 39

Broken Vows

December 13, 2015, Missouri

It only took a week for us to return to our nightly routine. Lincoln and I were fighting about his schedule again, and it instantly escalated to a battle of wills.

"Lincoln, I've had enough! Just do your homework!" I screamed.

"I can do it later. I'm going to my friend's house."

"Follow the schedule!" I pounded the sheet hanging on the fridge.

"I'm sixteen. I can plan my own life."

"No, you can't!" I couldn't fathom giving up the control.

Mitch tried to mediate. "Guys, knock it off! There's no need to keep screaming at each other. This is not a hard problem to solve. Sonja, let Lincoln write out his own schedule."

"Absolutely not!" My eyes shot a hole in Mitch. How dare he betray me. We were supposed to support each other.

"Sonja! Seriously, you have got to stop this! This is insane," Mitch said.

"I should've never asked you to help me. You just take things over until they're yours," Lincoln snapped. "I'm writing my own schedule. I'm not doing yours."

"NOOO!" I screamed. I was gripping at slipping reins. *How dare they take this away from me. How dare they torture me like this. I'm in so much pain; they should let me have this one thing. It makes me feel better.* With Alex and Rachael on missions, Lincoln's life was all the control I had.

"Sonja, you're done overseeing Lincoln's schedule!" Mitch backed Lincoln.

It was two against one, and all my control was gone.

"This is all your fault!" I shot a stiff finger at Lincoln and ran out of the room.

I felt like I was trapped in a building quickly catching fire; the flames climbed, and I could feel the heat at my ankles. My pain screamed its way through the windows, like pressurized heat blowing out the glass. I knew the only way out was to jump, so I ran to my bathroom, locked the door, unscrewed the lids to my medications, and swallowed hundreds of pills.

"Sonja, open the door," Mitch demanded. He rattled the doorknob.

I ignored him.

"Sonja!" Mitch screamed.

I could hear him trying to pick the lock, so I swallowed more pills faster, trying to guarantee success. I began to feel strange; my knees went weak, and I fell to the floor, straining to focus my eyes. I was sinking, slipping. My phone lit up with a text from Lorie. "Are we still going to dinner?"

My shaky hands grabbed my phone and texted Lorie. "Can't go. I just took a ton of pills."

I tried calling Allyson, Heidi, and my brother Mike to tell them goodbye. Heidi picked up first, and through sobs and slurred speech, I told her how much I loved her, then hung up.

I was dying. I felt it. My spirit screamed out, *Wait! Wait! I can't go. I'll never see my children again! Mitch—what will he do without me? What am I doing? My kids will be shattered if things end this way.*

I started fighting like hell to stay alive, but I'd already made a choice from which there was no coming back.

"Sonja!" Mitch pushed the door open.

Blurrily, I saw him run toward me. He held my head as he called 911. Lorie and her husband, Dean, ran through the door. I went in and out of consciousness as Lorie stuck her finger down my throat trying to make me vomit. Mitch didn't want Lincoln to see what was happening and wanted him gone before the ambulance arrived; Dean called his son to pick Lincoln up.

"Sonja, stay awake. We need to get the pills out." Lorie put her finger down my throat again. "Try to stay awake."

Ambulance lights flashed through the windows of our house. Bright reds and blues swirled against our brick house, waking up our usually quiet street.

I passed out, and Lorie stopped, afraid I'd end up choking.

As the paramedics rushed my body out of our house on a stretcher, neighbors stood on their lawns watching. Mitch rode with me to the hospital watching me remain unresponsive as two large IVs swayed with each bump in the road. Dean and Lorie followed in their own car. The hospital staff recognized us. They whispered, "It's the CEO and his wife," as the ambulance team pushed my unconscious body through the emergency room with Mitch at my side.

I was taken to the trauma bay in the hospital, reserved for the most serious emergency admissions. Mitch, Lorie, and Dean sat in the room with me while doctors and nurses tried to save my life. They cut off my clothes and began pumping my stomach. The doctors filled my stomach with charcoal, hoping it'd absorb some of the pills. I was put on a ventilator to make sure I didn't stop breathing. No one knew if I would live.

With suicidal ideation, there's a level of uncertainty that forced Mitch to be on guard, as he had very little control over me. When I was depressed, he took medicine in the house with him to work. Advil, cough syrup, everything. Opening cupboards and searching through the house to make sure he hadn't forgotten about pill bottles left in a junk drawer felt just as routine as taking a dog for a walk before work. Packing medicine in his briefcase couldn't stop me from going to the store and buying more to overdose on. But the activation energy it'd take for me to drive to the store dropped the chances. Removing an easy temptation lowered the risk.

People would tell Mitch, "Your wife is suicidal; you need to watch her more carefully!" But what about when your wife's *always* suicidal—should he stay home from work and watch me forever? When family came to help for a couple of days, they'd come in and think they were giving groundbreaking advice, based on the things they observed. "You should stay home from work today; she's clearly at risk." But the reality was I was always at risk. This wasn't a temporary situation. He'd never hold down a job if he stayed home every time I was having a bad day.

Mitch looked around at all his friends, and suicide risk wasn't a part of their marriages. But it played a large role in ours, and he knew as long as he stayed married to me, it always would. I had threatened suicide thousands of times, and hundreds of times it was so severe Mitch took extra precautions. When you avoid failure that many times, you can believe you're good at handling a situation, and that complacency can be dangerous.

That night, I'd found my medication in his briefcase, sitting in our bedroom closet, which he hadn't hidden well enough that day. This made him feel partly responsible.

Mitch told me later that he had been watching his sixteen-year-old son slowly fall apart for the last year under the relentlessly controlling environment my illness created. He loved me with everything he had, but he wondered about his role as a father, a protector. He felt he had not only failed me, but his son. The one thing he knew with certainty was Lincoln had to come first and he couldn't manage the two of us under the same roof.

I woke up three days later totally confused. I couldn't speak. *What's wrong with my voice?* I squinted. Everything was blurry. I couldn't move. *Am I paralyzed? Where am I?*

A nurse came to my side when she saw me wake up. "Sonja, you're in the ICU."

"Cazrex." I tried to speak, but nothing came out except scattered, unintelligible sounds.

The nurse got a piece of paper and a pencil. Barely holding the pencil, my hand slid across the paper, making a crooked line. I had no control over my limbs.

Was I in a car wreck? I wanted to ask them if I'd ever walk or talk again, but I blacked out.

"Sonja…Sonja," a nurse kept saying my name. I opened my eyes. I saw Mitch standing next to a team of doctors.

"Mitch, you're here." I struggled to speak louder than a whisper. "How bad was the car accident?" Everyone in my room stopped and looked at me. "Am I paralyzed?"

"You're not paralyzed." That was the question Mitch chose to answer.

One of the doctors stepped toward my bed. "Sonja, you attempted suicide. We think you took over one hundred pills. You're lucky to be alive."

It all came flooding back to me the moment he said it. *Oh my hell! I tried to kill myself!* I wanted to scream. That was the *one thing* I had made a pact with God about, and He broke it. Panicked, I looked to Mitch for assurance, but when I stared into his eyes, he had nothing to give.

"You're in no condition to be a mother right now," the doctor said.

What did that mean? What is he talking about? Being a mother was the only thing that gave me purpose.

"Sonja, Lincoln is moving to Utah. He's going to finish high school there. I gave him the option of living here with me in an apartment, but he chose to live with Uncle Chris and Aunt Leslie in Utah. I think being around his cousins and grandparents might be better for him right now," Mitch explained.

I felt my whole soul being ripped out. My sixteen-year-old son was being taken away from me. *Will he forgive me? Have I damaged him beyond repair? If I can't be a mother, who am I?*

"We'll be back to check on you tomorrow," a doctor said, then headed for the door as the others followed him out.

Mitch sat in a chair by my bed; he had a hard time looking at me. From his profile, I noticed the scruff on his face. He hadn't shaved for a few days.

"I love you," I said, breaking the silence.

He sighed and pinched the bridge of his nose. "I love you too, Sonja. I just can't do what we've been doing anymore." He looked at the tubes in my arms. "All this…chaos. I sat in this room with our son while you were unconscious. Lincoln asked me if his mother would live, and I had to tell him the truth—I didn't know."

"Mitch, I'm so sorry."

"For years you've leaned on me to fill you up, but nothing is filling *me* up. I'm so low that I'm even uninterested in living life. I've just been trying to survive and keep our family from coming apart. But now that that's happened"—Mitch shifted in his seat and took a breath—"I'm going to look for an apartment. You can live in the house. It'll be better for you to be around familiar things and not move."

"We're separating?" My heart fell to the floor, hitting the ground hard, sinking lower than ever before. I no longer believed in rock bottom.

"Sonja, I love you—how can I not? You're the mother of my children. Even with your illness, you've always put the kids first, and I've admired that about you. But I think it'd be best for both our long-term health if you learned to live a more independent life."

"What do you mean by *independent?*" I asked.

"Maybe you need to get a job—something that requires you to wake yourself up in the morning or shower more often. I just can't keep being the only person keeping things sane."

I knew Mitch's impending loss of Lincoln broke something in him. He loved me, and I loved him, but keeping the family together had been a huge motivator for him to push through the bad years. And now that motivation was gone.

"Are you going to divorce me?" I asked timidly.

"I'm not sure how this will play out. I haven't thought that far ahead."

"I'd understand if you do"—I swallowed—"and I'll let you go peacefully." It hurt to admit that divorcing me made sense. Unlike the one hundred pills, admitting I was a burden was hard to swallow. I looked at Mitch and saw him. "You've stuck with me through thick and thin, and I'm grateful for that. I don't want to cause you any more pain. But I will fight for you, our marriage, and our family. I love you. You're my soulmate and I'll do whatever I have to do to keep you."

"I'm struggling to believe things can be fixed," he said.

I reached my hand toward his, but he didn't move to bridge the gap. His phone rang.

"Yeah, Linc? All right. I'll be home soon." He put his phone in his pocket and looked at me briefly. "I have to go."

He got up, and every reason I had to stay alive walked out the door. I was losing everything that meant anything to me in one day. I was alone. No family. No God. No angels. I committed the one act I swore I wouldn't, and the consequences were more than I could bear.

CHAPTER 40

Calm after the Storm

The next day, I lay in the hospital bed without suicidal feelings. It felt foreign. I waited for the thoughts and urges to come, but they never did. I closed my eyes and enjoyed each moment. It felt wonderful.

"How are we doing today?" the hospital psychiatrist asked, walking into my room.

"Still not suicidal. My life's fallen apart, but I want to live. I don't understand it," I said.

"The doctors think you had a seizure in the ER, and that could've reset your brain like electric shock treatment does. But to be honest, we're not a hundred percent sure what happened," she said.

"I don't need to know how or why. I'm just so grateful I feel good."

"You're lucky to be alive without any permanent disabilities."

"That's what everyone keeps telling me."

"You have a lot of work ahead of you, though. I know your sister is dying from cancer, and you've been grieving her. But why grieve a person who is still living? Be grateful she is still with you and enjoy her while you can. Celebrate every day she is alive and leave the grieving for when she's gone."

"I never thought about it that way, but you're right. She's here today. I like that thought."

"Good. Now how are you handling your father's death?" she asked.

"I'm ready to forgive my dad for how he left."

"And what about your own suicide attempt? How are you dealing with that?"

"Didn't see it coming. I believed I'd never try to take my own life," I said.

"Yet dying is all you thought about. Can you honestly say you're surprised?"

"Yes."

"Why? You told everyone you wanted to be dead. Was that a lie?"

I stayed quiet.

"Your illness wanted you dead, but I'm asking if you—*Sonja*—wanted to die?"

I sidestepped the question. "I stayed alive for my family."

"True, but there's more. Sonja, you've been battling suicidal thoughts and urges for over two decades. That's one amazing battle. Why have you stayed alive? Dig deeper."

I choked up. The truth could no longer be hidden. "I wanted to live," I admitted.

The psychiatrist handed me a box of Kleenex. "We are not sending you to the psych ward since you are no longer a danger to yourself. But you need to get into an intensive outpatient program."

"I can do that."

As my psychiatrist left, my nurse walked in to check my vitals.

"My husband might be divorcing me," I told him.

"I divorced my first wife four years ago," he replied.

"Are you happy in your second marriage?"

"I am." He smiled.

"What if your first wife would've fought for you? Would you still have divorced her?" I asked.

"Absolutely not. I'd still be married to her. But she wasn't fighting for me or our marriage, and that was the problem."

"I'm going to fight for my husband and our marriage. Do you think he'll stay with me?"

"I can't really say"—he took the blood pressure cuff off my arm—"but I will tell you this: you're lucky to be alive. I'm a believing Christian, and people who kill themselves go to hell. You just escaped damnation." He patted my shoulder.

I knew I hadn't "just escaped damnation." All I escaped was death. The stigma around suicide and mental illness wasn't only perpetuated by those who knew little about it. Doctors working in that field were equally susceptible to bias, despite their exposure and knowledge.

At work, Mitch's boss, the vice chancellor of health affairs, and the chief medical officer, were the only people who asked how he was doing. The rest of Mitch's coworkers chose not to acknowledge his wife was lying in the ICU five floors above them. It seemed because it wasn't some physical ailment people could understand, it instantly became delicate ground no one would tread. Suicide is a difficult topic.

The hospital had put a fake name on my hospital wristband, but Mitch still felt the whispers, and many people stopped looking him in the eyes when he walked the hospital hallways. Some even outright avoided him. His presence made them uncomfortable, and although they were good people, their actions added to how alone he felt.

A leading psychiatrist told Mitch that if this happened again, not to bring me back to this hospital. He told Mitch that because he was CEO, he needed to take me to a hospital where people wouldn't know us. This disturbed me. I was ready to change. I realized keeping my suicide attempt a secret didn't help anything. Silencing trauma perpetuates stigma and isolation. Mitch almost lost his wife to suicide; he wasn't thinking about his public image. I wanted to use this opportunity to show mental illness is no respecter of persons or families.

The fact is it doesn't matter what race, religion, gender, age, or economic background you come from—royalty to the homeless—mental illness can affect anyone's family. This psychiatrist's words lit a fire inside of me. I no longer wanted to hide. I wanted to stand with the mentally ill.

"You ready to go, girlfriend?" Lorie smiled as she walked into my room. She had visited me every day and was my anchor, giving me the support I needed. As we drove home, I felt nervous to see Lincoln. He had only visited me when I was unconscious. I wanted to find a way to heal the wounds I had created. I was also anxious to be home with Mitch. I wanted to prove myself to him. I wasn't sure Lincoln or Mitch would give me any chances.

I sat in my empty house waiting for Lincoln to come home from school when my doorbell rang. I opened the door, and there stood a neighbor I had only talked to a few times in passing. I was sure that she and the entire neighborhood knew of my attempted suicide. The team of paramedics loading my unconscious body into an ambulance was hard to miss. I stood there without saying anything.

"I know you're not okay. Can I come in?" she asked.

"Sure." I moved to the side, and we sat in the dining room.

"How are you holding up?"

I instantly broke down. "Not sure. I'm losing my son. He's sixteen. And my husband's considering divorce." I took in a shaky breath. "I'm not sure where to go from here."

"When I got diagnosed with breast cancer, I thought my life would end. One night, I told my friends I felt like I was climbing my own personal Mount Everest, and I didn't know if I was going to make it. They told me, 'If you're climbing Mount Everest, then we'll be your gloves, your boots, and your jacket along the journey.'" My neighbor teared up. "There will be people who will surround you and help you climb your own Mount Everest," she said, giving me a tight hug before leaving. I was surprised and touched by her visit.

I went to my bedroom, anxious for Lincoln's arrival. Because of me, he had to leave everything he cared about—parents, home, tennis, debate team, and countless friends. It pained me to think back on how hard he worked the last eight months to make varsity and graduate early. Mitch told me Lincoln was strong, but even so, he cried when he told his tennis coach he was leaving. I couldn't help but think he resented me.

When I heard his backpack drop on the floor and the fridge open, I jumped out of bed and walked into the kitchen. He paused and looked at me. I wrapped my arms around his neck.

"Lincoln, I'm so sorry." I held him tight.

"It'll be okay." He stiffly patted my back.

"You really think so?"

"Yeah." He turned away from me. My heart snapped. The tears came, and there was no way to hold them in.

The doorbell rang.

"I'll be in my room packing," he said, checking a text message.

"Okay." I watched him go into his room. The doorbell rang again.

I opened the front door, and a man waited on the porch with my oxygen tank. I pointed to the rug, unable to get any words out, and he carried it in.

"It's a pretty simple setup," he said, setting it on the rug. "You'll want to make sure to turn this knob."

I continued to silently cry.

"And then move…" His voice faded out as he realized I was wiping countless tears. "Ma'am, are you alright?"

"Just keep going." I waved my hand for him to finish. My heart was breaking in the most painful way. I burst into a sob in the middle of his explanation.

He continued, "You'll use this at night since you stop breathing when you sleep."

I covered my face with my hands and slid to the floor.

"Ma'am, are you sure you're okay?"

I nodded, unable to speak through my tears. He handed me the instruction manual and wished me a good day. I closed the door and went into Lincoln's room to help him pack.

I ended up lying on the floor, unable to do anything but cry. I was paralyzed by sadness. How was anything ever going to be okay again? I picked up my phone and dialed Lorie's number.

"Lorie, we need to pack, but I can't," I cried. "I can't believe this is happening."

"I'm coming over."

Minutes later, Lorie walked through the front door and came straight into Lincoln's bedroom. She saw him stretched out on the bed texting, and me crying, helplessly moving hangers around but not accomplishing much.

"Okay, enough crying." Lorie clapped her hands. "Lincoln, you need a haircut, and I think we could all use some frozen yogurt."

Lincoln and I stared at her.

"Come on, you two. Let's go," she said.

Lorie corralled Lincoln and me into her car and drove us to Supercuts. We sat in the waiting room while Lincoln got his haircut. He chatted with the hairdresser as if nothing was wrong.

"Is he going to be okay?" I asked her.

"He'll be more than okay."

"But I did this, Lorie. He's going to need therapy. This is bad. I mean, really bad!" I started getting myself worked up again.

"You need to be strong for him, for your family," she said.

"It's not only Lincoln I need help repairing. It's my marriage. And Rachael and Alex don't even know yet." I hung my head.

"Just take it one day at a time." Lorie gripped my hand.

My crying tapered down, and all that remained were puffy eyes as I quietly ate my frozen yogurt. Lorie packed Lincoln's suitcases and set them by the front door.

That night when Mitch came home, I ran to meet him. "Hi, Mitch! Are you hungry? Should I make dinner for you?" I asked.

"No, that's okay. I'm just going to go to bed," he said.

"Well, how was your day?" I followed him toward our bedroom.

Mitch stopped me in the doorway. "I think it'd be best if we slept in separate rooms."

I took a step back. In all the years we'd been married, Mitch and I had never let a fight put one of us in a separate bedroom. Even after all the arguments and crazy things I'd done, Mitch allowed us to go back to the way we were after. This time was different. Mitch needed space. I tucked myself into Alex's bed, hooked up my oxygen tank, and tried my best to sleep as I awaited the dreaded flight to Utah the next morning. It was Christmastime and we were going to drop Lincoln off to begin his life without us.

—⁂—

On the plane, Mitch and Lincoln chatted, and I looked out the window, feeling I'd be the outsider this Christmas. We pulled into Mitch's parents' driveway, and I looked at the Christmas lights on the house.

His parents were tied at the hip, as seen in the details of their home. Their shared hobby of oil painting covered the walls—farm scenes signed by him and flower paintings signed by her. Two comfy chairs sat together in the front room by the fireplace where they spent their evenings, and stacks of books in the kitchen showed their shared love of French cooking. Mitch's dad, Lyle, was a lifelong student who, at age sixty, learned how to play the piano, and at eighty, started learning the violin.

"Welcome. Mr. Lincoln, you look like a man." Lyle's voice rumbled. He opened his arms to Lincoln. "Come here, my boy." Mitch's dad was a farmer with hard hands and a soft heart, and his mom, Lynne, was a gentle woman with thick white hair and manicured nails.

"Good to see you," Mitch said, hugging his dad.

"Sonja, it's good to see you." Lynne warmly turned to me.

"Sonja, come here, dear." Lyle pulled me aside into the living room. "I want to tell you that I can't even begin to imagine what you've been through, but we're here for you and Mitch." He put his sturdy hand on my shoulder. "I just wanted you to know that."

"Thank you." I looked into the familiar blue eyes Mitch inherited from him.

"We love you." His voice cracked, and he quickly patted my back and walked out, cutting off any chance for me to witness the tough cowboy tear up.

I wanted to believe he loved me. After all the pain I'd put Mitch through, I didn't see how there'd be any room for his parents to love me. I felt unlovable, and my dad was not here to tell me otherwise. I felt awkward around Mitch's parents. Because of the hard life my bipolar disorder created, I thought they pitied Mitch for being married to me. I was the difficult one, and now I was the wife who attempted suicide. I could only imagine the things they thought about me. Like any daughter-in-law, I wanted them to like me. I wanted them to think I was a good wife and mother, but I couldn't see how they ever could. Mitch's parents often made me feel like I was the problem in my marriage. The book they bought me, *The Proper Care and Feeding of Husbands* by Dr. Laura Schlessinger, as a gift spoke volumes of their thoughts about me.

I knew my parents saw my marriage differently than Lynne and Lyle. My parents believed Mitch put his career before me and our kids. From their perspective, Mitch blamed all of our marriage issues on my mental illness, which they thought was an easy out. My parents thought he didn't look at his own weaknesses and held a false persona of perfection.

The truth was, his persona gave me stability in a strange way. I needed him to be perfect. I was more than willing to take all the blame and responsibility. He struggled with vulnerability, whereas I struggled to let the people I loved be imperfect.

I carried my bag down the stairs and saw Mitch's and Lincoln's bags in the same room. It didn't come as a shock to me that Mitch still planned on separate rooms, but setting my bag in an empty room furthered the distance I felt between us. I wanted us to go back to normal, which I knew was a lot to ask.

"So, Mom and I are going to do some Christmas shopping tonight. Is there anything we should remember?" Mitch asked Lincoln. With everything going on, we never got around to making Christmas lists.

"I don't know." Lincoln shrugged. "Anything's good."

Like the functional, happy parents we weren't, Mitch and I drove to the mall together.

"What do you think we should get him?" I asked.

"There are a few places I want to stop that I think will have something he'll like." Mitch readjusted his hands on the steering wheel.

That was the most he'd talked to me since I came home from the hospital. His lengthy sentence excited me, giving me hope for a longer conversation. Maybe Christmas shopping for Lincoln would give him a reason to shorten the distance between us. We were still parents after all.

We walked into the mall, and every banister was laced with fake pine. A larger-than-life tree shimmered in the center of the mall with ornaments the size of my head. Even though all the candy canes and trees were fake, every detail was an effort to make Christmas become something real.

I pointed. "Wow, look at that tree."

"Yeah. It's neat." Mitch was polite but measured. He turned the corner and I sped up to follow him.

"Should we stop at Build-A-Bear?" I asked. "I know he's sixteen, but he still loves those things."

"I just…I need space away from you," he said.

Just like that, I was reminded of his fragility and how I had broken him. Maybe it was the cheerful people shopping around me, or how he talked to me in the car, or maybe it was the intoxicating smell of Cinnabon around the corner—but I really believed Mitch was going to let me back in.

"Okay." I swallowed. "Just call me when you're ready to leave." I turned around and sat on a bench under some plastic mistletoe. And just like that, I was reminded of my own fragility.

—m—

On Christmas morning, Mitch's parents made a beautiful breakfast. Buttery waffles, bacon, and fresh orange juice waited for us on the round glass table.

"Good morning, Christmas crew!" Lynne greeted us as we came up the stairs.

"Merry Christmas," Mitch said, grabbing a waffle. During breakfast, Lincoln's eyes continually shifted to the shiny boxes under the tree.

"Once we're done eating, we'll open presents," I told him.

He picked up his fork and started eating at lightning speed. "I'm done," he said.

Mitch chugged a glass of orange juice and moved to the tree. "So, these ones are yours."

Lincoln opened his Star Wars BB-8 robot and Build-A-Bear from Mitch and unwrapped the stack of clothes from me.

"Thanks, guys!"

"This one is addressed to you, Mitchell." Lyle handed him a small, wrapped rectangle. "From Sonja," he said.

I sat up, feeling a bit nervous. Mitch tore off the paper and pulled out a book. He read the cover aloud: "*Mitch Wasden's Missionary Journal.*"

"I finally had your mission journals printed in a hardcover book. I sent a copy to Rachael and Alex to read while they're on their missions," I said.

"Thanks, Sonja." He smiled, thumbing through the pages.

I sat awkwardly in my chair as Lyle looked under the tree for my gift from Mitch. It didn't take long for him to realize there weren't any others.

"Well, Merry Christmas, folks," Lyle said.

I was fighting *for* Mitch instead of fighting *with* him, but my efforts didn't seem to be making much of a difference. I knew his emotions were complex. I almost left him by attempting suicide, and now he was wary of getting close again.

Lincoln set up his BB-8 robot with Mitch while his parents took naps in their chairs, so I snatched the keys and drove to the cemetery to visit my dad's grave.

Snow capped the top of every gravestone, and poinsettias spotted the white ground with flashes of red. I took a deep breath and looked out my window at his grave. A Christmas wreath dusted in snow hung on it, and I could see his motto inscribed at the bottom: "Family first, nothing second." He loved us so much, and although he left the way he did, his love for his family was something I couldn't deny.

I stepped out of the car, walked through the fresh snow, and crouched down so I was eye level with his name. "Dad, it's taken me almost five years to get to a point where I could come and see you." Emotion swelled in my heart; tears flowed easily, and I didn't hold them back. "I forgive you for how you left us. Forgive me if I didn't do enough. We both got stuck with this illness, and I don't know how, but I'm going to do something good with it, for both of us." I leaned down and kissed his ice-cold headstone.

CHAPTER 41

Losing Lincoln

December 2015, Springville, Utah

We heard Chris and Leslie talking with Mitch's parents upstairs. They were here to pick up Lincoln. My heart stopped, and the three of us froze. This was it. "You got everything?" I asked Lincoln.

"Yeah." He nodded. Mitch and I grabbed some of Lincoln's luggage and followed him up the stairs to the main floor.

"Lincoln, you ready to go?" Leslie asked, hugging him.

I wanted to reach out and grab him back. I wanted to scream, "No! You can't have him! He's not yours to raise!" Mitch's brother and his wife were doing us nothing but favors, yet it stung like an insult, and the moment burned with heartbreak.

As I looked at Mitch and saw him crying, I realized I wasn't in this boat alone; we were unified in our suffering. I grabbed Lincoln and hugged him tightly. Lincoln started crying, too.

"I love you, Lincoln." I tucked my face into him.

"I know, Mom," he said through his tears. "Just get well. I'll be fine."

Lincoln's strength and fortitude were far beyond a sixteen-year-old. Mitch and I stood watching him get into the car with Leslie to start a new life. Chris stopped at the door, and Mitch pulled his big brother close.

"Thank you, brother." Mitch cried in his arms.

Chris held Mitch tight, and I knew their already close friendship grew closer. Chris was doing something for him that Mitch could not do himself: parent his child. Leslie brought us a lot of comfort, too. We knew Lincoln was going to be taken care of by someone fiercely loyal who'd love him like her own.

Mitch and I zipped up our bags and left for the airport. We didn't talk much the whole way home—something about suffering makes silence loud. We both knew there was too much sadness wrapped around this event to talk about it without crying, and we had both cried enough.

When we got home to an empty house, Lincoln's absence stung deeper. Mitch went into our bedroom, and I went into Alex's. There was nothing left to say. Lincoln was gone. We both lost our son.

CHAPTER 42

Dialectical Behavior Therapy

L orie did hours of research on bipolar disorder and found dialectical behavior therapy (DBT), which is a scientifically-based therapy with excellent results. I had never heard of it, but I sat in a DBT therapist's waiting room for my first visit. There were old and young people sitting alongside me. A mom with her two-year-old, a teenage boy listening to music, and an old man leaning back in a chair next to the fish tank. Everyone was here to meet with their psychiatrist or therapist.

Mental illness touches many lives. The National Alliance on Mental Illness says one in five people are affected by mental illness in a given year. Suicide is a leading cause of death in the United States; depression is a leading disability in the world. Do those suffering from one of the leading disabilities in the world receive the attention and funding that other leading disabilities receive? Do we attract the same level of public awareness, campaigns, fundraisers, T-shirts, and bake sales as other illnesses? People don't like talking about mental disorders. The topic is more of a conversation killer.

"Sonja Wasden," my DBT therapist called into the waiting room.

I stood and walked through the hallway of offices to my therapist's room. Tonya was in her forties and had brown hair and big eyes. She looked caring but stern, like a strong mother figure. I was ready to ask her the question I asked all my therapists and doctors.

"Do you know anyone with a mental illness that is living a normal life?"

"Yes. Tons," she said, matter of fact.

I was sure she misunderstood my question. "I'm talking about patients who deal with daily suicidal thoughts. Patients with the uncurable mental illnesses."

"Yes, I know." Tonya opened her desk drawer, looking for a pen.

"I'm talking *severe* mental illness—like people who can't get out of bed or who have enormous spending sprees. People—like me—who are living an impossible life."

Tonya crossed her legs. "Absolutely. Sonja, DBT changes people's lives. And there's no such thing as 'an impossible life.'"

She was the first therapist to give me a straight answer, and a positive one to boot. Every time I asked this question, the doctors all seemed unwilling to commit to a firm answer. I liked Tonya's confidence, but I was still skeptical.

"I've done ten years of therapy, and none of it has helped," I said. "I've been listened to, validated, advised, and scolded. I might feel good for a few hours after a therapy session, but my behavior and thought patterns never really change."

"I completely understand your frustration. I was going to quit being a therapist because I didn't see my patients improving. I felt like my job was worthless," she said.

"So, what changed?"

"I learned about Marsha M. Linehan's DBT program and its success. I got certified and have since watched it change people's lives. This is scientific, evidence-based therapy, and I know it works," she promised. "You put the hard work in, and you will get the skills to create a life not only worth living, but one you'll experience joy in." She looked at me more softly. "Do you want that?"

The single word—*joy*—left me dizzy. Never in my wildest dreams did I think I could have a joyful life. Her confidence gave me the first real hope in years.

"More than anything," I said.

"Then let's get to work." She smiled.

Tonya taught me the four key skills in DBT. First, mindfulness—the ability to radically accept things as they are and be present in the moment without trying to change it. Second, distress tolerance—the ability to tolerate negative emotions instead of trying to escape them. Third, emotional regulation—the ability to move through problematic emotions. Fourth, interpersonal effectiveness—the ability to communicate with others in a way that is assertive, maintains self-respect, and strengthens relationships.

These were all new concepts to me. I was finally going to learn skills to manage my illness instead of just talking about it. Tonya had me believing DBT could change the course of my life. I was determined to not only learn these skills but master them.

"We'll have weekly one-on-one sessions, a two-hour group class, and twenty-four-hour coaching available to you," Tonya said. "Use the twenty-four-hour coaching when you're in a crisis. You'll have my phone number, and I will always respond within ten minutes."

"So I should call when I'm suicidal?" I asked.

"Suicide is off the table. That is nonnegotiable."

"How do I take it off the table?" I always felt like that decision wasn't entirely up to me. It was my disease taking me over, and I had little say in the matter.

"Suicide is never an option," she said firmly.

"I've fought with everything I have and still ended up attempting it."

"Stop fighting your feelings. Pushing against emotions only makes them stronger."

"But what if I get in too much pain or go into another episode? I don't know if I can survive it."

"Look at the evidence. You've made it through every episode for over twenty years. Yes, you attempted suicide, but that's because you hadn't taken it off the table. You're sitting on this couch right now, in this room, seeking help to create a life for yourself. You not only want this—you have the determination to do it."

"But what if I don't believe I have it in me to go through another episode?" My confidence was greatly shaken after my suicide attempt. "I don't want any more episodes or painful emotions. I'm tired."

"This isn't about what you want," Tonya said, snapping me back into reality. "Lots of people have illnesses they don't want, but nevertheless, it's theirs to deal with."

She had my full attention.

"What're your thoughts on people who die of suicide? Like your dad?" she asked.

"I think they're at peace and out of pain," I said.

"How do you know dying by suicide doesn't put you in a different type of pain?"

"Well, that's just what I believe."

"The fact is, not you, I, or a single person living knows what happens to people who die from suicide. But I've often wondered if it would be another type of hell to watch your family suffer because of something you did and not to be able to apologize or comfort them. Imagine looking down on the family you left in pieces, and you can only watch. Wouldn't that cause pain, even to a heavenly being? When you hurt people you love by taking your life, there is no closure."

"But I think being bipolar is no different than having cancer. If the illness takes you out, it takes you out," I said.

"Yes, both are illnesses, but every illness affects people and families differently. I've done therapy with people who've lost someone to cancer and lost someone to suicide, and there's a different type of horror with the latter. That's just a fact. You'd change the course of your family's life. Do you want to be responsible for that?" She tipped her chin down to look at me.

"I've never thought about it like that."

"Well, it's time to."

CHAPTER 43

Appearances

January 2016, Columbia, Missouri

Mitch and I stepped into a glittering ballroom for a gala his hospital was sponsoring without so much as brushing arms. It felt important to put on a brave face and get the public awkwardness out of the way. I had nerves of steel as I mingled for hours in a room full of people aware I had attempted suicide. I shook hands with each one of them, meeting their curious gaze. I looked every bit the part in diamonds and a black velvet dress as we were greeted by the chancellor, deans of each college, and the president of the university. On the outside we looked like a perfectly dressed, happy couple, yet we were severely bruised and broken. Every person smiled at me and acted like nothing had happened. If I'd been in a car wreck and almost died, I knew people would stop to ask me how I was doing. It was painful for me to be there for that reason, and because Mitch and I were separating. But I would support him to the end.

"Are you ready to go?" Mitch asked. "It's getting late." These were the first words he spoke to me all night.

"Yes," I said. We walked to the car in silence, my high heels clicking on the cement the only sound between us.

On his way to bed that night, he stopped and turned to me. "Thank you for coming."

"You're welcome." I stood looking at him.

He walked into his bedroom, and I walked the opposite direction to mine. The appearance of the united couple ended here.

I knew to save our marriage, I needed to face the wreckage of my last episode head-on. The next morning when Mitch left for work, I went in our bedroom and dumped out the credit card statements from my dresser drawer. I read them one by one, forcing myself to look at the numbers. Taking in how bad my spending had gotten made it hard to identify with myself. I felt like there was me, and then there was this other person whose credit card bills covered my bed. I had to separate myself from that person to get through all the envelopes. I got a highlighter and marked the totals on each statement. Calling the creditors to see how I could settle my debts was an eye-opening experience. I'd need a lot of money to pay these off, and I knew Mitch wouldn't be a part of the repair. I made a list of ways to pay it off on my own.

Get a job.

Sell jewelry.

Although my list consisted of only two things, they were big things. Aside from being a phlebotomist, I hadn't worked outside the home for twenty-five years. I loved the White House Black Market clothing store at the mall, so I filled out an application online. My résumé was sparse for my age. I decided it'd be best to go in person and talk to the manager. She didn't know me, but the assistant manager did because I shopped there so much. They offered me a job as a salesperson, though I wasn't sure I could hold it down. I imagined myself coming in late, forgetting I had work, or arguing with coworkers and customers.

Mustering up courage and faith in myself was difficult, but as I took each small step forward, I started to regain my power. I wasn't getting well for my kids or Mitch. For the first time, I was getting well for myself.

I was two weeks into my job and doing well. I arrived on time and dressed professional.

"Sonja, can you steam these display dresses?" my manager asked when I arrived.

"Sure," I said. The black dress swung on the hanger as warm puffs of vapor erased all the small creases. I slipped the dress back onto the mannequin.

"Is Sonja working today?" a short woman named Julie asked. Julie had money to blow and trusted my style advice the last two times she shopped here.

"Hi, Julie." I poked my head out from behind the mannequin.

"Oh, thank heavens!" she huffed. "My husband planned a family vacation, and I need something nice to wear." A pair of pants caught her eye. "How about these?" she asked.

I smiled. "Go try them on. You know I'll be honest."

Julie slid the curtain shut and noisily struggled her way into the pants.

"I'm coming out!" she yelled. She stood in front of the mirror with her hands on her hips. "Hmm, is it just me, or do these make me look wide?"

"No, they look great!" my coworker cooed.

"Sonja?" Julie raised an eyebrow.

"They make you look a little wide," I said, "but try these." I handed her a few skirts with flattering cuts. After trying one on, she asked me to pick out shoes and jewelry to go with the skirts. She bought everything I laid out for her. I made nine dollars an hour, which wasn't making a dent in my debt, but I got so much more out of my job than a paycheck. I became one of the highest-selling employees in the store, which gave me the confidence I could provide for myself. I could function in the world independently.

To get me ready for my next big step, Lorie and I laid out my jewelry on the dining room table. The table sparkled with a massive array of diamonds and gold that looked too beautiful to part with. This was my treasure trove, and I was desperately attached to it. I put on a gold and diamond necklace.

"This really is pretty," I said to the mirror.

"Which is why it'll sell fast." Lorie was trying to keep me on track.

"I know." I took off the necklace.

We photographed pieces, and Lorie helped me put them on eBay. My gold Tiffany necklace and bracelet were bought quickly, but the no-name-brand stuff was difficult to get people to buy. I also sold to jewelry stores and pawnshops, and to help my cause, Lorie bought two bracelets from the pile. Most jewelry isn't an appreciating asset, so no matter what I sold, I lost money ultimately.

—⚬—

Mitch came home from work that evening and looked at the dining room table covered with jewelry. Trays of rings and bracelets glistened in stacks as I busily typed on the computer.

"What are you doing?" he asked.

"I'm selling my jewelry. Lorie and I have been working on it all week." I kept typing.

"What about your OCD?"

"Dialectical behavior therapy is teaching me how to get comfortable with being uncomfortable."

"And you feel like it's working?" He sounded a bit skeptical.

"Yes. But either way, I need to pay off my debt."

He didn't know what to say to my newfound clarity, but he seemed to be worried it was a temporary ploy to win him back.

"Why are you all dressed up?" he asked.

"I got a job," I said.

He froze. "What?"

"I'm working retail at White House Black Market in the mall."

"Wow. Congratulations," he said, still not moving.

"Thank you." I smiled.

—⟋⟋⟍—

Mitch and I scheduled counseling sessions for Lincoln once a week to help him heal. Lincoln's therapist, Sam, said he'd call to tell me how the meetings were going. I waited nervously by the phone until it rang.

"So how is he? Is the damage fixable? I did this. I'm to blame!" I got to the point.

"Slow down—he's more than alright," Sam assured me.

"What? Really?"

"Yeah, really. I've seen kids go through a lot less and completely fall apart. After talking with Lincoln, I know he feels valued and loved. You and your husband have provided your son with such a solid foundation, I can honestly tell you he's going to be fine. He's an exceptional young man."

"But he was raised by a bipolar mother," I said.

"First of all, you are more than your illness. Second, bipolar or not, you raised a great son."

I fell silent.

"Lincoln will triumph over this. This will give him the confidence he needs when life throws him more crap, which it will."

"Thank you," I said, and I meant it.

"He loves you deeply but is very scared for your well-being. You attempted suicide, which is a serious thing. There's work to be done, and he has experienced trauma. I'll continue to help him process this experience. You'll have to be patient, but I'm very, very optimistic about the outcome, and you should be, too."

I hung up the phone and said a prayer of thanks. Lincoln would be okay. But what about my marriage?

CHAPTER 44

Heartache

January 2016, Columbia Missouri

Mitch researched apartments online and took tours of the ones he was interested in. He wanted something close to work that allowed pets, in case he ended up getting a dog to keep him company, but said none of the available complexes felt right.

Mitch's work was to take care of himself and heal. My work was to let go of the past and not fear the future. I wanted to live in the present moment, even though it was filled with so much uncertainty. I was motivated to move on and build a better life. It was time to fill my days with the things I loved.

I grabbed a handful of art knives and squeezed a dozen colors out on my palette. My heart beat fast from excitement. I was going to paint for real and not just in my head. Dipping my brush in the paint, I pressed the crunchy bristles to the canvas and moved my hand freely. My art was colorful, loud, and chaotic—everything my clothes and house were not, but everything I was. I painted for hours, forgetting to eat, check the laundry, or think about my illness. The chaos inside poured onto my canvas, like it was sucking the venom out. I wiped my forehead, getting paint on myself, and looked back at my work, proudly. It was only through paint that I could make my pain beautiful. Unlike a mirror, or a diary, I could look my emotions in the face when they were on a canvas.

My alarm went off reminding me to leave for hot yoga. I rinsed my brushes and drove to my class. Tonya said daily exercise would help my mental health. Being told exercise would help wasn't new to me, but this was the first time I was giving it a real chance. I was a little nervous about doing yoga for eighty minutes in 105-degree heat, but I pulled into the yoga studio's parking lot regardless. I rolled out my mat in the dark, steamy room and faced the wall of mirrors. Everyone was lying on their backs or stretching, and as the new student, I copied.

A man in a tank top wearing his hair in a bun stood at the front. "Welcome, everyone. Take a few cleansing breaths and let's start in down dog."

He turned on some music, and I looked around to see what "down dog" meant. Our instructor guided us through many challenging and relaxing poses, and though out of shape, I enjoyed the fast-paced movements mixed with deep breathing.

At the end of the session, the instructor invited us to stand on one leg and slowly "grow our tree." He demonstrated by slowly moving his hands from his heart all the way up to his face and then stretching out his arms wide like branches over his head.

"Think positive thoughts in this moment, and let them fill your soul," he guided.

I balanced on one leg and brought my hands to my heart. I closed my eyes and waited there. My pulse raced in the quiet room, and I could hear my heartbeat drumming in my ears. I exhaled and brought my hands from my heart to my face and then stopped. I never stood in open stances like that. In fact, I lived in positions that were the exact opposite—curled up in the fetal position or sitting tensely in bed with my knees pulled to my chest and my arms close to my sides. This felt too vulnerable.

I looked around and saw everyone with their hands in the air, breathing deeply. I was the only one struggling with this part. I was amazed people were this open to life. It looked terrifying. I wrapped my arms around myself and went down to child's pose, forehead resting on the mat, folded over my knees. I wasn't ready to open myself up that way.

—ɯ—

Mitch pulled into the driveway after work and saw me dressed in all black, pruning my rose bushes. My cheek leaned into my phone screen as I talked on the phone. I was focused—my brow furrowed, and neck positioned deep inside the thorny bushes.

He got out of the car with his briefcase, and I looked up and gave him a huge smile and wave. He waved back and walked into the house.

I began to feel panicked and ran into the kitchen. I prepared a bowl of ice water and began dunking my face.

Mitch came rushing in the kitchen.

"What are you doing?" he asked, watching me submerge my entire face into the large bowl. I pulled my dripping face up and took a sharp breath.

"TIPPs," I said quickly between breaths. "It's a DBT skill for anxiety." I sank my face back in the icy water.

"Is it working?" he asked, watching my face sit beneath the water and ice cubes as I counted in my head. My wet face once again emerged.

"Yes. The shock of the ice water resets my brain when I'm in trouble. I'm learning skills, Mitch. I'm not fighting this illness or pleading with God to take it away; I'm learning to live *with* it." I dried off my face with a kitchen towel. He just stood staring at me, not sure what to say. I dumped the ice water down the sink and walked over to my chocolate cupboard. "Alexa, play 'Don't Stop Believing' by Journey," I called, getting myself a piece of chocolate before turning back to him. "Having an illness doesn't mean I can't enjoy life." I closed my eyes, savoring the chocolate.

The music pounded through the speakers. I danced and sang along as I unloaded the dishwasher. Mitch and I had so much history together that despite his current hesitancy, it felt natural to slide back into old patterns. He picked up a broom and started sweeping the kitchen, eventually humming to the song.

He looked into my eyes. I leaned closer, and he kissed me; memories of our first kiss came flooding back, along with the countless kisses over the years, ending on the memory of him kissing my forehead with my head in his lap on the bathroom floor. It was like our minds were linked as our lips touched and Mitch saw the same memory.

"No, Sonja. Just no." He shook his head, stepping away. Mitch walked back into our bedroom and shut the door behind him. There was instant pain. I knew his heart ached—it ached for me, but it also ached because of me.

I actively tried to repair the hurt between Mitch and me, but he was stuck. Something kept him from pushing through and openly loving me again. I knew my suicide attempt hurt him in ways he couldn't put into words.

The next day, Mitch came home from work to find me crying on the couch. *And we're back to normal,* he probably thought. I sat against decorative pillows, wiping away tears, writing in my DBT workbook. He sat next to me.

"You need something?" I asked, looking up from my book.

"Um, no. Do you?"

"No."

"But you're crying," he pointed out.

"Obviously." I rolled my eyes. "Mitch, I lost the privilege of raising our sixteen-year-old son. All I've ever known is being a mother." I placed my hand over my heart. "Even though we visit him, I have a lot of work to do to repair that relationship. My therapist said it's okay to cry, but I have to do my DBT homework to learn how to create better relationships. So I'm kinda busy right now. Can we talk later?" I squinted my eyes apologetically.

Stunned, he stood. "Uh, yeah, sure."

CHAPTER 45

DBT Group Therapy

February 2016, Columbia, Missouri

I hugged my latest toy store acquisition, a plush cat carrier with six tiny cats stuffed into small cubbyholes, as I entered the small, blue DBT group therapy room. I gripped the handle of the cage, realizing there wasn't a single open seat. I pulled a cat out of its cubby and held it to my face, closing my eyes.

Maybe I'll just skip this week. My hand reached toward the door.

"Oh, Sonja! You're fine, we're just a full class today," Susan, the therapist, said. My face must have revealed I was a flight risk.

"You can sit by me." A toothless old woman smiled. She scooted over on the small couch and patted next to her.

I paused, wondering how we'd fit.

"Come on." She patted again.

I said nothing, squeezing myself into the tiny space. I took a deep breath and greeted the old woman who introduced herself as Mary.

"Let's begin with our mindfulness exercise. Everyone, sit up straight in your chairs and place your hands on your legs, palms facing up. Now, close your eyes and take a deep breath. Watch your thoughts; don't push them away or judge them. A thought is just a thought, nothing more."

Susan hit the gong, and we began.

We sat in silence and my mind's predictable reel of negativity started to play. *You're worthless. Your life is impossible. You're weak. You can't do this. My* instincts told me to run and push these negative thoughts away. *You're a failure, you're going to mess up, you always say the wrong thing!* No amount of positive thinking drowned them out. They insisted on being seen and heard. The more I resisted them, the stickier they became. My therapist told me to label my negative thoughts, "sticky thoughts," so when they came I could say to myself, "Oh I'm having a sticky thought," instead of believing what it said.

Sticky thoughts are rude, they speak out of turn, they're mean, and they have bad manners, but when I embraced them, I set myself free from them. I learned when the repetitive, sticky thoughts came to open my arms out wide and say, "Hi, sticky thought, I hear you, I see you, come on in." They came and went, but I didn't judge them as good or bad. I learned not to assign meaning to them or spend energy deciding if they were true or untrue. These uninvited thoughts had no meaning other than the meaning I gave them.

The gong rang.

"Time's up. How'd it go?" Scott, the co-therapist, asked.

Ann, a woman with a big sunflower pen, began. "I kept thinking about my son. If it wasn't for him, I wouldn't be here trying to improve."

"How old is he?" I asked.

"Five."

"Wow, you're improving so early! Think of all the good years ahead of you," Mary told her.

"No, no, no!" Ann broke down crying and stormed out, slamming the door behind her.

I understood Ann not being able to think about the future. It was forbidden to talk about the future in my home. Mitch and the kids knew not to mention future vacations, my birthday, anniversary, or retirement plans. I largely lived one month at a time.

"I didn't mean to upset her," Mary told the therapists.

"You'll notice in group therapy that you or someone else can get upset. This is an opportunity for you and that person to practice skills," Susan explained.

"Now let's get back on track," Scott continued. "Biosocial theory answers the question regarding why some people have so much trouble controlling their emotions and actions. Emotional vulnerability is biological. It's simply how you are born, so there is no need to blame yourself. You may have intense emotions, but that doesn't mean you have to be at their mercy."

A man in his sixties raised his hand. "Mental illness is dangerous. I feel like a CIA agent, surviving life-or-death situations daily. I was very brave accepting my thoughts today. I successfully completed a high-risk operation." He folded his arms across his chest.

I spoke up. "I like that he said he was brave. My sister is dealing with cancer, and she's told that. I think people with mental illness need to be told they're brave, too."

"You're all brave to face your illnesses head on," Susan added.

"Alright, how'd last week's mindfulness assignment go?" Scott asked.

Mary began, "I planted a peppermint plant. Now, whenever I start to feel panicked, I go outside and water it or just watch it in the sunlight. I call it 'my panic plant.'"

Susan clapped. "That's great, Mary!"

"Sonja." Scott pointed to me.

"When I felt unsafe, I went on a walk and brought myself to the present moment. I focused on what I was doing right then, and I said to myself, 'Okay, I'm on a walk.' Then I started describing the things I saw around me. I noticed the purple flowers in my neighbor's yard and the blue sky without clouds. And as I kept describing things, my anxiety lessened," I said.

"Thank you, Sonja. That is a great example of being in the moment," Scott said. "By practicing mindfulness, we're able to pause, check in, and identify emotions."

For so long, my mental illness dictated my behavior. This simple introduction to mindfulness became a powerful ally. The idea that my emotions and thoughts were merely things that passed through me gave me peace and perspective. As I separated myself from my emotions and thoughts, I became a "watcher" of them. I didn't eliminate all my demons, but with practice, mindfulness allowed me to live above them.

CHAPTER 46

Honesty Please

Mitch and I flew to Utah to visit Lincoln, and seeing his new life was painful and comforting. He had friends, traditional family dinners, chores, therapy, and a balanced routine. I felt if I had gotten help sooner, I could've provided all those things. If I could go back in time, I would have figured out my mental health before bringing children into the world, but here I was, a woman doctors deemed unfit to be a mother.

On the flight home, I turned to Mitch. "Why didn't you hospitalize me earlier? It would have been against my will at any time. But obviously you had the power to do it and you didn't."

"How dare you! I have taken care of you for years."

"How dare *you*! It took you years to hospitalize me even though my parents begged you to do it and even offered to help."

"I've been on the bipolar roller coaster sitting next to you, and I never left. I never threatened divorce. I stayed."

"I never left either."

"Yes you did." He ground his teeth. "You attempted suicide."

"I fought hard for our family!"

"You threaten to divorce me all the time!"

"You let your children's mother not only suffer for too long, but allowed me to be their main caretaker as a sick person. You did not protect me or them!"

"And neither did you! If you died, you'd have abandoned our children and me. Just because the doctors were able to save you, doesn't change the fact that you tried to leave us."

"I needed help."

"You refused all the help I brought you!"

"Because I was *sick*. I wasn't thinking clearly! Your mind works just fine. What's the real reason you didn't get me help sooner?"

"I was young. I didn't understand what we were dealing with."

"In the beginning, yes, but for twenty years? You work in the healthcare field, for God's sake."

"I tried."

"Not hard enough. Even after my suicide attempt, what programs did you research for me? You have a PhD; you know how to research. It was Lorie who found DBT therapy and got me a therapist. Did you ever even do a Google search?"

Mitch snapped his seatbelt off and stormed off to an empty seat in another row. He was fuming, and from a few rows back I stared at the back of his head wishing I could see inside.

"Sir, you need to move back to your seat," I saw a flight attendant tell him. Reluctantly, he sat back into the seat next to me, not looking at me.

"I love you, and I'm fighting for this marriage," I said.

"*And* you attempted suicide, and I lost my son."

"Please forgive me. I'm fighting for you, but we need to have a more honest relationship. I feel like you didn't put me first—even if you see it different, this is how I feel. You put your career, your image, your reputation first. I was the afterthought. Tell me I'm wrong."

Silence.

"Tell me the reason you didn't get me help earlier." I took his hand.

"I was broken," he stiffly admitted.

"I was broken, too."

He kept his gaze pinned on the seat in front of him.

"Why Mitch, why? Was it the stigma?"

"I don't care what people think."

"Really?" I looked at him shocked. "You can't stand it if I bring up your flaws or weaknesses. You're furious if I say a word to anyone that puts you in a bad light. You *need* people to think you're perfect, and a mentally ill wife didn't fit that image."

"You needed me to be perfect, too. You needed a solid person to rely on. Someone without cracks."

"Yes, there is truth to that, but that shouldn't have stopped a father from getting his wife help so she can be the best mother to his children. Mitch, what about our kids? What about Lincoln?"

He removed his glasses. "I failed you. I failed them. It wasn't only you who wanted to keep your mental illness a secret. I wanted it, too. I worried my boss would think that I wasn't capable of being CEO if he knew my wife was bipolar. I worried I wouldn't get that next promotion. I didn't want to be judged."

"I can understand that. I feared being judged, too. Stigma is what kept me from resisting help and accepting I had a mental illness."

Mitch took my hand.

"Mitch, I've learned so much in my DBT classes. You did the best you could with what you knew at the time. And so did I. We both need to go back and give our younger selves a hug. When you know better, you do better. And that's what we can do now."

Stigma—that's what kept both of us silent, and that silence not only almost took my life, but my family's well-being.

CHAPTER 47

Fighting for Love

February 2016, Columbia, Missouri

Having just got back from Utah, Mitch and I went grocery shopping for the week, and like a moth to the flame, I hovered at the flower department.

"Do you want some flowers?" Mitch asked.

"You wouldn't mind?"

"Not at all." He pushed the cart toward me.

"Thank you," I said, setting baby pink roses in the cart. An unconscious smile spread across my face.

"I'm not exactly buying you flowers," Mitch said for clarification. "This isn't a romantic gesture. It's part of our grocery budget."

I smiled. "I know."

It had been months. Mitch still hadn't moved out, and I wasn't sure why. He sat on his bed, going through apartment brochures. I didn't know why he hadn't pulled the trigger. He just kept looking at apartment after apartment without signing any paperwork. Something was holding him back, and I needed to win him over before that something got resolved. I knocked on the bedroom door and walked in.

"Mitch, I need to talk to you."

"About what?" he asked.

"I need to apologize to you. I'm taking ownership of this illness, which I haven't done in the past. I've forced you to carry too much of it and then blamed you when I didn't feel it go away. I lashed out instead of accepting responsibility." I took a big breath. "Dialectical behavior therapy is changing my life. I know now, this illness is mine to manage. It's not your responsibility. I didn't do anything to deserve this illness, but nevertheless"—I threw a finger in the air—"it's mine to take care of!"

"Wow," he whispered. He'd never heard me talk about my illness this way before. There was a clarity in my eyes he hadn't seen in years.

"I've been so angry that I have an illness I failed to see there are thousands of people with crippling illnesses doing life; I'm not the only one. I'm not being picked on." I grabbed his hand, and he let me. "I want to fight for this marriage. We've had children together, done careers; you've been to hell and back with me. I want to come out the other end better for it. Now that I'm learning how to take responsibility and manage my illness, we have a bright future."

He took his hand back. "I'm not—"

"Let me finish." I stopped him. "I need you to know you can walk away from this, from me. You can leave this illness and never deal with it again." I stared him down. "I will let you go because I love you, and I will be okay. I don't need you. I want you. But until you serve me divorce papers, I will fight for you." I left with those words hanging in the air.

—⁂—

A few weeks later Mitch went to sign a lease on an apartment. I was on the verge of losing my husband. I drove straight to the nearest Walmart and thumbed through the greeting cards. I found a card two feet long and one foot wide with its very own giant envelope.

It had a sleepy puppy on the front and big letters that read, "Get Well Soon."

I poured out years of tender feelings into the larger-than-life card. I ended the card with, "I know having a sick wife makes you sick, too. I hope you get well soon and remember how much I love you." I taped a picture of me inside. It was one my college roommate took before I went to surprise Mitch in the middle of his history class to ask him on a date. She captured me laughing in pure happiness, something Mitch hadn't seen in years.

Although long years together brought aging and complexity into our lives, I knew not-so-deep down we were the same starry-eyed kids who fell for each other's smile and longed for each other's kiss.

I drove home rehearsing what I'd say. Gripping the large card, I found Mitch in the kitchen.

"Mitch!" I said, gathering my courage.

"Sonja, we need to talk," he interrupted.

I panicked. *Oh no, he's moving out soon.*

"Is it about you moving out?" I forced myself to ask.

"Yes. I went to sign the lease today—"

"Wait!" I shouted. "Just wait. Read this first, before you say anything else." I pushed the giant envelope forward. "Just read it."

Mitch opened the letter, and we stood silently as he read it. He teared up, not saying anything for a moment as he gathered his voice.

"Thank you." Choked up, he leaned over and kissed my forehead.

"Did I change your mind about leaving?"

"No." He laughed.

"What?" I furrowed my brow.

"When I went to sign the lease today, I felt it was the absolute wrong thing to do. I walked away from it. I'm staying here with you," he said.

I hugged him in shock. "You know, I was prepared to bake your favorite oatmeal raisin cookies every day to win you back."

"Hmm. Cookies would still be a good idea." He held up the photograph I placed in the card. "I always loved that picture of you."

"I want you to put it by your nightstand, so you remember me that way."

"I thought about what you said. How you're learning to manage your illness. If this DBT therapy really is changing your life, I owe it to our family to see this transformation through. I want us to come out of the hard times better for it, too." He pulled me back into his arms. "Choosing you just feels right; from the moment I met you, it always has. You're worth standing in the fire for," he said. Staying together was the legacy we wanted to leave for our kids. Even when the most tempting option was to leave, we found a way to stay.

CHAPTER 48

24/7 DBT Coaching

March 2016, Columbia, Missouri

Early in my DBT progress several memories began to flare: details of graduate school, Rachael's birth, and my pregnancy with Alex. The recurring nightmares of our time in Michigan often plagued me. The details were never far away: the apartment walls, the lack of prenatal care during my first pregnancy, the needles, the tubes of blood, the newborn diapers, and the constant financial stress.

Moving to Albuquerque, New Mexico, for Mitch's first job, being four months pregnant with Alex, and getting the first prenatal care at four months pregnant had weighed heavily on me. On October 23, 1996, I delivered Alex in the middle of the night, and Mitch went home after the delivery to sleep. He returned the next day at 7 a.m., dropping off a two-year-old Rachael, still in diapers, before he hurried off to work. He had paternity leave but chose not to use it, wanting to secure an upcoming promotion. As I was changing Rachael's diaper on my hospital bed, Alex crying in the hospital crib, a nurse came in and said, "What the hell is going on? You just delivered your baby six hours ago. Where is your husband?" These painful memories were hard to let go of.

"Morning, cutie," Mitch greeted.

I opened the fridge and pulled out a carton of strawberries. "Mitch, in Michigan, when I was pregnant with Rachael, and then Alex, why didn't we go on welfare?"

He stood next to me, putting his bowl into the sink. "Sonja, lots of women work while they're pregnant."

"And most of them have health insurance or go on welfare. I was seven months pregnant with Rachael and with Alex four months pregnant and I hadn't seen a doctor."

"Ugh, this again? Why are we reliving the past?" He sighed.

"I'm not. I just feel like you've never acknowledged how traumatic that was for me. We gambled with Rachael and Alex's life. Something could've really gone wrong!"

"But it didn't," he reminded me.

"That's not the point! It was still a dumb decision."

"Are you blaming this on me?"

"No! I'm blaming us!"

"I'm sorry we were poor graduate students. It wasn't an ideal situation, but we were doing our best."

"And neither of our parents stepped in to help us!" I wanted him to feel the panic I once felt. "I would never let my kids be in that situation."

"Our parents did the best they could," he defended.

"I want you to admit we were young and dumb. I don't want you to relive the past. I just want you to acknowledge it," I pushed.

"You always regret the past. Just leave it alone."

"Maybe I keep going back because you continually sweep it under the rug and act like it never happened. If you'd just admit we've made mistakes—"

"I don't think that would change anything," he interrupted.

"To this day, it makes me sick. It makes me feel like we were unfit parents. We had no business having children if we couldn't afford them. We weren't being responsible."

"Well, everything worked out."

"But it doesn't always. What about after I had Alex and you left our two-year-old daughter in my hospital room for six hours to go to work? The strain of lifting Rachael caused my stitches to rip, and I got a serious infection!"

"Why can't you just let the past go?"

"I want us to look each other in the eyes and say we made mistakes."

"I'm more interested in the future. What are we going to do today to make better decisions?" he countered.

"I can't trust we'll make better decisions if we never acknowledge we've made bad ones! I swear, you need DBT therapy! You don't know how to validate!" I sobbed. I immediately called Tonya in a frenzied state. "Mitch isn't validating my point of view. I want to run out of this home and never come back! He makes me escalate!" I yelled into the phone.

"Sanja, Sanja," Tonya calmly mispronounced my name. I had her on speaker. "Do you have your stuffed animals?"

"No."

"Crying hysterically isn't going to get you anywhere."

"But Mitch won't validate my feelings!"

"Sanja! Stop. Where are your stuffed animals?"

"In my room."

"Okay. Go get them. We don't want to end up in the ER. Now, I don't want you interacting with Mitch."

"Because Mitch just escalates me!" I said.

"No, this isn't about Mitch. This is about you learning to interact with the people in your life, in your environment, skillfully," she corrected.

"I'm trying!"

"Okay, you're at a ten. I want you to do TIPPs. Go put your face in ice water and call me in ten minutes." She hung up.

Mitch filled a bowl with ice water and set it on the counter for me. I dunked my face. *One…two…three…four…five,* I counted in my head. The shock from the icy water pulled my thoughts away from my frustration. Wet hair hung around my face, and the cool air hit my cheeks like a minty, effervescent breath. I leaned over the bowl and cried. I needed more dunks. I wiped my hair away and went back under. *One…two…three…four…five.* I did four more dunks and dried my face. I got into bed with my stuffed animals and texted Tonya: "*I'm at a 3 now. TIPPs worked.*"

"Sonja?" Mitch knocked at the door.

I didn't say anything. He walked into our bedroom and sat at the edge of the bed.

"I want to validate you. You're right. We did make mistakes. And if I could go back and change things, I would." He paused. "I don't want to acknowledge it because it's hard for me to admit I did something that hurt my wife so badly and didn't take care of our children the way I would've liked to. It's really painful to acknowledge that." He grabbed my hand.

"That makes sense. I know what it's like to own hard choices."

"That's one of your strengths, Sonja. Owning your mistakes is something you're really good at. You're humble and teachable. I need to learn from you."

"Thank you for saying that." I smiled.

"We're a team. We've been to hell and back. Can we work on building our beautiful future?"

"Yes." I squeezed his hand. "And thank you for validating me. I won't bring it up anymore." I kissed the top of his hand. "We're a good team."

Mitch saw I was making considerable efforts in not only our relationship, but to pay off my credit card debt, so he helped me come to settlements with the creditors. The silver lining in this ordeal was my credit score got trashed, which stopped companies from sending me more offers. Mitch and I came to the agreement the best way to manage our finances was to separate them completely. To this day, I don't own a credit card; I operate purely on cash and a debit card. Mitch gives me a weekly allowance and comes with me to buy any big purchases. I have not had a spending relapse since.

CHAPTER 49

Breaking the News

March, Columbia, Missouri, 2016

Rachael returned from her mission, and Alex came home a few months later. We had told them Lincoln moved to Utah to spend time with cousins since he felt lonely being the only child at home, but now it was time to tell them the truth.

Rachael and I drove to the grocery store, and I felt now was as good a time as any. I turned down the radio.

"Rachael, I have to tell you something," I awkwardly started. "While you were on your mission, I attempted suicide. That's the real reason Lincoln moved to Utah."

There was a long pause as Rachael processed what I said. "Are you serious? Like, you actually almost died?" She creased her eyebrows.

"Yes."

"Why would you do that?" she yelled. "Of all the times to leave, you chose when Alex and I were gone? We'd come home motherless! What would Dad do? We'd all feel completely abandoned. Do you have *any* idea how suicide would wreck our family?" She got quiet. "No. Of course, you do. You know *exactly* how horrible that would be."

321

It was true, and it stung.

"I don't want to die anymore," I tried comforting her.

"How do you expect me to believe that? My whole life has felt like one sick game of jack-in-the-box. We've all been tiptoeing around the idea you could disappear one day and never come back," she snapped.

I pulled the car off to the side of the road and waited a moment before saying anything.

"God chose me to be your mother, even though I'm sick. Rachael, you haven't only been my daughter, you are one of my favorite people in this world." I sighed. "If there's ever been a time to believe I'll live to be in my eighties, it's now." I looked at her. "I mean it." I pulled her into my arms, and she grabbed me tight.

"I just don't want to lose you," she cried. "I still need you."

"I know," I said, wishing I could go back in time and make my suicide attempt disappear.

—◦—

Alex left for college before I told him. I struggled finding a time to bring it up. He called me one day full of questions, and I knew I couldn't avoid answering them.

"Mom, I know there is a reason behind Lincoln finishing high school in Utah. What is it?"

"Alex, I think it's something I should tell you in person," I said.

"That could be a while. Just tell me."

I took a deep breath. "Last December, while you and Rachael were gone, I attempted suicide." Silence filled the space between us, and after a long pause, he asked, "How'd you do it?"

"I took a lot of pills and ended up in the ICU."

More silence.

"I forgive you," he said. "Are you okay now?"

"I've never been better. I love you. You know that, right?" I hoped he believed me.

"Yeah, I know. I love you too."

In September, Alex texted me pictures of banners BYU put up for Suicide Awareness Week. It was Alex's way of letting me know he was thinking of me and acknowledging I had an illness. He kept his emotions so concealed I didn't know how he really felt about my suicide attempt, and I probably never would.

CHAPTER 50

Two Truths

Columbia, Missouri, 2016

While most people want to avoid the emergency room, I loved it. When my anxiety got out of control, they'd give me warm blankets, apple juice, and an IV of Ativan to calm me down. I began to rely on it. Tonya was helping me develop better coping skills. We put a routine in place: chamomile tea, hot baths, mindful meditation, ice packs, and the occasional Barbie princess movie.

I woke up with the same anxiety waiting for me that I usually escaped while I slept. I wanted to run to the emergency room, but I needed to learn how to master my emotions and thoughts, not just drug them.

I looked out my window at the rain splashing the cement. The tree leaves dripped, refreshed by the sudden shower. The rain looked so inviting, so gentle. I walked outside barefoot and stood under the opened sky. Rain splashed on me, no differently than the plants, the roof, the streets, and I liked feeling a part of it all. The rain held no favorites.

I sat in the anxiety, welcoming it as it rose in intensity. *You're allowed to be here,* I said to the anxiety. *Get comfortable with the uncomfortable.* Two truths could be true at the same time. I was enjoying myself, and

I was in pain. I breathed, held my head up higher, stood a little taller, and let the rain pour down on me as my anxiety raged. I stood on one leg and felt like I, too, was planted in the front yard. I bent my neck to the sky, reached my arms over my head, and grew my yoga tree. I experienced radical acceptance—a point at which you stop trying to fight your feelings and allow yourself to have them. I stood there, arms wide open, as the rain drenched me and the pain softened.

Mitch opened the front door. "Sonja, what are you doing? You're drenched. Come inside."

"It's working," I whispered, stiff as a statue.

"What's working?"

"Shh!" I stayed as still as possible, not wanting to disrupt the moment.

The anxiety moved like waves crashing against me, receding out to the ocean and pulling pieces of my pain out to sea with it each time until it slowly faded out. The feelings went through me like my internal weather, but they no longer defined me. So many times, I had reached out to touch a moment but felt locked inside myself. Now, I had the key to let myself out: DBT.

The next day I ran up to Mitch. "Let's go walk that trail everyone says is so pretty," I said, snatching the keys off the counter.

"Okay, like right now?" he asked.

"Yes, right now." I grabbed his hand.

My senses had been shut down for so long, I felt like I had just been cured of blindness and I wanted to see everything.

Mitch put the car in park, and we stepped out onto the trail, holding hands. I looked up at the canopy of trees glowing green under the sun. My illness was so quiet I could barely hear its whispers. All I heard were the birds and our shoes crunching over the gravel.

"Feeling the way I do today, I could live to be a hundred," I said, reaching my arms out to the sun. I constantly opened my arms as I walked now. This new openness to life was liberating.

"Normally, you say you feel like you're one hundred inside, so would that make you two hundred?" Mitch joked.

"I still feel aged by life, but I don't feel like I want it to end," I said. We crossed a bridge and I stopped to look over the railing at the rushing stream.

"It's good to have you back." Mitch leaned into me. "You left me for a long time, but I knew you were still in there."

I finally gathered my courage, put on a brave face, and asked the question I'd been too afraid to ask most our marriage. "Why did you stay with me?"

Mitch looked at the ground as he thought for a moment. "I've asked myself that question hundreds of times. Was I staying for the kids? Was I staying out of duty? To be honest, I stayed because before the chaos we had a good marriage. I remember the girl I married. I still love that girl, and I hoped one day she'd come back to me."

I looked up at him. "Do you feel like she's back?"

"In some ways. But I think after everything you've been through, you're a wiser version of yourself. The positive naiveté is gone but not the innocence."

"I wish this could last forever," I said, dropping a leaf into the water. I couldn't believe the woman smelling the air and enjoying the chirping of the birds was the same woman who, weeks prior, painfully inched her way through the minutes of the day.

I rested my chin on my hands, looking over the bridge one last time. I felt the beauty of the trees and the stillness of the breeze. I knew this moment wouldn't last. Pain, anxiety, and medicine side effects would still be a part of my life, but these beautiful moments made it all worth it. The more I used DBT, took my medication, and got comfortable with being uncomfortable, the more I realized nothing was changing but me.

CHAPTER 51

Weddings

February 2017

In preparation for Rachael's wedding, I baked over a hundred cookies and filled three hundred chocolate cups with vanilla cream with the help of Allyson and her daughters. Allyson's cancer treatment worked, and she lived past the two-year mark, which far surpassed what doctors had predicted. Even though her future was still unknown, I was determined to enjoy every moment I had with my sister. With more than five hours spent in the kitchen, we became dessert-making machines. I scraped the last of the cream out of a bowl and plopped it into a cup.

"I'll wash the bowl. Go put the cups in the fridge," Allyson told her oldest daughter.

"Wait! There are still two chocolate cups left! We need to make another batch of cream." I frantically grabbed the bowl from Allyson.

Allyson rolled her eyes. "We're not making another batch of cream for two cups."

"Just one more batch. I'm worried we won't have enough desserts for the open house!" I panicked.

Allyson rested her hands on the counter, crushing the chocolate cups under her palms.

"Oops," she said.

We started laughing, and the tension I'd felt about the wedding snapped as easily as the chocolate cups. I carried a bowl of Juicy Fruit gum to the reception and set it on the table by the entrance. Although my dad wouldn't be at the wedding, I made sure to make him part of the details. I even wrote my speech on a yellow legal pad.

The reception was indoors, but it felt like we were in a garden. Soft white and cream rose petals weaved around dark green garland, filling the room with the intoxicating smell of fresh flowers. Tall, silver vases held massive white flower arrangements on the tables, and the seven-tiered cake had a staircase of white roses ascending to the top. A dozen chandeliers sparkled from the ceiling, and as the clock struck 1 p.m., pretty dresses and friendly faces filled the reception hall. Everyone stood as Brett and Rachael walked in and sat at their table draped in a garland of roses.

Mitch stood at the mic. "So, I'm the father of the bride, and as most of you know, it's overwhelming to see your children get married. I was reminded of a story that, when I was a missionary in Scotland, my companion told me: 'You know, Elder Wasden, the harder you work, the prettier your wife will be.' And several years later, when I married Sonja, I realized he was right. So, I'm sure Brett's parents are happy to know that Brett was the hardest-working missionary in all of Europe." Mitch shared several endearing stories about Rachael and prepared Brett for their life together. Brett and Rachael danced, cut the cake, and—before I knew it—were about to run through a crowd of people to their car.

"Rachael, wait!" I yelled.

She stopped, looked back at me holding my arms open, and ran into them.

"I'm going to miss you," I cried.

"I'm not going anywhere, not really," she said, hugging me tighter.

"I love you." I wiped my eyes. "Now go, before Brett leaves without you."

She squeezed my hand before heading off with Brett through the cheering line.

"And just like that, they're gone," I said to Mitch, watching their car drive away.

"I trust him with my daughter," he said.

"This was a day I dreamt about for years." I leaned into Mitch.

Only six months later, beautiful flowers and delicious food were prepared once again, this time as Alex married his best friend, Kelsie. She was happy, calm, and had never experienced depression. I joked with her that I was clearly standing in the wrong bus line in heaven and should have joined hers.

Their special day was held in a white shabby-chic building. Baby pictures of them hung on twine over a wall, and grilled cheese sandwiches were served with chocolate chip cookies, two of Kelsie's favorite foods. I watched Alex beam throughout the day and hold his bride tight. I danced with Alex for the mother-son dance and cried my way through it. There's something about weddings that makes you feel like you're losing something, even though you're gaining so much more.

"Two kids married," I said to Mitch.

"And one to go." Mitch rubbed Lincoln's head.

Lincoln was tearing up.

"What's wrong?" I put my arm around him.

He hugged me fully for the first time since he left home. "Nothing's wrong." He held me. "It's just, you're alive. You're here."

CHAPTER 52

Retirement Party

November 24, 2017

Thanksgiving was the first holiday with Rachael and Alex's spouses, and we wanted to do something special, so we rented a cabin in the mountains near Sundance, close to all of them at BYU–Provo.

Our car zipped along tree-lined roads as flocks of wild turkeys scattered. A soft, orange glow seemed to coat everything as the sun set.

"Wow, this looks nicer than the picture!" Mitch said, pulling up to the cabin.

I clicked my seat belt off and looked up at the tall cabin.

"I'll get the bags. You go on in," Mitch insisted.

I opened the large, wooden door and saw all my kids and Mitch's parents waiting for me. The room was covered in streamers and balloons, and a big sign above the fireplace read, "RETIREMENT PARTY."

"Happy retirement, Mom!" Lincoln hugged me.

"What's all this?" I asked.

"You always said once you became an empty nester, you wanted a retirement party, just like anyone with a full-time career would get.

So…now that Lincoln's in college, we thought it was time to celebrate!" Rachael said.

Alex handed me a stack of letters. "We each wrote you a letter, but you can read them later."

"Wow." I teared up. I felt a rush of overwhelming love, the type I thought was impossible for me to experience. I felt they not only needed me, they wanted me in their life despite all the hurt I had caused. I went to sit on the couch with Alex and Kelsie, but Lincoln stopped me.

"You sit here." He pointed to a chair at the front of the room.

We played a game the kids organized: Who Knows Mom Best? We all sat around answering quiz questions like, "What was Mom's most recent Internet search?" or "What's Mom's favorite magazine?"—to which the kids accurately replied, *People*.

As we laughed and talked, I realized my family was happy. And so was I. Mitch often referred to our family as a tribe, and that was exactly what we were: a group of people so tight and loyal, we were like an army that had been in a foxhole together and came out alive. Nothing could sever us.

Mitch handed me a long red box and my heart pounded. Jewelry had been the source of so much contention in our home, I doubted he would ever give me another piece again.

"Sonja, I'd like to read you my letter, but first, open your retirement gift," he said.

I opened the skinny, rectangular box, and diamonds sparkled back at me. I recognized the bracelet instantly. It was an Art Deco bracelet that was part of an estate sale. It was the most beautiful piece of jewelry I had ever seen. Mitch stood behind me, his right hand on my shoulder, and read the letter:

Dear Sonja,

Happy retirement from twenty-five years of dedicated service as CEO of Wasden Enterprises. You have often said you feel like you're a hundred inside. You're close but not quite there. If you add up each of the kids' ages—twenty-three, twenty-one, and eighteen—plus the years you've been married, you get eighty-seven years—not quite a hundred. To commemorate all those years of service, we wanted to give you something that is as old as you feel but has found a way to—just like you—be timeless, stunning, and beautiful. It was made during the 1930s Art Deco period, exactly eighty-seven years ago. This bracelet is like you in one other important way. Each diamond was formed through years of heat, pressure, and refinement.

You will always be a mother. You are only retiring from the children's laundry, tennis practices, art lessons, and tutoring. Now it's your time to embark on dreams you selflessly put on hold while you focused on the most important thing: raising great children. I love you and would pick you again. You were chosen for me.

Love always,

Mitter

There wasn't a dry eye in the room. I was emotional, but more than that, I was grateful. Was I still ill? Yes. Was I still a powerless victim of my illness? No. Not anymore. I could've freed myself at any time and at any moment. I never realized I held the keys to my shackles. Everything I needed, I had within me. I didn't need to move or get a new husband or make more money or lose weight. The people around me didn't need to change. I needed to change the way I interacted with myself.

I no longer believe I'm living an impossible life. Now, instead of asking therapists and doctors if they know of anyone with a mental illness who has a life worth living, I can ask myself. And the answer is yes, I do know someone.

Me.

END OF BOOK ONE

Afterword

Sonja's ongoing journey required a trial-and-error process of several medications, treatment dosage combinations, therapy, and skills development to find what worked for her specific mental health issues. This process required trust and patience as she worked with her team of doctors and therapists. Many who face mental health challenges struggle with medication adherence and keeping appointments because results are not as quick as they would have hoped for or medication side effects feel unbearable. By trusting the treatment process, taking her medication, doing therapy, and remaining dedicated, Sonja has created a life worth living.

Sonja is one of today's most insightful and inspirational mental health speakers. She has traveled the country, speaking with Fortune 500 companies, nonprofit organizations, government officials, advocacy groups, and top media outlets about the importance of mental health. Sonja has been a member of *Newsweek* Expert Forum. She has become a devoted mental health advocate. Sonja does advocacy work with drug addiction recovery programs, homeless shelters, firefighters, police officers, veterans, women's prisons, students, and others.

Oprah Winfrey graciously participated virtually in one of Sonja's mental health book club's discussions to inspire the inmates at Central California Women's Facility, the world's largest women's prison.

Sonja has published op-eds in publications such as, *HuffPost*, *The Washington Post*, *Newsweek*, *The Hill*, *Ms. Magazine*, *KevinMD*, *NAMI (National Alliance on Mental Illness)*, *Oprah Daily*, and others.

Sonja and her daughter, Rachael, were invited to give a TEDx talk at HartlandHill. She has shared her story on local news across all fifty states, including national news, *CBS This Morning*, and *Tamron Hall Show*. *CBS This Morning* correspondent Dr. Tara Narula said Sonja's story was "one of my most sacred and special I've ever done." Her memoir, *An Impossible Life*, is an Eric Hoffer Grand Prize Winner.

Sonja continues to be a passionate mental health advocate and loves creating open, inclusive, and educational conversations around mental health. She has had the privilege of sharing her story and message of hope with millions.

BOOK TWO COMING SOON

A POSSIBLE *Life*

> *"I went out on a journey to prove, despite having a mental illness, I could be successful. I didn't know what success looked like for me, but I was willing to try everything until I felt the success equaled the pain I had been through."*

RACHAEL SIDDOWAY AND SONJA WASDEN

The Impossible Series

An Impossible Life: Sonja's Story
A Possible Life: Sonja's Journey to Success
An Impossible Mom: Rachael's Story

For family pictures and more information go to
sonjawasden.com

Follow us on Instagram @impossiblelives

Mental Health Messages of Hope

**From people who gave Sonja hope
along her mental health journey!**

Mental Health Message of Hope
Jenn, ER Nurse, Who Helped Save Sonja's Life

Dear *Impossible Life* Reader,

When I found out that Sonja was looking for me, my first thought was, why? After all these years, I was still someone she thought about. It reminded me that we may have a huge impact where we think we've had none. In almost two decades of nursing, that was a first for me. We never get to see the afterwards. Thankfully this afterward, Sonja had a wonderful outcome!

It's ok not to be ok. And when you're not ok, please remember, there are people out there who will help you fight when you don't have any fight left in you. Your story is not over.

Jenn

Jenn
ER Nurse, University of Missouri Hospital

Dear *Impossible Life* Reader,

I was a first responder at Sonja's father's suicide and have attended many other suicides and deaths in my sixteen-year career as a police officer. One thing I have found is that in every case, there is someone left behind who deeply loves the deceased and would do anything to bring them back. No matter how insignificant you think you are or how much pain you feel, you need to know that you are loved and that your life is worth living. There are people in your life who need you here and are willing to help you through your struggles. You are stronger than you realize. Don't give up hope!

Officer Jacob Simmons
Lindon Police Department

Dear *Impossible Life* Reader,

I would like to let anyone who is having thoughts about suicide know that you are not alone. Many people have felt that pain at some point in their life. I became a police officer to connect and reach out to people who are struggling. People's lives matter! You don't have to navigate this life alone. I know that it may be hard to talk to a police officer who is a stranger, but I also know that most of us wearing a badge want to take all the time in the world to help someone who needs it. I chose this career to help make a difference, and there is no better way to help than just being able to be there for someone who is having those thoughts. Always know that there is no problem too small or insignificant. We are only one call away. We want you to call. We want to help you, and we care about what you are going through. Please take a deep breath and call.

Phillip Bringhurst

Lieutenant Phillip Bringhurst
Mapleton Police Department

Mental Health Message of Hope
Rebekah, Sonja's DBT Therapist Post ICU

Dear *Impossible Life* Reader,

I met Sonja at a point in her life when she was a shell of a person, full of despair and nothing left to muster up the strength to take a step forward. What she didn't see was that beauty, love, and grace were still there, just hidden away and difficult to find. I see this time and time again in my practice. Clients come in and voice they have lost their way and a future has become but a glimmer or even worse, all desires have been replaced with a dark, empty hole.

Sonja's personal story in this book is a chance for you, the reader, to realize the light of hope does exist, even in the darkest of nights. By definition, hope is the wish or desire to have a certain thing happen. While this is a start, hope can also be undefined because it simply has taken on a meaning far beyond a wish. Hope can be a strand of strong energy pulling you through a challenging moment, day, week, or year. Hope can be what you turn to in order to accept there could be a different path.

Each time I had the pleasure of meeting with Sonja, I would remind her of what my mentor taught me: "two truths can be true at the same time." This idea suggests that we can be in despair and still have hope; we can be lost and found all at the same time. Often what is called for when you are suffering is complete surrender to what *is* in the moment. Surrender does not equate to "it is fair, just, or okay"; it simply means whatever is here is here, and before you can move on, acceptance or full surrender to the now must occur. Surrender, acceptance, and hope are all the same.

Sonja is a great example of realizing she had a choice; stand still and continue to fester in pain and suffering or search inside herself for the life worth living that was there all the time. I am fortunate to know Sonja and will always be grateful I walked alongside her on her journey to wellness. If you remember nothing else from her work, please observe the power of hope that is already inside of you.

Remember, there is another moment just around the bend and full of life to give you if you want to take it!

Rebekah Freese
LCSW, PhD

Mental Health Message of Hope
Sharon, Who Gave Sonja Her First Job Post ICU

Dear *Impossible Life* Reader,

In January 2015, while managing White House Black Market, a women's clothing store, Sonja boldly walked up to the counter and said, "I would like part-time work, but I haven't worked outside the home in over twenty years."

I thought, *this woman has style and carries herself with confidence.* She was so put together, I wondered, could she sell, or would she intimidate the average customer? I found that she was an excellent sales associate and had a way of making her customers feel great about the way they looked as they made their purchases.

As I continued to work with Sonja, I found she was friendly and talked about her family but mostly kept her personal life private. I had no idea what she had gone through or what it took for her to take that first step into our door to ask for a job.

What might have seemed like a small thing to some of us was Sonja's first big step to her amazing future of healing and helping others. Having hope is the first step toward healing; the next steps will be easier.

Sharon Viles
J. Hilburn Men's Personal Stylist

Mental Health Message Hope
Laurie, Sonja's Mental Health Prescriber

Dear *Impossible Life* Reader,

I applaud you on your efforts toward mental wellness. You are a resilient soul; I know this because you've invested time to read messages of hope from others that have gone before you. You are not alone on this journey; in fact, you are surrounded by a community of people who stand in solidarity with you, believe in you, and genuinely want you to be your best self. In order to move forward with hope of feeling better, we must first reframe the way we think about mental health treatment and then learn to set boundaries to maintain mental wellness. The key to success is to embrace and protect the internal metamorphosis that you are setting in motion.

Change can be hard. It takes guts to identify that you need help and then courage to both ask for and accept it. Let me be clear: if you have had mental health symptoms, addiction, or have an official mental health diagnosis—there is, in fact, *nothing* repellent about you. You have a medical condition that needs to be addressed (with therapy, medication, treatments, etc.), much in the way one would address high blood pressure or diabetes. When neurotransmitters are misfiring in the brain, this happens for a huge variety of reasons (heredity, head trauma, substance misuse, emotional abuse, etc.). Treating the symptoms does *not* in any way constitute a personal weakness. You are not diminished, less than, unreliable, or in any way, unworthy.

Learning to take care of yourself is one of the keys to getting better. You must decide that today is a new day. If anyone in your inner circle makes you feel ashamed for seeking help, they are most likely not playing for your team. Recognize this and start setting boundaries. Remember, the *only* people who are upset about your personal boundaries are those who profited when you had none.

The reason so many of us struggle with boundaries is that we never learned or weren't permitted to have boundaries in key relationships. Many of us have had parental figures or significant others who were perhaps mentally unwell themselves and felt threatened by the development of boundaries. As a result of this, many of us have never learned how to advocate for or value ourselves.

During this journey, you may have to make changes as you move toward wellness. You'll start recognizing those supporters who belong in this new life you're creating and identify those who don't fit as well as they previously had. You'll invest in your own stability by attending appointments, perhaps taking medications, and participating in daily activities that reinforce your self-worth. You'll grow more protective of your happiness and begin to realize that any situation that costs you your peace of mind is just simply too expensive. You may encounter obstacles as you grow, but the more you invest in yourself the greater the chance of success. That glowing spark of developing self-care turns into self-respect, which can then catch fire into a loving relationship with yourself. Once you value *you*, others will as well.

This next chapter is your own personal story. You are the author, editor, and publisher of how the world will view you. You are not defined by mental illness, addiction, hardship, abuse, or past challenges. Your narrative is your own, and someday I can't wait to read all about it. I'm proud of you for taking the time to invest in, respect, and love yourself.

Laurie LaVon Clair, PA-C

Laurie LaVon Clair
PA-C, MSPA, Medical Director

Mental Health Message of Hope
Laura, Sonja's Therapist

Dear *Impossible Life* Reader,

> *"Hope is the thing with feathers—*
> *That perches in the soul—*
> *And sings the tune without the words—*
> *And never stops—at all"*

This familiar verse in Emily Dickinson's poem, *"Hope" is the thing with feathers*, written in 1891, sits in a simple frame in my office facing the couch. Perhaps my clients read it, perhaps not. For myself, the words resonate through every hour that I sit with individuals who come through my door seeking support for all manner of suffering: *HOPE never stops at all.*

There is a point in most sessions, when the story has been told and the pieces sorted through, that I invite my client to close their eyes, focus on the long exhale, and let their attention sink down into their body, where memory and emotion are stored. Life is full of challenges and painful realties. It can feel confusing and difficult and even unfair at times. But don't despair! It is these same painful experiences that offer us an opportunity for learning and healing growth. Life will keep giving us the lessons until we learn what we need to learn.

And as Sonja powerfully shares, there is always help along the way. There is always hope. It is inside the very core of your being. *And it never stops at all.* Wishing you love along the journey!

Laura

Mental Health Message of Hope
Peggy, Sonja's NAMI Friend

Dear *Impossible Life* Reader,

What message of hope would I want to shout from the rooftops if I had the chance? Based on my experience as a family member of loved ones over the past twenty-five years who have experienced the darkest depression and the most paralyzing moments of anxiety, I can't say I know how that feels, but I can say I know the overwhelming helplessness that comes from loving them and not being able to make it better.

Watching them experience the fallout from their illness—ranging from failing grades to failed relationships to incarceration and hospitalization—I know how badly I wish I could wave a magic wand and make it all go away, to help others understand that this is an illness, not a choice.

My message of hope is that a mental health diagnosis is not the end of anything, but rather the beginning of a lifelong journey that will have ups and downs, twists and turns. But it is not a journey of only darkness and despair. It will have moments of great light and love. If you learn about your illness and help your loved ones to learn as well, you can find support and empathy rather than judgment and withdrawal. If you seek support, you can receive it. If you are vulnerable, others will be vulnerable in return.

My message of hope is don't be afraid. There are many of us who understand, and we are here with you.

Peggy Huppert

Peggy Huppert
Executive Director
NAMI Iowa (National Alliance on Mental Illness)

Mental Health Message of Hope
Annell and Dale Hiersche, Sonja's Inspirational Friends

Dear *Impossible Life* Reader,

I am Evelyn, and my husband is Don in *An Impossible Life*. I have a mother who was schizophrenic, and so is my husband, Dale. My mother refused medication and ended up leaving the family through divorce. When my husband received his diagnosis, I gave him an ultimatum of taking and staying on his medication or losing his family. He chose to stay on his medication. Because Dale chose to stay on his medication, we had a third child, and now have two beautiful grandchildren. He has held down a full-time job that provided enough financial resources that I was able to stay home with my children.

After receiving his diagnosis, I made a decision not to hide his illness, in order to help stop the stigma of mental illness. Having grown up with a mentally ill family member, I remember the shame of telling people about it. I didn't want that for my children, so when the circumstances are appropriate, I share his diagnosis. Mental illness is not something people choose.

Mental illness is the same as any physical illness like heart disease. When I told Sonja about his illness, I didn't know about her struggles and she didn't know about mine. I don't remember the conversation and why I shared that information with her. Since Sonja has left Baton Rouge, I have been diagnosed with depression. I am taking medication and seeing a therapist regularly to help me with that.

My advice to anyone experiencing mental illness is to educate themselves on their particular illness. Seek out the best medical care you can find, and build a support system of therapists, friends, and family. Then live your best life! You can have a happy, satisfying, successful, and fulfilling life. We are cheering you on!

Arnell Hensle

Dan Hierlh

Mental Health Message of Hope
Ben, Sonja's Spiritual Leader

Dear *Impossible Life* Reader,

My cherished friendship with Mitch and Sonja began several years ago when I served as one of their church leaders.

One night, Mitch called and asked me to come to their home, as Sonja was having deep suicidal ideations. It was clear that even as she is a powerful voice and advocate for those with mental health challenges, she was facing a battle herself. Through tears we prayed together, pleading with our Father for His divine love and assistance. Sonja was strengthened to persevere and overcome that season of despair and darkness until she regained hope and light.

Many years ago, my brother Chris gave me a small picture of him and me running a marathon together. It is obvious from the picture that I was pretty worn out and certainly struggling more than he was. The inscription under the picture reads, "Happy is the man who, during life's most challenging endeavors, glances to the left or right, to see a brother striding by his side and conquering with him." This is one of my favorite gifts, as it captures our struggle together. There are many who can stride with you through your darkest moments—a family member, friend, neighbor, or religious leader. Seek for others who can help you see yourself as you are becoming. If you can't find this person or group, look outward, and you will find them.

Jesus Christ declared his mission is to "heal the broken hearted, recover sight to the blind, and set at liberty those that are bruised." Through His love and grace, we can overcome. No matter our past, our brokenness, our ongoing trials and challenges, He provides healing and hope.

Go forward, and "run with patience the race that is set before you" with hope in His grace and your love for others resonating in and through you.

Benjamin Studling

Dear *Impossible Life* Reader,

I would say to anyone who is struggling with mental illness the same thing I have said many times to Sonja. Things may seem dark at times, but there is always, always light ahead, even if you can't see it right now. You are stronger than you realize. There are things that can be changed. And the things that can't be changed, forgive them. You may feel broken, but your broken pieces can be mended and fashioned into something even more beautiful than it was before. Your life has value, and your possibilities are infinite. You are treasured. You are loved.

Mental Health Message of Hope
Joe and Christy, Sonja's Brother and Sister-in-law

Dear *Impossible Life* Reader,

When my wife, Christy, and I were married, we believed our future was only limited by how big we could dream. We mapped out our life and started down that path full of confidence, hope, and excitement. More than thirty years into our journey together, we've now realized that we were naïve to the realities of the twists, turns, peaks, and valleys that life throws at all of us. As we reflect back, we are grateful for that naiveté, as there were many days the only way we could move forward was to look past today and have hope that tomorrow would be a brighter day, which it so often was. Our greatest loss was that of our daughter Anna, who valiantly and courageously fought cancer from the age of three until ten, when she passed away. There have been other genetic health challenges that have impacted the quality of life for several of our children. Our own personal family has also dealt with the struggles associated with mental health illness, with many of those struggles publicly known and many being fought privately. Essentially, we are no longer naïve to many of the most difficult challenges life can throw at all of us, which have caused us some very dark and hopeless days.

So, what has sustained us? Our family is a family of faith, and regardless of the challenge we have been faced with, we have turned to our faith to provide us hope. One of the leaders of our faith, Elder Jeffrey R. Holland, has provided a quote that we would like to share with those reading this message that summarizes the hope that sustains us.

"Whatever your struggle, mental or emotional or physical or otherwise, do not vote against the preciousness of life by ending it! Trust in God. Hold on in His love. Know that one day the dawn will break brightly and all shadows of mortality will flee. Though we may feel we are 'like a broken vessel,' as the Psalmist says, we must remember, that vessel is in the hands of the divine potter. Broken minds can be healed just the way broken bones and broken hearts are healed. While God is at work making those repairs, the rest of us can help by being merciful, nonjudgmental, and kind." — *Like a Broken Vessel, 2013*

It is truly our prayer that regardless of what hardships life has or will throw at each of us, we will all find hope through whatever channel it is made available to us. That hope might come through a family member, personal relationship, professional advice, medical care, a divine spiritual connection, inspirational messages, or through a myriad of other means. We simply cannot stop seeking to find the means that will sustain us during those dark times and give us hope in a brighter tomorrow.

Joseph Nemelka

Christy Nemelka

Mental Health Message of Hope
John, Sonja's Brother

Dear *Impossible Life* Reader,

Having experienced painful and traumatic events in my life, I needed hope in order to endure and eventually heal from these traumas. I needed to find "my why," so my suffering could cease to be suffering by finding its meaning. Viktor Frankl's idea that those who can have a why to live can bear almost anything has guided me in such a way that I eventually found "my why," which is love and service. This has given me the hope and courage to endure my darkest moments. Like Sonja, I try to use my life experiences to give hope to others who are suffering. It is possible to not only survive but thrive. Find your "why!"

John F. Newell

Mental Health Message of Hope
Allyson, Sonja's Sister

Dear *Impossible Life* Reader,

What do you do when you have a parent, spouse, sibling, or friend who suffers from debilitating mental illness?

It is heart wrenching watching someone you love suffer, not knowing how to help or what to do. My father died from suicide; it was devastating. The thoughts, *What could I have done differently? What could I have done to save him?* would constantly bounce around my brain.

Now, as I reflect on my experience with him, I would have done one thing differently. I would have mustered up the courage to sit in the fire with him. I would have to be brave going down into the darkness with him, and just being there with him. I would not pressure him or point out all the good he had in his life. I would just sit calmly with him in the fire, gently holding his hand. I would look him in the eyes and say, "I see you. I am so sorry you are suffering. I'm here with you."

I recognize that perhaps this could not have changed the outcome; my father still could have lost his life to suicide. Nevertheless, I wish I had been there, really been there, in his suffering.

So now, when my sister Sonja calls me, struggling and praying for relief from her suffering, I try to truly be there with her. I want her to know, *I see you. I hear you. I know it's hard. I'm here.* Sonja's life is an incredibly difficult life to lead, but as she has shown it's possible to have a life worth living.

Allyson Davidson

Mental Health Message of Hope
Rachael, Alexander, and Lincoln, Sonja's Children

Dear *Impossible Life* Reader,

Our lived experience with our mother has shown us the immense power people have to rise above their darkest hours. Her life has not been an easy one. She has faced challenges and obstacles that many of us could not imagine. Yet, despite everything that she has gone through, she has never given up.

It is through her example that we have come to understand the true meaning of hope. Hope is not just a feeling or a wish. Hope is a choice. It is a decision to keep going, to keep striving, even when everything around you seems impossible.

So, if you are struggling, if you feel like the odds are stacked against you, remember our mother's story. Remember that hope is a choice, and that you have the power within you to choose hope over despair. Keep pushing forward, keep striving, and know that you are not alone.

My family is currently living what we once hoped for but didn't think was possible. There is hope!

Mental Health Message of Hope
Mitch, Sonja's Husband

Dear *Impossible Life* Reader,

Losing hope is easy; holding on to hope is hard. When you witness the person you love most on Earth experience thousands of dark days in a seemingly never-ending succession, it's natural to ask God questions like "Why? What does this level of suffering accomplish in the universe's grand plan? When is it enough?"

Of all Sonja's accomplishments and accolades, the one I am most in awe of is her ability to cling to faint and misty threads of hope with the grit of a prisoner in a mental war. How can I not love that? How can I not forget my own sleepless nights, mental turmoil, and tears when I see her courageously carrying a load an order of magnitude greater than mine?

Sonja's hope and optimism have given her another gear that has allowed her at times to narrowly escape her mental health battles. Her hope and faith have propelled her forward to learn skills, to try dozens of medications and dosages, and to attend hundreds of therapy visits, all because she believes she can have a life worth living. Hope spreads when it's shared with others, and there are few groups who need hope more than those battling a mental illness.

Sonja's desire from the moment she wakes up to the minute she goes to bed is to share her story of hope with those who have lost hope. Please join with my sweet wife, Sonja, in sharing a message of hope with others.

Your Message of Hope

Write your Message of Hope on this page and pass this book along!

Mental Health Resources

Emergency Number

Call **911**
Open 24 hours a day, 7 days a week

Suicide & Crisis Lifeline

Call or text **988**
Open 24 hours a day, 7 days a week

Crisis Text Line

Text **HOME** to **741-741**
Open 24 hours a day, 7 days a week

NAMI HelpLine

Call **1-800-950-6264** or text **HelpLine** to **62640**
or email **helpline@nami.org**
Open Monday - Friday, 10 a.m. –10:00 p.m., ET.

Made in the USA
Monee, IL
23 April 2024

57186933R00225